OUT INTO THE DEEP

By
MARK RUTLAND

Printed by

ADVOCATE PRESS
Franklin Springs, Georgia

DEDICATION

— Jesus and Alison —

He gave her to me. She constantly draws me closer to Him.

Table of Contents

Launch Out .

Chapter I
Launch Out . . .

INTO THE DEEP

Jesus' heart broke for them. They were so hungry. The seething multitude hung on His every word. They all wanted to touch Him. Those in the rear pressed forward like famished children.

As the throng pressed upon Him, the Lord decided to take refuge in a boat. Such a floating pulpit would offer Him the opportunity to teach them without being forced backward into the water. One young fisherman, Simon Peter by name, was willing to oblige. Simon nudged his boat out a bit and balanced it with his oars while Jesus preached. He listened along with the rest until suddenly Jesus turned from the many, as He was wont to do, and fastened His eyes on Peter. In ministry to the many, Jesus was never too busy for the one. In the feeding of the five thousand, Jesus never forgot the woman at the well.

"Simon," He said, "launch out into the deep and let down your nets for a draught."

Those few simple words threw the young fisherman into confusion. A thousand protests filled Simon's head. What did this — this rabbi know of fishing? Does a carpenter have some secret insight on fishing that **he** — a mere lifelong professional fisherman — had missed? Also, he was exhausted, from having fished all night and discouraged from having taken nothing. Anyway, who ever heard of daylight fishing in the Lake of Tiberias? Even a carpenter should know better than that!

Yet His gaze — those eyes — those penetrating, fathomless eyes seemed to answer all Peter's objections. The words themselves were disturbing. ". . . out into the deep . . . , " What did that mean? He knew and yet felt he did not know. It made him somehow slightly afraid. Still, disobedience appeared unthinkable. Peter's feeble protests finally trailed off. "Nevertheless, Lord, at thy word . . ." Peter said with more of resignation than faith in his tone. The act of naked obedience albeit without gushing enthusiasm, was all the Lord required, however, and Jesus smiled as the little craft plowed toward deeper waters.

From the helm, Peter stared at Jesus' back. Why did he feel as if Jesus were watching **him**? This whole thing was becoming more disturbing by the minute.

No sooner had the dragnet been spread than the obvious activity of a large school churned the water. In minutes, Simon's nets bulged with fish. His booming laughter punctuated his shouts to his partners. Ha-ha, he thought, I have **never** seen anything like it! One catch like this a month, and my whole future would change. As he hauled in the nets hand over fist, laughing and shouting as the fishes' shining, little bodies flopped into his boat, his eyes met once more with the Master's. In that second, his future did indeed change.

Through that one, brief morning encounter, Simon's life was to never again be the same. He laid down his nets, left the security of his livelihood, and "launched out into the deep." He would never — **never** forget those words. In miracles, in ministry, in betrayal, in darkness, in resurrection, at Pentecost, in death — once in the deep with Jesus, there was no going back. From his trade and tradition to riot and revival, that morning on Galilee's lake, a fisherman launched out into the deep and became a fisher of men.

I am persuaded that the abiding call of the Spirit is to **launch out into the deep**. The Holy Ghost has declared Himself at unalterable enmity with the status quo. Wherever we are spiritually, God's call is for us to move on. Choose your own metaphor — higher ground, a closer walk, another step, or a higher path — it is the call of the Holy Spirit to greater growth and maturity through obedience and faith. The command to "launch out into the deep" is simply the insistence of the Lord that we go on with Him.

Now, there is something inherent in the human heart which resists the deep places. The lust of the flesh is solidly on the side of safe harbors and the shallow security of self-indulgence. Anything that contradicts the instinct for self-preservation, even the voice of God, the flesh perceives as threatening. The great struggle of the human spirit is between "business as usual" under the dominion of self, and "the deep places" with King Jesus. Everytime any nation, people, denomination, congregation, or individual chooses safety over the call of God, hope for a more excellent vision dims a bit.

A member of the board of a certain holiness camp meeting wrote me demanding to know if I spoke in tongues, implying that if the answer were "yes," an invitation to speak (already tendered me), would be summarily withdrawn. I resisted the temptation to give him any satisfaction on the question, but the point remained. He did not want his sacrosanct set of "holiness" doctrines called out even slightly from the theological shallows to which he had become accustomed. If I announced my topic at such a camp meeting to be "Tongues: A Genuine Gift," many there would refuse even to listen. By the same token, I could stand before many Charismatic prayer meetings in America and announce my topic was "Suffering in the Life of the Believer" and ninety percent would turn me off before I began. Undoubtedly someone would shout, "Out in the Name of Jesus!"

Everytime the Lord offers to teach us anything new or to take us where we have not been, we react like petty, panicky children. Perhaps the whole Christian experience can be understood best in terms of trusting Jesus in uncharted waters. He is loathe to teach us the same lessons day after day. The Lord's dream for us is "glory unto glory." He is Master Pilot. There is not a reef or shoal hidden from his eyes. The grandness of the Christian Adventure is not for those who play it safe. The deeper the water — the bigger the fishes!

The Spirit of the frontier is but a flickering candle in much of contemporary Christendom. We are being deluged with a veritable passion for nice, safe, unchallenged, shallow-water religion. Satisfied with dabbling in the surf and satiated with the vicarious thrills of the cinema, we are in danger of becoming shoreline Christians. By turning back in fear of pain or danger or distress in the crucible of obedience, we run the risk of the miniaturization of a soul that was meant to be fitted for the skies.

It is this lust for security that is behind the damnable contemporary plague of divorce and abortion. If a circumstance or relationship promises even the hint of pain, where the American answer was once to press on with courage, it is rapidly becoming to abandon ship and all hands.

"Until death do us part" has become a ghastly joke in America. As soon as a rough spot presents itself, divorce is the only logical solution. The idea of "launching out into the deep" place of a relational storm has become simply unthinkable. Sometimes, I suppose, courageous and committed Christians have no options in divorce. Much more often, however, divorce is simply the path of least resistance.

Likewise, abortion is the most cowardly brand of murder in the world. All this talk of sparing the lives of endangered mothers is a ludicrous rationalization for the murder of nearly 1.5 million babies who had the unmitigated audacity to be inconvenient or embarrassing. That, not any health question, is the deciding factor that sentences a small nation of innocent babies to death every year in America. Because their parents, or at least their mothers, are more ready to do murder than to experience a "deep place" of embarrassment in their own lives, infanticide rages like Black Death in a "Christian" country.

It is important, however, to remember that Jesus did not call the fisherman into the deep to drown him, but to bless him. What a wretched story it had been, indeed, if the Lord had taken Peter into the deep and deserted him. We must remember that the great haul of fishes Peter took that day was a great, practical, personal blessing — to **Peter**! Peter's profession was fishing and the bulging nets translated to him as shekels. Oh, the liberty to obey which graces a heart utterly persuaded of God's good intentions. When Peter obeyed, despite his screaming muscles and a night of fruitless self-effort, Jesus opened a world for him that he had never dreamed of in Capernaum. In the deep place with Jesus, Peter found the great pain of crucifixion. He also found the power of Pentecost and the exultation of the crown of life.

Everyone's "deep place" is peculiarly his own. At various stages of each life, the "deep places" change as well. Hence, the whole process of grace is a marvelously intricate work leading the lost to salvation, the saved to sanctification, and the saints into service. Even beyond that, however, the Holy Spirit is constantly at work in the lives of even the most devoted believers to break away every confining letter and every blinder. The Lord leads us through the gardens of blessing and deserts of affliction alike for one purpose. Every idol must fall. Unloving, unburdened believers bound in the creeping vines of petty parochialism and self-centered insularity must be set free to win the lost at any cost.

In an age where a split-level in the suburbs, two Buicks and membership in a local country club has become a virtue, the Lord is challenging the very heart of this generation when by His Spirit He says, "Launch out into the deep . . . ."

Chapter II
Launch Out . . .

INTO THE FIRE

The American dream was mine. I held it in my hand like a captive bird and felt its beating heart against my palm. The flutter reassured me that regardless of what befell others, success was **mine**.

My high school graduation was a night to remember. It was as profoundly American as rodeos and toothpaste. My family and my girl beamed as I received not only my diploma but a variety of awards, both athletic and academic. It was a high school career to be envied — president of the student body, high academic honors, and participation in several sports.

Two weeks later, to the day, I entered the University of Maryland's summer school and made three A's. A year later, I married the girl, Alison Permenter, who had sat with my parents and proudly watched me graduate. Married at 19 and 17 and desperately in love, we were happy — really happy.

We worked hard. Alison took a job as a clerk at an electronics laboratory. I took a full course load at the University and worked at a variety of part-time jobs. These included teaching tennis, apartment maintenence, teaching in a private school, driving a bus, chauffeuring, managing a gym, and bagging groceries three nights a week until 1:00 a.m. in a black, all-night grocery store on Rhode Island Avenue in the District of Columbia.

For two years, we didn't even own a car. The hard work and the penury was never very galling. The ersatz couch we fashioned from an army cot covered with blankets was more fun than sacrificial.

My degree was to be Public Relations and my ambition was to go as far in politics as I could go. The meagerness of our life-style, the frugality, the extra jobs, and the hard hours seemed more than appropriate to my conservative politics. I became an officer in Young Republicans and was offered a scholarship (which I refused) by Young Americans for Freedom in return for taking the Presidency of the University of Maryland Chapter of YAF. It was heady stuff rubbing shoulders with congressmen and senators and the new Governor of Maryland, Spiro Agnew. The way seemed open before me.

Yet, something kept yapping at the heels of my ambitious dreams. A nagging, bothersome, secret knowledge that I was going in the wrong direction fast, haunted the back rooms of my heart. Political ambition gripped me hard. I wanted that life-style and all I saw that it offered. It appeared so very **attainable** — except for one thing, that is.

Years before, as a young teenager in North Florida, I had had an experience with Jesus Christ that I just couldn't quite seem to shake off. A young student from little Asbury College in Kentucky was hired as a summer Youth Director at First Methodist in Port St. Joe, where my family and I attended.

We were a church family in every sense of the word. From my bedroom window, I could look directly across the street and see the friendly lights of the First Methodist Church. My father taught a Sunday School class and my mother was president of the Women's Society. My early dates were church hayrides and MYF beach parties.

It never occurred to me that I was not a Christian. I came as close to living right **in** the church as was possible. With the awakening of adolescence in my body, sin struck like a thunderbolt. Sexual lusts consumed me, and with success at athletics came locker room language, smoking and surreptitious drinking. I suppose that mine were fairly innocuous sins compared with the orgiastic frenzy of today's youth, but they were sufficient to reveal one thing to me. Something was wrong. Now, suddenly, the warm Methodist lights acroos the street made me uneasy about myself. Fun seemed further and further afield, while home and church were a growing inconvenience.

Jack Taylor, the new Youth Director, hit our youth group like an A-bomb. Young, attractive, tanned, and athletic, he used his

13

genuine humility and humor to great advantage. We went, did, played, and "activitied" at an unprecedented pace. It was powerful gravity to pull a straying adolescent back to the Church. All the while, Jack presented the claims of Christ frankly and calmly.

By summer's end, I was acutely aware of my sins and my need for Jesus Christ. In August, Jack took the whole group to a youth camp in Blue Lake, Alabama. There, I had to face the preacher's firm and clear insistence that death without Jesus meant eternal hell. This message scraped agonizingly across my raw nerves until one August night in the suffocating heat, I stepped out from the back row and made my way up the center aisle.

As I walked up that aisle, wanting only forgiveness and salvation, a very shocking and alien thought pushed its way into my mind and insistently demanded attention. It was like an announcement, a declaration of self to soul. I nearly said the words aloud as I walked toward the front.

"I must preach. I am to be a preacher. This is what my life is to be."

A preacher?! The thought was amazing to me. Even as I prayed with Jack at the altar to ask Jesus into my heart, the urgency of the thought grew. By the time the prayer of faith was finished, I felt compelled to share the thought with Jack.

"Now that you're saved," he answered, "God has the right to direct your life. Let me pray with you."

He placed his hands on my head and began to pray. He prayed that either God would lift the sense of the call or confirm it. Then he prayed that having done, God would never release me from it. He urged the Lord to melt any disobedience on my part with unmitigated force on His part. "Break him, bend him, take eveything he holds dear," he prayed, "until he obeys the call and claim on his life. In Jesus' Name, Amen."

Such ruthlessness in prayer was remarkable to my conservative, Methodist heart. It made an indelible impression on me and frightened me more than a little at the moment.

Alas, however, both the intimidating effect of the prayer and the conversion wore thin all too quickly. The good seed found little root system and soon I was left with barely a tattered remnant of faith. That which remained only served to naggingly convince me that the sinful, backslidden, wasted exist-

14

ence I was living was wrong. It was still strong enough to make me miserable about my sin, but not nearly strong enough to make me change.

As had been so very frequent in my childhood, my father was transferred again. This time, the change from Florida to Maryland came during the winter, very soon after my church camp experience.

Maryland seemed to offer the possibility of leaving the whole thing behind. Not one soul except Jack (whom I was not to see again for fifteen years) knew of my call to preach. Perhaps in Maryland's snow-covered countryside, I could forget the fevered prayer at an Alabama altar.

I found that the prayers at the altar could **not** be forgotten. They could, however, be suppressed. I blanketed the experience under a high sheen, lacquered surface of sin and frantic high school activity.

Jack was gone. The big, cold Methodist Church in Maryland was as dead as a stone and I knew not one single born-again Christian in the new high school.

In neither of the Maryland high schools I was to attend, would anyone have imagined that I had **ever** claimed to be "born again." A new school, a new church which brought absolutely no conviction to bear on my life, and a new girlfriend that neither knew nor cared anything about my brush with Jesus — these were the elements of my happily backslidden life.

Before we married as teenagers, Alison Permenter, my cheerleader girlfriend, attended a Youth for Christ convention in Atlantic City, New Jersey. It was there that Alison was fully, soundly converted. It proved to be one of the most durable and affecting conversions I have ever witnessed. Everything about her life changed. I watched with real pain as the cute little pagan with whom I had fallen in love, developed a mature love for the Christ I had deserted.

At one point, she had even made the proper Biblical decision to break off with me. Then, during the summer we were apart, she had a supernatural experience in prayer that was to change everything. The Word of the Lord came to her, revealing that I had been called to preach. Only God's Spirit could have done this. Not even my parents knew of this "dark secret."

Never mentioning to me the prayer experience or the revelation she had had, Alison and I reunited and dated steadily until she graduated from high school. Her consistent witness and the obvious change in her life spoke not only to me but to the entire community.

She was probably the most popular girl in her school. When she resigned from the cheerleading squad because it was an "unwholesome atmosphere," many were infuriated. Her faculty sponsor even called her parents. The statement it made about the seriousness of her commitment to Christ was unmistakable.

When, in her senior year, she was elected homecoming queen, I was convinced it meant that many others, as well as I, saw that she was an exceptional young woman. She wore the little crown gracefully and gave all the glory to Jesus Christ.

After our wedding, I came heavily under conviction that I was Satan's one hope in her life. The fear of dragging her down began truly to haunt me. Finally, one afternoon, I turned once again to the Jesus of my youth. He met me with precious grace and open arms. I felt restored to the fellowship I would never before have admitted I even missed. I also felt something else. I heard that same insistent voice that had boomed in my ears as I walked the aisle of the youth camp. "Go and preach. Go! Preach!"

A man has a sort of triumphant joy, nay, a veritable soaring spirit when he thinks, for just a fleeting moment, that for once in his life, he knows something his wife does not. Deep inside, he knows that it is hope against hope; but, nonetheless, he clings fearfully to that pathetic, little shred of optimism. He approaches the moment of the announcing of such a gnostic treasure with a kind of mystic wonder.

My wife, a gentle, Mother Earth smile in her eyes, dashed my hopes. It was only then that she shared from her little diary the revelation God had granted her in prayer.

She rejoiced so sweetly with me, however, over my renewed commitment to Christ and my determination to be obedient to this newly admitted call, that it took some of the sting out of it.

Two years later, upon graduation from the University of Maryland, I enrolled at Candler School of Theology at Emory University. The two years as a declared "future preacher" had been years of spiritual stagnation. Except for our youth work at a local Methodist Church, I had no source of true Christian fellowship. Alison and I floundered in a sea of constant church activity with absolutely no depth. I had no prayer life, very little understanding of Scripture, and almost no sense of abiding victory.

These things compelled me toward the Methodist ministry: 1) An unquestionable call of God. I could not hope to understand it. I did not pretend to particularly like it. Yet, I could not deny it. At times (many times, if I am honest), I was quite the more assured of my call to preach than of my salvation. 2) A growing conviction in the truth of evangelical theology. Based more upon experience and vaguely remembered sermons from my youth in Florida than upon up-to-date reality in my own personal relationship with God, this conviction was at the core of my life at that time.

I **knew** that salvation was by faith in the atoning work of Christ. I **knew** that. I knew that the mushy liberalism and social-gospel message that seemed to engulf the Methodism of the late 60's and early 70's was insufficient. **That** I knew for sure. What I did **not** know was **power in my own life**.

I used to believe the great problem in the Church to be the "liberals." The liberals I thought to be the great, grey nameless "They" that were ruining the Church with wrong-thinking and wrong theology.

Now I believe that to be an error. I do not believe that the occasional "liberal" could hurt the Church if she were, on the whole, saturated in the Holy Spirit. The great disaster of the contemporary Church is not the liberals. The real danger is dead, unctionless, unanointed, powerless, effete, watered-down orthodoxy. The true contemporary tragedy in the American pulpit is not the advocate of liberation theology (though, that is tragedy enough). The modern horror story is the dull-eyed, passionless, pathetic company man, whose compromised ministry is baptized more in complacency than in power.

In a very real way, my evangelical "theology," if you wish to call it that, was hardly more than a natural outgrowth of political conservatism, Methodist traditionalism, and a true, but shallow salvation experience. I "believed" that Jesus was the only Way in much the same way as I had believed that Barry Goldwater was right.

The real menace hindering the outbreak of another American revival is never the wild-eyed Marxist Jesuit spouting pop theology, nor is it the seminary jade calmly announcing that God is dead. The more nefarious foe of a spiritual awakening is the slick professional who substitutes charm for unction, compromise for conviction, ecclesiastical politics for spiritual power, and church growth techniques for revival prayer. He is a pitiful husk of a preacher. He is a superficial, virtually useless "den mother" whose preaching has no power to convict or to convert. His ministry, despite the earmarks of success, leaves a trail of starving congregations with swollen bellies and unmet cravings. He is personally popular, powerless and pathetic; tasteful, tactful, and tepid. His preaching is inoffensive and ineffective.

My own life became the consummate nightmare of moral inconsistency and spiritual powerlessness. I kept telling myself that I would "get it together." I lived in the hope that something (I had no idea what, but "something") would come along and change things. Nothing did!

Yet, in spite of these things, I considered myself an evangelical's evangelical, when I was appointed to the Little River UMC in Woodstock, Georgia. Out of step with the liberalism at Candler, I took great satisfaction and fulfillment in the local parish work there. I plunged into it with a passion.

Due in part to my bad attitudes, and in part to the Spiritual bankruptcy there, my years at Emory's Candler were, on the whole, wasted. I found Candler to be a pseudo-intellectual community of lost souls, baptized in arrogance, drunk on their own importance and totally ineffective at training folks in any realistic ministry. We quibbled in theological senility over questions that affected no one, argued about Caesar Chavez (who remembers him now?) and tore each other to ribbons in required, gut-grinding discussion groups.

These last were brazenly labeled "Supervised Ministry," but here were less ministry than emotional terror squads.

Oh, the sweet oasis of my little country church! The love and gentleness and reality I found there were like an island of sanity in a gurgling sea of academic madness.

I did not so much pastor there as they just adopted my wife and me. When I arrived at the Little River Church, I had never been to a funeral, only one wedding (and I was nearly in shock at that one), and had preached only five times in my life. My wife, at age twenty, was nearly as young as some in our youth group, and appeared sixteen. For all the pretended sophistication of my twenty-two years, there was hardly any hiding the stark fear in my eyes when I went in the pulpit. There was absolutely no denying the fact that there was not one man on the administrative board as young as I was, or who knew as little about church business.

Yet for all the twelve-minute sermons filled with useless quotations by German theologians; for all the crazy, half-baked ideas; for all the misplaced, youthful enthusiasm; for all the inabilities and ignorances, that rural Georgia congregation poured on the love. They overlooked so much that was bad and pretended they could see plenty of good through a generous camouflage.

A particularly precious memory to me is the weathered old face that belonged to a farmer named Bill Keheley. By the time I met him, Mr. Bill had seen nearly 100 years of preachers come and visit on his front porch. I do not know why he took me on as a special project. He seemed to consider it his sacred duty to rub the varnish off this young pretender to the title of pastor. He did it with such loving tenderness and with such obvious good intentions, that it hardly hurt at all, and with such wisdom that I am still grateful today.

"I been waiting for the right day to show you something important," he said, "come on by here, will you? It's important."

He met me in his driveway and escorted me away from the house and into the pasture. We walked the muddy fields while he talked about his cows like they were pets. I, meanwhile, city-born and bred, was far more concerned with trying to avoid what his "pets" had left in the wet grass. Finally, he stopped his reverie and pointed to my feet.

"Look at yer shoes, Preacher," he said.

"Yeah, swell, Bill, " I muttered. "Did you bring me here to ruin my shoes?"

His eyes peered into mine for a moment before he said, "Now remember this. The people don't trust a preacher that ain't never had no mud on his shoes."

Then he smiled his little shy smile and turned to the house, leaving me standing in his pasture. I think it was his way of trying to minister a little reality to a smug. young, pseudo-intellectual seminarian.

It was also at Little River that God began to work in my life in a new way. There are two ways that God can bring a man to brokenness. The first is to simply strip him. God can take away in a single hour all that a man holds dear, until in desperate brokenness he turns to God. On the surface, that seems to be the more ruthless way.

The other way is to bless Him. And **that** can really break a man. God began the blessing process with a torrent. Blessings literally filled my little world.

The church began to grow. We added members at an unheard of rate for that church. A traveling youth choir of about 40 voices sprang up where there had been only a handful of bedraggled teens. All the signs of a good, healthy, evangelical church were there from new Sunday School classes to new ball teams. Contemporaneity certainly certifies as spiritually fit any church with rising attendance and winning ball teams.

In the midst of all this public heaven, I began a private descent into hell. I fell into the darkest, blackest, most depraved sin of the ministry. I did not run off with the choir director. He was well over 50 and not all that attractive to me. The fact is that God can often deal with the sins of the flesh more easily than the sins of the spirit. The man living in chronic adultery knows he is a sinner, but such a revelation may not be so readily apparent to the habitual gossip.

The most debilitating sin of the ministry is not moral turpitude. It is ambition. It was to **this** that I fell. The broad path for me was ruthless, cold-blooded, cold-eyed ecclesiastical ambition. I wanted to "get ahead."

Looking back on it now, I realize how ridiculous it was. Hardly to the end of my first appointment, only one year out of seminary and yet, peering relentlessly toward the goal of advancement through a now almost coincidental fog of actual ministry. I began to talk about "moving up in the conference." What can that even mean? That is an irrelevancy in the mouth of one ordained in the Name of Him who had not where to lay His head.

I studied the Conference Journal. I knew who was up to move, who had paid his apportionments and who had gotten a raise.

One particularly painful memory is of being with a group of young pastors discussing the sudden death of another. He had left a young widow and three children who had to move out of the parsonage. Did we ever once get on our knees and pray for her, or the children, or the church? Absolutely not! We coolly discussed the chain of mid-year moves this would open, and who might advance as a result.

I became consumed with a passion for bigger churches, more prominent positions, and more prestige. The modern, American, denominational church is a highly sophisticated corporate structure, replete with "presidents," "vice presidents," and "star salesmen." There are also significant and obvious rewards for advancement. This is a heady intoxicant for a young preacher. The pecking order is clearly defined and the method of advancement is, though unstated, orderly and understood. Sam Rayburn said of the congress, "If you want to get along, go along." That's about it.

The one great "sin" which the structure will not tolerate is not adultery. With a repentant posture and some time for the storm to blow over, that can be weathered. And it certainly is not ambition or greed. Hardly! The one unforgivable, intolerable transgression against the structure is boat-rocking. Cause a stir, trouble the waters, challenge the status quo, and wear the Scarlet Letter.

I determined I would do whatever was neccessary to "scale the utmost heights, to catch a gleam of glory bright." And I soon realized that a modest evangelicalism was no hindrance to the land of higher steeples. Nice, safe conservatism, a kind of Oxford, buttoned-down evangelicalism is comforting to folks and does not inordinately discomfit the hierarchy. I pursued it with a passion!

Such ambition is a horrible sin because it robs a local congregation of its perfect right to expect a pastor who will minister to them where they are. As soon as a church becomes, for any pastor, a stepping stone, he forfeits all spiritual authority and the people are sheep without a shepherd. And he is a pastor without a church from that very moment. It is a hellish sin.

It is one of the great and more regrettable sins of my life that I left that church with a lie in my teeth. I personally requested that the District Superintendent move me. Then, by hint and innuendo, I let it be known that the mean old District Superintendent was making me leave.

Dr. Charles Boleyn's telephone call one night late in the spring seemed to be exactly the opportunity I had hoped for. He invited me to be his associate pastor at Oak Grove United Methodist. Dr. Boleyn was a former District Superintendent and was now pastor of that prosperous North Atlanta congregation. Fellow ministers advised on every hand that it was a marvelous opportunity, not only for advancement at that moment, but for being identified with that kind of church. That was music to my ears.

I returned Dr. Boleyn's call shortly later and eagerly. As I hung up, I ruminated warmly on the perfect way things seemed to be breaking out. I bounded into our bedroom where I found my wife sitting up in bed, reading the Bible.

"Well," I proclaimed buoyantly, "That's it. We're going to Oak Grove. This is a big step for us."

She quietly turned her Bible down on her lap and slowly, almost painfully raised her eyes. "A big step?"she asked. "Mark, I'm confused. When you first started out, all you talked about was preaching the Gospel and seeing people saved. Now you say we're taking a 'big step.' if this is a 'big step,' then where are we going?"

The accusation cut deep and hurt feelings and wounded pride boiled over. I flew into a veritable rage.

"You just can't stand for me to have any success, can you?" I shouted. "To tell you the truth, I'm sick of your sanctimonious, 'holier-than-thou' routine."

I stormed out the door in a rage that was to become a constant and fearsome part of my next year and a half. It was in **that** happy frame of mind that we arrived a month later at one of the largest Methodist churches in Georgia.

Yet, at Oak Grove, God continued His blessings. It seemed as if everything turned to gold, not at the touch, but at the glance. I surveyed my little world and found myself exactly where I wanted to be.

There remained, however, a new and insatiable emptiness of my life. It devoured endless hours of work and consumed leisure time with a ferocious appetite. Restlessness was at its heart and anger was its fruit.

At the end of my first eighteen months at Oak Grove, I was forced to one inescapable conclusion. Something was wrong

—very wrong — in my Christian walk. Regardless of how many times I "rededicated my life to Christ," things seemed to be getting worse.

In the summer of 1975, our first child, Travis, was born. I panicked at the added responsibility. Fear, sin, and an unpredictable anger that kept my wife constantly on edge became terrifyingly constant in my life. In the evenings, I became a pacing, sullen, withdrawn hermit; before church members, I remained warm and good-natured. The strain on our marriage was like a Goodyear stress test, and soon we were at the very breaking point. Separation seemed inevitable.

I could not seem to fill the hours in my days. Supposedly full-time at the church, I began teaching creative writing on the side, refereeing two nights a week and all day Saturday and coaching every Church athletic team I could. Insomnia became a curse and when I did sleep, I was haunted by horrible, violent nightmares. Soon followed the telltale seasons of deep, morbid depression. Those for whom depression has never been a reality cannot conceivably know its horror. I do not mean times of feeling flat emotionally because this or that went wrong. By depression, I speak instead of a great black cloud which inexplicably looms up, out of the swamp and engulfs its victim in a paralyzing nightmare of the soul.

Finally, the restlessness would not be satisfied. At night, I would wait until my wife was asleep, and then leave the house. Many nights I have gotten in my car and driven until it was impossible to drive further. Circling Atlanta on its perimeter highway (I-285), time after time, I would drive until fatigue came. After sleeping in my car for a few hours in some empty parking lot, I would go to my office, shave and go make visits in the name of the Church.

Sins I thought I had conquered in junior high school came crowding back into my life. Victory seemed so unreal to me that I became quite skeptical of it, not only in my life, but in the testimonies of others.

One of the real mistakes in judgement common to most backsliders is the assinine notion that sin can be negotiated with. My good friend, Dr. Henry Gore, a fabulous musician (and head of the math department at Moorehouse College in Atlanta) sings a song which says it well. "Don't let the Devil ride, 'cause if you let him ride, he's gonna want to drive."

I found myself at 28, an ordained elder in the United Methodist Church, struggling, not only for my sanity and my marriage, but for control of my own life. I knew I was losing. Then finally, predictably, I fell to the most desperate kind of sin. I developed a secret life of real depravity and the carefully manicured public appearance of an upstanding and theologically proper evangelical pastor. Looking back on it now, I cannot imagine how I hid any of this from my church.

In the midst of such inner turmoil, God brought His message of full salvation to me in a most unlikely way. If I had discussed theology with Dr. Charles Boleyn for five minutes, I never would have gone to Oak Grove.

If there was anything I hated worse than a "liberal," it was a "Charismatic." I adamantly denied any such experience as a "second work of grace." I mainly lumped all the Charismatics, Pentecostals, and Westleyan Holiness types together and dumped them in the same garbage pail. (I still maintain they all have more in common than they choose to admit.)

I saw myself as preaching a nicely laundered, highly palatable, conservative evangelicalism. I was a Southern Baptist in Wesleyan sheepskins. I considered the Holiness and Charismatic ilk to be an embarrassment to all "true defenders of the cross." I mean, there we were on the firing line against the **liberals**, and all the theological dingbats were just making the battle tougher.

At Oak Grove, I found in the senior pastor the shock of my life. I expected him to be the typical "business as usual" ex-District Superintendent. Instead, I discovered 14 carat, solid gold, 100 proof, Holy Ghost Charismatic. To add to my consternation, he was on the Board of Trustees of the already suspect Asbury Seminary in Wilmore, Kentucky. As a District Superintendent, Dr. Boleyn had experienced what he called "baptism in the Holy Spirit." I did not even like the sound of it.

He began methodically, calmly, to try and introduce me to an awareness of the validity of such an experience and I responded with an absolutely unteachable spirit. I stonewalled. He kept up a steady flow of books and tracts. Some I thumbed through, others I discarded with hardly a glance.

The tapes were even more regular. The fresh pile of cassettes on the corner of my desk each Monday morning seemed like the leavings of some electronic animal having passed through in the night.

I remained, however, impervious. My carefully manicured, evangelical theological hide proved impenetrable, and my personal life worsened steadily.

By the fall of my second year at Oak Grove, I realized I was flirting with a nervous breakdown or worse. Thoughts of suicide became almost obsessive as the sense of ruthlessness and deepening depression, coupled with a rapidly degenerating marriage.

I now believe I was under attack by what might be called a "spirit of suicide." Thoughts of self-destruction came almost daily. Once, while making a pastoral call, the lady I was visiting left me alone in the living room for a moment. I discovered a child's toy pistol lying on the sofa beside me.

Something of my state of mind is revealed in the casual, absent-minded way that I put the plastic barrel in my mouth and cocked the hammer. How embarrassing to find myself looking down the barrel and into the quizzical stare of a four-year old. One can only imagine what must have been in his mind to see the preacher in such a posture.

In November, while on family holiday at my parents' home in Middle Georgia, I smuggled one of my brother's pistols into the woods, but was overtaken with such a fit of shaking, that cowardice prevented what good sense could not.

The proverbial straw that snapped things came in late November. A teenager in my youth group overdosed. I stayed at the hospital until he was out of physical danger. When he was placed in a room in the psychiatric wing, I agreed to stay with the boy. He vacillated dramatically between nightmare hallucinations and brief stages of clarity. One moment he was pointing, in horror, at snakes crawling out of the woodwork, and the next, he was clutching at me and pleading for help.

"Help me, Mark!" he would beg. "Help me, please. Don't let them come back. Pray for me. Why won't you help me?"

In his demon-haunted eyes, I was finally confronted with my own spiritual and emotional poverty. The absolute penury to which I had come was awful to me. I was filled with a self-contempt that is inexpressible.

"I can't help you, son," I said, wrenching myself out of his grasp, "I can't help myself."

At 3 a.m., in the hospital parking lot, I sat staring at my

dashboard. I decided to finally do it. I remember reasoning out that if I could make it look like an accident, it would be better all around. It was as if day dawned. Satan truly comes as an angel of light. I was clothed in a sense of well-being. I knew I had finally made the right decision.

I went onto the freeway and sped my car toward some overpass pylons. The last time I checked the speedometer, I was passing 85 MPH and climbing.

"Now," I thought, with relief. "Just turn the wheel and you are out of this thing."

I do not know what happened next. There is a period of time — five minutes or an hour, I can only guess — completely blank to me. When I came to, I was through the underpass and parked on the shoulder of the road. The car was turned off and the emergency flashers and brake were on. God had intervened! I think God simply would not have it so.

Both relief and fear flooded me at once. I was instantly drenched in a cold sweat. My hands began to shake and I was nauseated. I got out of the car and began heaving violently.

"My God," I thought, "I am totally cracking up. I nearly did it. Oh, God," I cried out, "help me. Please, God, help me."

Grasping for straws, I determined that I would resign my Methodist orders and leave the ministry. I feared scandal almost as much as suicide and I knew that I was wide open to a variety of charges.

The method of Grace, however, was more marvelous than I knew. God moved on the heart of Dr. Boleyn, my senior minister, along with a handful of other Spirit-filled pastors, to put together a conference on the Holy Spirit. Directing it totally toward ministers and importing speakers from out of the area, they found an amazing response. One hundred and fifty pastors registered. But not I.

The very title of the Conference irritated me — **Conference on Power for Ministry Today**. I did not know what a conference on the Holy Spirit was, but I did **not** like the sound of that. I told Dr. Boleyn I could not attend because of a shortage of funds. He paid my way!

Trapped, angry, frustrated, and apprehensive, I showed up late for the opening session. John Wesley wrote that he went to the Adlersgate prayer service "reluctantly." If he felt half of what I did as I went through the doors of the Atlanta Ramada

Inn, he had an unparalleled gift for understatement. I hated the Conference, the motel, the other registrants and the day I was born for having brought me to such a sad state.

I harbored fleeting hopes that the speakers themselves might redeem the situation. The brochure I was handed dashed these miserably. The first was Dr. David Seamands, pastor of the Wilmore, Kentucky, United Methodist Church. He, the flyer gaily informed me, was closely connected with Asbury, also in Wilmore, and was one of the leading contemporary spokesmen for Scriptural Holiness. He was to be sharing the platform with none other than Dr. Ralph Wilkerson of the Melodyland Christian Center in Anaheim, California, one of the best known Charismatic churches in America.

I read the brochure in in sheer horror and utter disbelief. Surely, this was just a nightmare. A **Holiness and a Charismatic**! My God, I shuddered, what if someone should see me here?!

At the registration desk, I found one Lawrence Lockett. Lawrence later became my pastor and one of my closest friends. At that time, however, I thought the man was absolutely daft. I had heard through the grapevine that he was having healing services in his church. That alone was sufficient evidence in my book to have him committed.

"Hello, Lawrence," I mumbled, feeling like a lamb in a slaughterhouse. "How are you?"

"Well, I've got a little sore throat," he answered brightly. "But, I'm believing God to heal me at this Conference."

"Sore throat," I thought. "You don't even know what a real sore throat is. If I could get over that table, I'd give you a sore throat." Instead of responding, I managed a reasonable facsimile of a smile and took my name tag in bovine resignation to the fate that I knew awaited me in the conference room behind him.

One hundred and fifty pastors jammed the conference room. The only seat in the house was on the **front row**. A nice little man in spectacles sat beside me. He seemed filled with nervous energy as he thumbed through his Bible.

"We're going to have a great Conference," he said softly with a smile, patting my arm reassuringly.

"Right," I muttered, a tight-lipped smile flitting across my face for a split second.

Later, the speaker was introduced. "Now," said the moderator, "it is my pleasure to introduce a former missionary, a great pastor, and a great preacher — Dr. David Seamands."

The bespectacled little man beside me patted my arm again. "Now, pray for me," he said as he rose to go to the pulpit. I could feel the hot breath of the hound of heaven!

"My topic tonight," Dr. Seamands began, "is sin in the ministry." His sermon, using Samson as example, charted out the debilitating effects of sin on a preacher. I thought my wife had called him in Kentucky. The longer he preached, the more obvious I thought it must be to all there he meant me. He might just as well have pointed at me and proclaimed, "Here is the perfect example of just the kind of backslidden wretch of which I'm speaking." My face burned and at each jab of his finger, I slunk lower in my chair.

I have heard laymen speak of "having their toes stepped on." That little man lacerated me with a bicycle chain. By the time he had finished, all my posturing and self-defense mechanisms were totally useless. Slain by the breath of his nostrils and quivering on the front row, I clung to the hope that the benediction would surely, finally come. He did not give an invitation that first night and I got out of there alive swearing I would never go back!

My wife was still awake when I returned that night. On the twenty minute drive from the Conference, I had managed to summon enough of the old anger to arrive home full of bluster. We had sung a few hymns, heared a testimony, prayed (in English, I might add), and heard a sermon. Yet, Alison's innocent question, "How did it go?" brought a raging tirade.

"You would not **believe** what went on down there!" I ranted. "Craziness, Alison, craziness! They can call themselves Methodists if they like but they are just a bunch of crazy Pentecostals. You would really not believe what went on down there."

Finally, I stated my response to the craziness of such "goings on." "I am not going back, either," I declared! "I don't care if Dr. Boleyn did pay my way, I don't have to sit through all that." Calming only slightly, I continued. "Anyway, I couldn't go back if I wanted to. I simply **must** mow the lawn **tomorrow**."

Thank God my wife had the good sense not to point out that it was **December 5!**

28

The next morning at 8:00 a.m. sharp, I cranked my lawn-mower. I wore a heavy jacket and gloves. I could see my breath in the wintry morning air. They never said a word to me, but I suspect the sight was not wasted on my neighbors — one a Baptist and the other a Catholic.

After four or five frigid trips up and down the yard, it began to dawn on me that no grass was blowing out the side of the mower. "What am I doing?" I thought. "This is crazy! I am not **going** to be intimidated about the Holy Spirit by a bunch of jackleg Pentecostals. I know about the Holy Spirit," I reasoned. "After all, I have a four credit 'A' at the graduate level in the book of Acts."

I parked the lawnmower, showered, changed and started out of the house. My wife leaned out of the kitchen with a springtime lilt in her voice and asked, "Decide to go back?"

Absolute fury comes the closest to describing what I felt then. I never understand women. Why can't they just leave it alone? I had on a three-piece suit. Did she think I was going to change the oil?

I slammed the door on my car until the windshield rattled. "I just hope someone asks me about the Holy Spirit," I screeched into the Ramada's parking lot. I jerked the door wide, ready to open fire.

The morning session had just ended and the preachers were all astir. Something was up. I asked a fellow pastor what had happened in the morning meeting and he grabbed my lapels, "Oh, Mark!" he said, "Jesus has healed me and baptized me in the Holy Spirit." I could have been no more shocked if a frog had jumped out of his mouth. That was not this man's kind of language. It was certainly not the way I talked. I began to feel my defenses crumbling.

In the next session, I sat on the **back** row. Ralph Wilkerson was to speak and I did not want to be up front. I had never seen a real live Pentecostal up close but I knew I didn't like them. I cannot now remember for sure what I thought he would do. I suppose I had apprehensions about his rolling on the floor and foaming at the mouth. I **do** know that I knew an Asbury Holiness like David Seamands was bad enough — but, after all — what kind of man names his church Melodyland, for heaven's sake?! I did not want to get too close.

His message on "fullness" was, however, a pleasant suprise.

I listened intently for anything weird, but it really sounded rather like any other sermon on the Holy Spirit I had heard. At least, the **words** were much the same. Something in Wilkerson's confidence, and his calm assurance of God's power, I found tremendously winsome. At the end, he closed his Bible and said, "Now, I don't like to talk about the Holy Spirit in an objective way without experiencing His power. I'd like to just minister in the Spirit for a while."

He began to minister in the gifts of the Spirit in a way I have seen since in my own life and others. I had never seen anything even close to it before that day. Wilkerson, in the power of God, began to point to men whom I knew, sometimes stating clearly their physical afflictions and praying for them to be healed. Some were healed instantly. These were fellow clergymen that I claimed to love. If I had been asked only moments before if I wanted them sick, I would certainly have said "no." When they were healed, however, I was furious. Jesus came crashing through the paper walls of my snug little theological box and I was angry at the inconvenience. For years, I had declared a sort of threadbare Jesus with enough grace to forgive us, but hardly enough power or the inclination to do anything more. Now the room seemed to be **full** of a God of miracle power. Wilkerson himself was ablaze with anointing.

I burst out the door, down the steps, and into the parking lot. Anger, doubt, and confusion wrestled within me for control. For reasons I could not then understand, I returned to the conference room, only to leave again, return, and leave yet again.

Just as I started to leave, for what I swore would be the last time, Wilkerson made an unusual announcement. "Someone here has a Word of Prophecy, now. I am going to ask him to give it."

The words startled me. I had never in my life heard anyone speak of a "Word of Prophecy." I had studied I Corinthians in seminary. What did I think it meant? I cannot now recall. I thought, "If we're going to do a Word of Prophecy, I'll stay."

A less likely candidate I could hardly have imagined than the modest "liberal" who stood. His face was bleached and his voice was paper thin. "It's me," he said, spreading out his hands and facing us. "I'm not sure I understand this, but I know God wants me to say something." Then, closing his eyes and taking added force in his voice, "There's going to come a revival in North Georgia and it's beginning now in this room."

When he spoke those words, something happened in that room. The ambiance of the entire conference suddenly, violently shifted on its axis. The power of the Holy Spirit filled the room. A sense of deep conviction seemed to fall on us all.

My secret burden of conviction, sin, depression, fear, and anxiety suddenly seemed crushing. I could not escape the haunting accusation of my own life and wasted ministry. Tears filled my eyes and then gave way to great racking sobs. I dropped to my knees as if felled by some unseen hammer blow. As the weeping grew in intensity and the struggle to stop more futile, I felt more and more conspicuous. I later heard that it was happening all over the room. But at that moment it seemed that 150 pair of ordained eyes were all glued on my back.

Claude Smithmier, a Spirit-filled pastor came and knelt beside me. "Wouldn't you like for me to get one of the speakers, Mark?" he asked gently.

"Yes, Claude," I babbled, fearing that the nervous breakdown I had been dreading was beginning in earnest. In a last show of pride, I was just about to request the Methodist, when Claude departed too quickly. He returned with Ralph Wilkerson.

I steeled myself. I braced against any high-pressure Pentecostal manipulation. Instead, he did the one thing I could **not** resist. He put his arm about my shaking shoulders and he said, "My brother pastor, I love you."

If he had said anything but that, I could have resisted. If he had said any of the things I was expecting, I certainly would have been forearmed. If we would all cease trying to shake tongues out of folks and allow our words to be more informed with love, perhaps more people might receive the Holy Spirit.

"Oh, no." I blubbered. "Don't call me pastor! You don't know the condition I'm in. My life and ministry are shipwrecked. I —I'm living in terrible sin. I'm not even sure I'm saved anymore."

Wilkerson looked me hard in my eyes and then spoke with a fatherly love that I longed for. "You're a Christian. I perceive that you've prayed the sinner's prayer until you're sick of it. You just have no power. Don't you want to receive the Holy Spirit?"

Everything in me rose up against that suggestion. I hated the very sound of it — "receive the Holy Spirit" indeed! The echoes of every pitiable sermon I had ever preached against the second work of grace loomed in my ears. Every denial of miracles, every scorning word about the Gifts of the Spirit, and every mocking word against the Charismatics and the Asbury Holiness crowd filled my mind.

Yet, when I spoke, I heard myself say, "Yes! Oh, God, yes. Please help me to know this power. I want to receive the Holy Spirit." I knew my spirit had finally answered instead of my prideful, egotistical intellect. I was broken in my brokenness and the shattered pieces were finally at the feet of the Master.

Wilkerson led me in a simple prayer of full devotement. Something like, "Lord Jesus, be my Lord. I give You everything. My house. My family. My possessions." I repeated each phrase without hestitation until he prayed, "And I give You my ministry and my future. Send me anywhere."

That stuck in my throat. I knew that was very near the heart of my sin. Even more than the certainty in my life. It had always been "my ministry" and "my future." If I truly gave it to Jesus, I might spend the next forty years in some nine-point charge in South Alabama, labeled as the "Conference nut." I sensed intuitively that I was tottering on the brink of kissing my chances of being elected Bishop good-bye.

The Lord gave grace and somehow I knew that 40 years in a nine-point charge with the peace of God would be infinitely better than the high-steepled hell I was in. Just as I finished that prayer, Dr. Ralph Wilkerson reached out his hands and laying them on my head, he said with authority, "Now, receive the Holy Spirit."

In that very second, the Lord Jesus Christ poured His sanctifying grace into me in a visitation of divine presence I had scarcely ever dreamed of. I was, in that very moment, literally immersed, drenched, filled, baptized in the Holy Spirit I had blasphemed in my ignorant pride. Oh, glory to God! No tingling. No sense of electric current. No "waves of liquid love." Just the most exultant in-rush of peace, forgiveness, grace, and power I had ever known. I **knew** that the Comforter had come. The sweet Holy Spirit of Jesus had taken up residence. Receive the Holy Spirit? I did! I surely did.

Since that December 5, 1975, God has shown me miracles,

gifts, signs, and wonders. Six weeks later, my wife received the Holy Spirit. The immediate transformation of our home life was a daily miracle. My parents were soon filled with the Spirit. I have preached in many countries, travelled far, seen thousands saved, watched the crippled get up and walk and the mute speak. I have seen things the proven which I preached against for seven years.

Despite all this, however, any man anywhere who asks me what difference the sanctifying flame of this baptism has made in my life, I would not answer with any of these. I would simply say, "I am a happy man."

I suppose it doesn't sound like much of an answer, but it is **my** answer. For one who spent so long, so unhappy, it is a great work of grace.

John Wesley said, "The people are unhappy because they are unholy."

I do not have all the victory I want. I do not even have all the victory I have seen. What I have, at this writing, is more victory than I ever knew or preached was possible for a great part of my ministry.

Now there was no looking back. I had seen and tasted the River of Life. I knew immediately that I could never, ever go back again to the tasteless, unsalted "slough of despair" in which I had languished for so long.

What lay ahead I could never have imagined. All that really mattered, though, was that the nightmare behind me was swallowed up in Victory.

Chapter III
Launch Out . . .

INTO THE VINEYARD

The massive chandeliers suspended from the cathedral ceiling stared down at the heads of Oak Grove's regular Sunday morning congregation. What they saw was exactly what they saw every Sunday.

The ponderous notes of the pipe organ summoned the robed choir to their loft. The senior and associate pastors took their respective places and the rather sodden proceedings were underway.

The worship service that morning was probably not memorable for most there. But it is fixed in **my** memory. I had been baptized in the Holy Spirit only two days previous in a moment of almost terrifying grace. I could tell that my wife was watching me. I could see her stealing sidelong glances when she thought I did not notice. I knew it had been a shock to her when I returned from a conference which I had attended with clearly articulated loathing to then announce that I received an experience she had heard me preach against for seven years. Her response to this sudden, shocking change in me was what a State Department Communique would call "guarded optimism."

But as I had walked the few blocks to Sunday School that first Sunday morning after, nothing could dilute the giddy happiness that seemed to fill my whole world. The early December chill made me think of the morning only three days before when I had attempted mowing dormant winter grass in an effort to elude the conviction of Dr. Seamands' sermon. As I walked, I breathed a prayer. "Thank You. I have never before known such happiness. Thank You. But help me, **please** help me, not to be silly."

It had been years since I had felt so comfortable in His presence. The beauty of the colors that morning struck me. I realized only then how the grey cloud of depression had so veiled even my perceptions of the world. It seemed as if not only I, but all the world had been bathed. I was a young colt on a frosty morning, barely reining in the wild impulse to run and kick up my heels.

The morning service began, however, and I had not had time to think of what all this meant. I was the liturgist and Dr. Boleyn was to preach. I started the Apostle's Creed as always.

"I believe in God, the Father Almighty . . ."

I read on, the congregation droning along, but as I approached one familiar passage, my voice suddenly boomed out, "I **Believe** in the Holy Spirit!" I noticed several heads lift. One of the teenagers in my youth group stared up in naked curiosity.

Not exactly a momentous service in the history of Oak Grove. But for me, it was a soaring, exultant profession of faith. Now I knew. It had not been the over-emotionalized reaction of a neurotic trapped in a highly charged conference. The experience of the Holy Spirit baptism translated quite well outside and beyond the conference room. I did — I **really did** — believe in the Holy Spirit. Creedal recitation had given way to personal **reality**.

I had, furthermore, not just experienced the Holy Spirit in a hothouse moment. I now saw that a whole new life had begun. I had no possibility and no intention of turning back.

That night in the evening service, I preached on the Holy Spirit. It was not the first time. It was, however, the first time I preached out of the resource of a specific experience of grace, inviting others to receive it.

It was a simple sermon on Luke 11:13 which I ended with a brief testimony of the weekend conference. I had not calculated on anyone responding to that first invitation to receive the Holy Spirit. But eighteen did! As they knelt at the altar, I suddenly realized with a shock, I had not the least idea how to pray with them. When Dr. Boleyn heard me announce rather faintly that those at the altar should move into the church parlor, I could feel his eyes on me. As those eighteen dutifully arose and filed across the hall to Oak Grove's posh wedding parlor, I said a hurried benediction and followed them.

Dr. Boleyn intercepted me in the hall, "What are you doing?" he asked. "Why didn't you help those people?"

"I don't know what to do," I answered him meekly. "I guess I need you to teach me. I hadn't expected anyone to respond."

Only moments later, after Dr. Boleyn led those seekers in prayer, I found myself laying hands on people to receive a blessing which I had openly denounced only four days earlier.

The time between December and June were "Judy Holiday" months. I constantly felt like I was born yesterday. In every Bible verse, I saw the freshness of Adam's first dawn. Preaching vaulted from clever oratory to something much more akin to internal combustion. Prayer began to thaw out and for the first time in my life, I began to **want** to spend time praising and worshipping God.

When my wife was baptized in the Holy Spirit, our marriage knew a healing grace beyond our wildest dreams. Some may say that such overnight changes in life and ministry are overstated. And I would be the very first to admit that God and I still have unfinished business. It is, however, neither drama nor oversimplification to state that I was dead and Jesus raised me up; I was blind and He made me to see. Life simply changed. **Everything** about it changed from preaching to sex; and as far as I could see all in that spectrum was made gloriously **better!**

I began almost immediately to search for some theological handles on this experience. Something had happened. I knew that. And I knew that it was something glorious and wonderful and that this was of and by the Holy Spirit. Beyond that, I knew only that all my theological underpinnings had been swept away by a riptide. The conservative, evangelical, vaguely Calvinistic, dispensationalism to which I had clung for years, now seemed staid and insufficient at best, and probably downright idiotic in the face of the spiritual hurricane into which I had stepped.

Haunting Christian bookstores and libraries like the phantom of the opera, I prowled in search of help. There I found them. A whole battalion of warrior princes to whom I had never been introduced: Samuel Chadwick, Andrew Murray, Samuel Logan Bringle, A. W. Tozer, Leonard Ravenhill, and E. M. Bounds.

There were others, also, and a liberal sprinkling of contemporaries. For spice, there were testimony books by men like Harold Hill and Demos Shakarian. Yet, from the beginning, God seemed to be combining in my heart, a marriage of charismatic-holiness theology. I still believe this is where the movement of the Holy Spirit is and needs to be today.

There are some sad, blind spots and unfortunate legalistic prejudices in the classical holiness movement, especially toward the Gifts of the Spirit. And there are some obvious superficialities in some of the charismatic diggings.

If the fire and power of the Charismatics were to be informed by Wesleyan discipline and holiness-thought, it could well be the catalytic agent of yet another great awakening. The trick, of course, is for this to happen without dampening the blaze.

If the Charismatic and Holiness encampments would lay aside their petty suspicions of each other and join hands, the result could well be Holy Ghost revival.

Perhaps the truly suprising part of these early months "in the Spirit" was the immediate immersion into the ministry of a new kind. Almost from the day of the Ramada Conference, I was invited to preach or teach on the Holy Spirit or testify on my experience with Him. I was reminded of a wall plaque I saw once in an engineering firm.

"Last week I cuddent spell ingeanear — and now I are one."

The movement of the Holy Spirit among the Methodist preachers at the conference was bigger news than I or anyone else there had imagined. In an extraordinary bit of yellow journalism, an Atlanta newspaper's religious page blurted out in headline form that 150 Methodist preachers had been baptized in the Holy Spirit. This conference was later mentioned in **Love Covers** by Paul Bilheimer.

Soon, I was giving testimony at churches, revivals, and conferences at an astonishing clip. It seemed that a United Methodist pastor who confessed Spirit baptism boldly was a considerable novelty. It is news when the very one who had gone to Damascus with papers from the Chief Priest to arrest the Charismatics and bring them in chains had returned, saying, "I also am a believer."

I remember meeting one pastor at the entrance to a Holy Spirit rally in Milledgeville, Georgia, where again Ralph

Wilkerson was to preach. "What are **you** doing here?" he said with blatant inflection. Before I could answer, we were pressed inside by the crowd. I know his shock at seeing me there at all was magnified when Wilkerson called me up to give a testimony!

One group which was a great blessing during this time, and continues to be, was the Full Gospel Businessmen's Fellowship International. I believe them to be one of God's chosen instruments for revival in our generation. God has honored them with miracles because they have honored His miracle power.

I was freely accepted with none of the smug "I told you so's," that I dreaded. The refreshing esprit de corps among these laymen enveloped me. They took me from Chapter to Chapter to give my testimony. The experience in the ministry I gained in that period paid a thousand dividends. Nothing in the seminary or the pastorate had prepared me for the kinds of ministry into which God was plunging me. Those early revivals and conference meetings were "on-the-job training" in how to pray with the sick, how to lead people into baptism in the Holy Spirit, and proclaim a fullness of the Gospel I had never before preached. Such facets of ministry ought to be taught in seminary. Young people should not graduate from seminary without knowing at least something about how to give an altar call or employ Gifts of the Spirit in counseling or in conducting a healing service.

God took me from the Ramada Conference almost directly into a "remedial Seminary of the Holy Ghost." My teachers were the works of Ravenhill and Tozer and my laboratory was dozens of revivals and conferences.

The immediacy of the change in the tempo and power of ministry with the coming of the Holy Spirit was a wonderment to me. The youth group at Oak Grove which already had a good basis in evangelical faith, responded to the sudden about face in their associate pastor like metal shavings to a magnet. The beginning of revival in that group was sudden and powerful. Our spring youth retreat was only a few months after my own personal experience. About 40 senior highs jammed my sister's lake cabin in South Georgia. I shared the first night on the need for holiness of heart and life. This was to become the most sacred and precious theme of preaching to me, but was then, painfully new. I approached the teaching with the obvious timidity of a neophyte lacing it all liberally with my testimony. The young people listened eagerly but quietly. The next morning, my wife taught on prayer and at the end of her lecture, that lovely electricity filled the air. As we prayed, first one, and then another, began to weep. Prayers of repentance were called out, sobs racked young bodies and that day nearly all of them were baptized in the Holy Spirit.

Out of that small group on that retreat, there are, at this writing, eight in serious, Spirit-filled, full-time ministry, either as pastors or missionaries.

In June of that year, as Methodist pastors do, I transferred from associate at Oak Grove to Midway United Methodist Church as pastor-in-charge. This small congregation proved to be a significant appointment for me in at least one way. The congregation was fully acceptant of a Spirit-filled minister and there was no resistance to the holiness message. Prayers for healing and baptism in the Holy Spirit as well as salvation became a regular and accepted part of Midway's church life.

Even more important to the future the Lord had laid out for me, these loving people were extremely generous with my time. I was free to accept as many outside preaching engagements as I felt led. They never once complained. Later, I really put this to the test.

I had never before seriously considered any other mode of ministry except pastoring. Billy Graham and Oral Roberts had always seemed to me like some kind of ecclesiastical mutations. **Real** ministry was the pastorate; the **Methodist** pastorate. That was **all!** The Biblical notion of differing gifts — pastor, teacher, apostle, evangelist — gave way completely to my tradition which identified only **Methodist Pastor** as genuine ministry.

As I began to discover an anointing for evangelism and teaching in a new way, I also felt the stirrings of the Holy Spirit within for a new direction in ministry. I took more and more satisfaction in the revivals and conferences and felt less and less fulfilled as a pastor.

I found God's power in those early revivals like an ocean breeze in a dry and parched land. Those saved and filled with the Spirit had been touched by God in a way that I had not believed possible only months before. I began to see the sick healed by prayer. I began to learn the rudiments of ministering in the Gifts of the Spirit.

Day after day, I felt God stirring a dream in me for preaching and teaching full-time in revivals and conferences. The idea was alien to me **and** so scary that I scarcely entertained the notion at first.

Rev. Tommy Tyson (from whom I learned so much) was in a conference in Atlanta. Late one evening in his hotel room, once again with Dr. Charles Boleyn and several other veterans of the 1975 Ramada Conference, I shared the dream for the first time. I was shocked to find an immediate positive response from those present.

For nearly eighteen months, I struggled with the dream. I would lay it aside, turn away from it forever, only to pick it up again. The idea of walking away from the solid security of the Methodist pastorate (parsonage, appointment, salary, etc.) into such abysmal insecurity looked to me like going over the waterfall in a barrel.

With a few notable exceptions, this fear was aggravated by most of those with whom I talked.

"How will you eat?"

"What about your family?"

"You'll be back to the conference with your tail between your legs begging for a church and you'll have to start all over again."

Thank God for my wife, who greeted the possibility with her usual calm faith. "The only thing I ask," she said, "is that you know for **sure** that this is God's will."

Suddenly like a shadow out of the past, Jack Taylor, the summer Youth Director from Asbury who had brought me to Christ, burst again onto the stage of my life as he called me to come to Tarpon Springs First United Methodist for a youth revival.

There, very timidly, fearing horribly the rejection of this gentle man that I loved so, I shared the dream. "I'll help any way I can," was his reply. Because I find it so difficult to express the struggle I was going through on this issue, I find it almost immpossible to put into words the joy I felt at such a precious, simple acceptance.

Finally, almost distraught at the struggle to be able to tell my wife **and** myself that I knew "for sure," I began to pray, in what was for me, a most peculiar fashion.

I asked the Lord to confirm it through someone who knew nothing of my struggle. I prayed that such a someone would just walk up and say, "God says you're to go into evangelism." I prayed it every day. "Lord, either take this burden away from me or confirm it."

Absolutely no defense is offered for the unorthodox prayers in this book. I have never pretended to be George Mueller. I am convinced that if I cannot recommend such a prayer (which I don't), I can recommend a God of such infinite grace that He would condescend to hear such a prayer.

Sitting at a table at a Full Gospel Businessmen's luncheon in Atlanta in January of 1977, I prayed the prayer yet again as I had for nearly three months. This time, I prayed it less with faith than fatigue. At the close of the meeting as I stood to leave, I came face to face with Gilbert (Tom) Sawyer. We were to become friends, but in 1977 we were more like acquaintances.

"Brother Mark," he beamed, "How great to see you! We were praying for you last night at my house."

"For me, Tom, I appreciate it," I said.

He put his hands on my shoulders and said quite evenly, "Mark, we felt led to tell you that if you're considering evangelism, the Lord says go ahead. Leave your church and go."

Not, I suppose, a memorable moment for him. For me it was absolutely spine tingling. Tears sprang into my eyes and I dropped straight back into my chair. It was a thunderbolt! It was the answer to months of turmoil, agony, and prayer. I had prayed in about as juvenile a manner as possible and God, in His infinite grace, had answered exactly as I had asked.

Through the months to follow, the call to evangelism became even clearer and the vision seems to be still coming into sharper focus, but that glorious confirmatory word has never faded even for a second.

Through the remainder of that winter and spring, my wife and I continued to pray and seek counsel, but it was settled in our minds. The anointing on the ministry of evangelism and teaching seemed to immediately quicken after we made that inner commitment.

Only a week later, I shared the concept of team evangelism with a close friend, John Bohlayer.

"It sounds great," he said. "I like the idea. But what are you going to call it?"

This very question had crossed my mind more than once. Alone in my office, I would sometimes say **The Mark Rutland Association** into a mirror. It sounded silly and I felt that if I could not take it seriously, perhaps no one else could. But no alternative occurred to me.

When I answered John boldly, "The Trinity Foundation," I was more suprised than he. I had no memory of ever thinking or saying the phrase before that moment. It sounded perfect! Not the ministry of one man but a team — a foundation to preach, give, serve, teach, and evangelize.

A week later, while speaking at a Holy Spirit rally in Porterdale, Georgia, I was given the offering. The following day, I deposited the entire amount, $103.28, in a bank account named the Trinity Foundation. The bank teller's request for a list of the corporate officers caught me short.

"Uh — how many do you need?" I asked with an ineloquence born of total ignorance of such matters.

"All that you have," was her curt reply.

I coolly listed myself as President and Secretary and my wife as Vice-President and Treasurer. Drawing myself to my full height and ignoring her raised eyebrows, I marched out of the bank as though I had deposited a million dollars in a Swiss bank account.

It was an inauspicious beginning, to say the least, but I refused to allow my spirits to be dampened by a supercilious bank employee.

As my steps to leave the pastoral ministry became more definite, the responses of others became more pronounced. I was disappointed that my fellow clergymen had little encouragement for my plan.

It should not have been. Until I began to seriously consider a specialized type of service, I had understood ministry solely in terms of the local pastorate. It is extremely unfortunate that many modern pastors regard evangelists with suspicion and fear, assuming an adversarial position instead of embracing and using this complementary New Testament gift to advantage.

More than one pastor friend has asked me why I **"left the ministry."** The modern evangelist among the mainline denominations is a square peg in a round hole. He is often branded offhand as an iconoclast or malcontent who "couldn't make it" in the pastoral ministry. Sometimes the evangelist is even considered a troublemaker because his methods or means may vary from standard Sunday morning procedure.

Once, on the third night of his revival, one pastor ordered me to cease giving altar calls! When I refused but offered to go home and let him finish the week, he shouted that I was trying to embarrass him before his congregation. Another pastor in North Georgia asked me to cancel a scheduled revival in his church. I said, "No, Brother, but you are certainly free to do so." He promptly informed his congregation that he had received a letter from me canceling. When the discrepancy came to light, several families left the church and I was charged with being divisive.

One humorous conversation came several years later when a pastor met me in a restaurant to inform me that serious charges had been laid at my door. I was flabbergasted when he asked, "Is there any truth to the rumor that you are about to proclaim yourself a bishop and start ordaining preachers?"

"No," I replied, "that's absurd! I'm skipping right over the small stuff like bishop — I'm calling myself an Apostle and start consecrating bishops."

He suprised me with a burst of laughter, then, getting control of himself and casting a wary eye around at the other patrons, he said, "My God! Don't joke, Mark, you're in trouble."

The perennial controversy, rumors, and charges always seemed to come to nothing, however, and God's anointing on the revivals seemed to grow yearly. I thank God for the encouragement and love of **many** wonderful Spirit-filled pastors. Their support and faith in my ministry were rewarding. The fellowship of such true-hearted soldiers of the cross has been one of the great joys of my life.

The invitations also grew. It became evident that soon I would have to decide between evangelism and parish ministry. I went to the District Superintendent with my hopes for full-time evangelism.

"What I want to know, Sir," I asked, "is — will you help me?"

I still laugh today when I remember his answer. "Yes," he said, staring into my eyes. "And I'll tell you why. I don't know who you are. Someday you may write a book, and I don't care to be remembered as the guy who stood in your way."

He not only did not stand in my way, but proved to be a tremendous help. He met with my entire congregation to work out an arrangement for me to continue as pastor while pursuing evangelism at the same time. He appointed my wife, who had earned a Methodist License to Preach, as my associate pastor. The church, in turn, hired a youth minister and a choir director and gave me permission to be away up to three weeks a month!

This amazing agreement afforded me the luxury of time to make at least some kind of preparation for being without salary or parsonage. What grand encouragement I found in that church! Instead of begrudging my time away, they honestly saw themselves as making an investment in a wider work.

In my last year at Midway, I preached 29 revivals, in addition to the pastoral work. The pace, I thought killing at the time, proved a mere warm-up for the years to follow. Since 1978, I have averaged 450 sermons a year, including one year of more than 500.

I would not trade the fatigue and hectic pace of that first year (or the years since) for ten thousand decades of leisure. That year, though exhausting, was worth a seminary education.

One lesson came to me at a tiny church in Alabama. I had finished two weeks in Kentucky and Mississippi only the night before and driven all day to get there. Winding back a dirt road, I drove up before a small white-framed chapel draped in evening shadows. I was weary and the sight of the handful of cars and pickups in the churchyard seemed a dreary one indeed. I peeked through the window at about twenty elderly people sitting silently waiting for service to begin. The greying pastor leaned against the piano listlessly thumbing a tattered Cokesbury hymnal.

I was filled with self-pity. I determined to make a little homily on love and try to find a motel, when the Holy Spirit brought me up short. The Word of the Lord was so clear to me in that moment, and so arresting, that I have never forgotten it. "The moment you are too big to minister to a few, you are too small to minister to many."

Occasionally the road has brought some painful moments. I had to leave for a revival in Waycross, Georgia, with my wife dreadfully sick. Alison's fever was so high, she probably should have been hospitalized. We had to farm the three children out to friends. When I wavered, my wife was firm.

"I'm going to call and cancel," I said.

"No, you're not!" she said, forcing herself up on one elbow. "We've always been in this together. I'll be fine. Now you go. Don't worry about the kids. They think it's a vacation."

I looked at her there, flushed with fever, trembling with weakness and smiling bravely past a splitting headache. I knew again what a priceless treasure I had in her. By His grace, I have never missed a preaching engagement due to sickness. The pace has been unbelievable. There have been times when my body, mind, and spirit had a difficult time arriving at the same place at the same time. I once awakened in a hotel room and couldn't remember where I was. I lay there, looking around at a hotel room that looked like a thousand others. After only a few moments I remembered, but in those few moments, I had quite a panicky feeling.

Through it all, however, I have seen the providence and power of God as I never dreamed I would. My clearest recollection of those early years are ones of **revival**.

Chapter IV
Launch Out . . .

INTO THE WINE

His sobs and shouts pathetically ripped the air in the packed chapel as he plunged up the aisle toward the altar.

"Oh, my God," he cried out. "Oh, my God! Help me."

He did not kneel. He collapsed. The altar shivered under the weight of his huge, muscular body. His response was to prove a match to dry tender.

The early evening had hardly suggested the spiritual outpouring that midnight. This, like all other United Methodist Men's retreats, was filled with hundreds of businessmen in boyish good spirits. Ralph Freeman's stunning tenor voice and beautiful spirit electrified the men and they responded by singing the hymns with enthusiasm.

The MC for the evening was a tanned physician, grinning good-naturedly at his own obligatory doctor jokes and the camaraderie was good. When the platform speaker began, however, the proceedings took an immediate and obvious nose dive. A professional public speaker from the Midwest, his message was on a Spiritual plane with the tasteless "mystery meat" and instant potatoes served earlier in the cafeteria. It was obvious from the onset that he was accustomed to making brief, well decorated motivational talks to the Kiwanis clubs and touchdown banquets.

In front of these eager, spiritually hungry laymen, he was about as stirring as chopped liver. His tired one-liners and pathetic theological pronouncements drew naught but stoney stares. His understanding of Christianity seemed to be an absurd mixture of broad-minded tolerance, middle-class Americanism, and musty quotations from Tennyson.

The man seated next to me suddenly said, a trifle too loudly for comfort, "Brother Mark, this man's not even saved!"

The scheduled late night chapel service was an attempt to introduce a Spirit-filled type of worship experience into the program of the men's weekend and I had been asked to speak. Since only a handful of diehard "Charismatics" were expected to attend any service that would not even begin until 11:00 p.m., the small chapel had been chosen as the site.

I arrived at the chapel to find it packed with men and filled with an air of anticipation. Almost as many as were inside jammed the windows and doorways outside. When a steady rain started, I had no doubt that we would immediately lose those huddled at every opening. A few umbrellas sprang open but most just stood in the rain. If anyone left, I did not see them.

The anointing upon the gathering was powerful. The testimonies were fresh and the praise was more lively and genuine than many of these men had ever seen. Ralph Freeman, Henry Gore, and Les Connell sang before I was to preach. Instead of preaching, I simply gave my testimony. As it always was and is for me, sharing those deeply personal, immensely troubled years of suicidal depression and spiritual blindness was salt in an old wound. The sting of the memories combined ruggedly with the naked humility of telling these nightmares to strangers. As He had done so many times before, God honored it. Magnificently!

Those men hung desperately on every word. Their eyes! I have noticed so many times that when the anointing of the Holy Spirit is very powerful in a service, the room seems to be full of hungry eyes. Tears coursed down the sin-hardened faces of the tired businessmen. It is a scene I have never forgotten. When I gave the invitation for salvation and baptism in the Holy Spirit, there was a sort of corporate pause. It seemed as though the hundreds of men drew a collective breath in anticipation of the next forty-five minutes of spiritual power.

Suddenly that burly truck driver plummeted down the aisle, shouting as he came. In seconds the old chapel was all movement and sound. Dozens of men, equally, if not as visibly broken as he, filled the entire altar. Others fell on their faces in the aisles and across the front. Men pressed in from the outside.

The sounds of weeping, praying men were bathed in sweet praise as Les Connell led in choruses. Before the last of them departed for the cabins, nearly a hundred men and at least six pastors had prayed for either salvation, baptism in the Holy Spirit, or both!

A hundred miles north of Atlanta is Canton, Georgia, a modest county seat town. It is an unremarkable, quiet mill town on the edge of Appalachia. The First United Methodist Church is a stately brick edifice just off the town square. The congregation seemed to epitomize middle-class, traditional Methodism. The equally traditional sanctuary with its padded dark wood pews and unused balcony seemed an unlikely site for Holy Spirit pyrotechnics. They exploded, however, almost from the call to worship.

The Sunday morning service was stodgy and the pastor seemed on edge. We had first met in his study just moments before the service. His opening line was unforgettable.

"I'm no Charismatic," he said, "and everybody I've talked to says I'm crazy to let you in my church. But my evangelism committee wanted you. Do anything or preach anything you want. I'm leaving here at conference. This church is in such a shape now I expect you could only help."

I stole a quick glance at Les Connell, my song leader. He is a precious Christian with an almost unflappable spirit. His thin smile and deep blue eyes were as inscrutable as ever. Oh God, I thought, please help me to be more like Les. He never seems to be shaken by **anything**.

"Let's believe God for a revival," was all I managed.

A flash of irritation went across the pastor's face and for a second he was silent.

"Yeah, fine," he said.

One brief perfunctory prayer later, we were out and into the service. What we found there I hardly expected. I was immediately aware of a good spirit in the house. The people were jovial and responded well to Les' song leading. Someone, I thought, has been praying here.

Among the first to the altar at my invitation was this same petulant pastor, Newton Scott. He broke there before God as sweetly and as finally as I have ever seen. His wife was beside him.

When I knelt before them, he said, "Brother Mark, help me.

48

I'm filled with anger and pride and hurt. My marriage and my ministry are both about shot." I certainly identified with **that**.

"We have even been separated," his wife said. "I came to church this morning hoping **something** would happen in this revival."

The middle-aged pastor and his wife received the baptism of the Holy Spirit together that morning and God's healing power touched that marriage in a precious way. The Spirit of Christ filled his ministry and his home at that very moment.

When the others at the altar had been dealt with and prayed through and the last praise chorus had been sung, the tearful pastor stood before his people.

"I've got something to say, now," he said, wiping the last tears from his eyes. "Today I have received the Holy Spirit. I've got a brother who has been talking to me about this for years. I always thought it just wasn't for me. Today, I can say, it **is** for me. My life, my marriage, my future, and my ministry all date from right now. I feel like I've wasted 35 years of ministry. I'm sorry. I'm sorry for the years I've wasted here. But now I'm ready to start."

"Praise the Lord!" he suddenly shouted. "Praise the Lord!" I looked at his wife with tears streaming down her face. She embraced a woman in the church with whom I later discovered she had been in a daily covenant of prayer. I looked over the faces of his shocked congregation. Men were wiping their eyes. Many were embracing.

"Put the word out," the pastor continued. "God's doing a new thing here."

Evidently they took him at his word. That night, the balcony was filled to overflowing. Some had come out of curiosity, and some in sincere desire to see a move of God. Even more had come as a result of the invitation of those who had caught fire that morning.

I have seen this as a necessary pattern of continuing revival anywhere. Revival is fire. If the flame is to continue, fresh wood must be added. Those who are touched in one service must become a Holy Ghost press gang with an absolute passion to see others inflamed as well. It is my experience that a very real part of any true outpouring of the Holy Spirit is a fresh hatred for unfilled pews and empty balconies.

That hatred certainly packed Canton's First United Methodist Church through those nights. Each evening's congregation grew in number and in liberal response to the messages. Service after service, the altar filled with seekers.

A respected physician in the town came only to pacify his Christian wife. On Sunday night, Jesus caught hold of Harry's heart and saved him gloriously. On Tuesday night, he was baptized in the Holy Spirit. Thursday's healing service found this very doctor moving about behind those seeking healing prayer. His excitement and eagerness at laying hands on the sick were obvious, but I also picked up on something else. When our eyes met over the head of one seeker, I saw what I took to be confusion.

"Are you OK?" I asked him.

"Yeah," he said sort of vacantly. "I'm fine. It's just — just that I don't know myself anymore. Sunday morning I hardly believed in God. Now I'm laying hands on my own patients for healing."

Among the many visitors at these revival services was the president of a nearby college. He was an ex-missionary and an old friend. Charles Stanley of First Baptist in Atlanta had been scheduled for that semester's opening convocation. When Stanley cancelled, the college president asked me to fill in. Since the convocation fell on the Wednesday of the revival, I was happy to accommodate.

Twelve students at that college chapel service were baptized in the Holy Spirit. Four others accepted Christ as Saviour. They responded to their own blessings by bringing others. Among those in the altar that night at Canton were seventeen students from Reinhardt. On Thursday night, twenty-three more students crowded the altar.

After the service on Thursday, I met with some students and faculty from Reinhardt to encourage them to bring others for Friday's final meeting. One professor borrowed a church bus and herded in sixty-seven Reinhardt students. The forty or fifty who responded that night brought the total number of college students in Canton's altar in three nights to more than eighty. This was in addition, of course, to the church members, townfolk, and visitors. Revival, like fire, has the wonderful property of spreading from rooftop to rooftop.

Lindale, Georgia, a suburb of Rome, is also a mill town. The town is row upon row of tidy white houses laid out neatly around a central mill, rather like the tents of the Hebrews around the Tabernacle. In many such mill towns, the Methodist church is a benign participant in the status quo. Not in Lindale!

Pastor Gene Collum, a Spirit-filled man of genuine and uninhibited faith, intended to see REVIVAL! Seldom have I worked alongside a pastor with such a thirst for a genuine move of God among his people. He mounted a great prayer campaign and mobilized his people to fill their sanctuary with those in need of the Gospel.

A series of services scheduled to run five nights burst into flame and ended only two weeks later. In those two weeks, 135 souls came into the Kingdom and 140 received the Holy Spirit. News of what was happening in the Lindale church spread faster than we could have dreamed. Visitors came seeking God's power from Alabama, Florida, and Tennessee. Pastor Collum was moved by the Spirit to open a 24-hour telephone line to receive prayer requests. Calls came from several states including Hawaii and God gave some miraculous answers to prayer.

In all the thrilling excitement of a revival, individuals and splendorous little moments tend to be forgotten in favor of more generalized memory. Often one exits such sessions of refreshing with a kind of golden glow that recalls the ambience and not the specific victories. Two of the Lord's sweeter blessings in Lindale simply refuse to be lost in the shuffle.

A little boy of about 10 appeared in the altar one night for prayer. His eyes were red and swollen with conjunctivitis. They looked absolutely awful. The boy was one of those touching waifs who, without any benefit of parental direction, seem somehow aware that God is the answer to all his needs. In every church I pastored, I saw them. They are pathetic little hungry ones that walk from trailer parks and ride church buses trying to find God in spite of the madness of their homes.

"I heard there was a meeting here, Mister," he drawled. "An' I come. Here I am."

"Good for you," I smiled.

"Well, I guess what I need tonight is my eyes fixed," he said as matter-of-factly as if he had called to a teacher for assistance on a stubborn math problem.

My initial reaction was to lecture him that only God can heal

51

and deny any power in myself. But as I stared into his sad, little eyes with their bloodshot whites and infected membranes, I knew he did not want or need a theology lesson. He just wanted help, and he had come to the clearest light he could see.

Pastor Collum, several others, and I laid hands on the lad and prayed. Almost immediately, his eyes began to heal! When he opened them, they were obviously better. Right there! The light in his eyes showed he knew something was happening.

"Are you saved, Son?" I asked as gently as I could.

"No, Sir."

"Pray with me now and give your life to Jesus. He'll save you right now," I said.

He softly prayed the sinner's prayer with me. "Thank you, Sir," was all he said. We embraced and he left.

It was only the next evening that we heard about him. He had awakened the next morning completely healed and deeply aware of his salvation. For hours he walked the streets of Lindale alone knocking on door after door and to everyone that would listen, he simply declared what God had done for him.

One woman tearfully reported to me his visit to her house. I opened the door and there he stood.

"Yes, what do you want," she said.

"Don't want nothing," he said."I just wanted to show you what God has did fer me. Last night, I went down to the revival at the Methodist church with pink eye real bad. God healed me! Then he saved me. If I died right now, I'd go to heaven."

"Well — uh, that's fine, isn't it?" she stammered.

"Yes, that's fine," he said, with that terrible bluntness of a ten-year old. "Are you saved, Lady? Please come tonight."

She did. That night she took Christ as her Saviour and told me the story. "A little child shall lead them." I weep to think of all the poor pastors pouring hours into Madison Avenue schemes to motivate unsaved, unsanctified congregations to take part in visitation programs. But let one little lad get a touch of supernatural, Pentecostal power on his life and he will show them all up for the hollow frauds they are.

One morning in Lindale's local restaurant, Pastor Gene Collum and I were served by a waitress hobbling about like a lion with a thorn. Each halting step brought a grimmace of pain to her face.

"It's broken," she moaned when she saw us. "I fell in the

back and heard it snap. The pain is awful but I just **can't** go to the hospital until the breakfast rush is over."

Rev. Collum and I, along with two or three others, prayed for the girl then and there. At the close of the prayer, she tentatively put pressure on the foot. Gradually joy and surprise spread across her face as she put her full weight on it. "It's gone," she gasped. "The pain is gone! It's healed. It's really healed." She literally skipped with joy.

Nothing would do but that she tell the whole thing to every customer all day. She had no doubt that God had healed a broken ankle on the spot. All I know is that she was hurting before we prayed and she was dancing after.

It should be clear that these are prayer-bought seasons of refreshing in local churches — not mass crusades put together with the benefit of an evangelistic organization and a large budget. I have found such a sense of the **reality** of God's power in His taking hold of small, awkward, unpromising situations and bringing a victory, not necessarily a headline, out of what seemed to afford only defeat.

I have found a precious delight in seeing the revival power of God move in unlikely settings.

While preaching in Sunday services at the First United Methodist Church in one southern city, I accepted an invitation to conduct an early afternoon meeting at a tiny church in the countryside. There was just barely time to hold a 3:00 p.m. service and make it back in time for the one at 7:00 p.m.

I prayed while I drove and felt deeply impressed to preach a salvation message and give an altar call.

When I arrived, I found a total congregation of twelve elderly folks. The airless little building was stiffling in the August heat. Several bottle flies and wasps cavorted overhead with a good deal more energy than the congregation displayed. The service was utterly lifeless. Why people continue to attend such crypts is beyond me. I thought it a victory that no one was stung by a wasp.

All my resolve to give an altar call for salvation dissolved in the face of the dozing stoicism of twelve ancient faces and the lay pastor with less life than the bottle flies. The Spirit remained emphatic as always in His insistence upon obedience. Hardly ever in the history of the church has a preacher given an invitation with less faith. But God is careful to watch over His Word and to perform it.

All twelve present knelt at the altar. As I went from one to the next, I heard them each say essentially the same thing. They were all church members and all were baptized. Several had been charter members of that church. Yet none had ever been born again! Oh, the rejoicing as all twelve wept around that altar and prayed together, in unison for salvation. And, oh, how I wept, too! Sometimes I think my whole life can be understood in terms of learning to trust God when I can see nothing. It seems, also, that I am a slow learner.

The "bottom line" in meetings is souls. A small city crusade in Dalton, Georgia, taught me a great deal. The crusade had been put together by laymen and drew both good crowds and the ire of pastors. I had more trouble and grief with the mainline pastors of Dalton than any place I have ever been. One precious Methodist pastor gave his support. Apart from him, the only others pastors in the rented hall were Pentecostals. One large Methodist church in town even refused to allow the **nursery** to be kept there.

The crowds were excellent, however, and grew each night. Our children's crusade in an adjacent auditorium drew nearly 300 children. The response at the altar in the main auditorium was a magnificent manifestation of God's power. We watched as Jesus healed, saved, and delivered.

I especially recall two touching moments. One of the altar counselors came to me, white-faced, after the service. He gingerly held a pistol in his hand. A young man on his way to commit suicide had come into the balcony that night and there Jesus sought him out. At the altar, he gave his life to God and his revolver to the counselor.

Equally as touching was the night a woman waited until the hall was empty of all but a few counselors and staff. Gee Sprague, our youth and music evangelist, brought her down front where we were getting ready to lock up.

Her poverty was obvious and that painful dullness of eye betrayed her mental retardation even before she spoke.

"This young lady wants you to pray with her," Gee said. It was no suprise to me that she had approached sensitive and gentle Gee. He has always had such a sweet, "Barnabas" nature.

"I ain't saved," she announced.

"Why didn't you come at the altar call?" I asked.

"Oh, no," she said in shock at such a suggestion. "I couldn't do that. Them folks wouldn't want us in thar alongside them."

The humility and simplicity of her answer was an arrow in my heart. I felt that arguing the tolerance of the other seekers was useless.

"Come, then," I said. "Come now and kneel here with us. **We** want you here and Jesus wants you."

"What about my brother?" she asked. "He wants to be a Christian, too."

"Where is he?" Gee asked.

"Back there," she motioned with a toss of her head. "He'll come if'n I call him. He's retarded. Me, too, if you didn't know. Since our people died, we stayed together. He can't work but I do." This last brought the slightest note of pride to her voice and eyes.

"Go and get your brother," I said.

She motioned with her hand and from out of the shadows at the back came a pitiable young man in an ancient army surplus trenchcoat. It must have been three sizes too large and hung about his body tent-like. A shapeless hat hung low over his brow and the three or four days of scraggly growth on his gaunt face would have given him a rather fearsome countenance had it not been for his little boy eyes peering out so guilelessly. He came slowly to stand by his sister.

"Do you want Jesus to come into your heart?" I asked.

He nodded carefully and we all three knelt at the deserted altar. I wish I had a photograph of Les and Gee and several counselors and me kneeling in that darkened auditorium leading a retarded brother and sister in the prayer of salvation. The young man barely moved his lips, only whispering the words after me. I wondered if he understood anything of what was happening. When we stood up he said his first words.

"Now when I die, will I go to heaven with Jesus and see my Mommy again?"

"Yes, you will," I assured him.

He slowly took my hand and shook it up and down twice very firmly, just as his Mommy had taught him, I'm sure.

"Thank you, Mister," he said.

Those two came back every night. They sat quietly on the back row of the balcony. They did not want to intrude.

Sometimes in a revival meeting, it is what happens after the benediction that is the most memorable. At the Marietta, Georgia, camp meeting one night, I was standing near the altar telling a group of friends goodnight. Gradually, the Holy Spirit made me very aware of a girl in her twenties, listening just on the edge of that group. She had one of those hard, painted faces that seemed to just announce SIN to the whole world.

I turned to her and looked her right in the eyes. "You need Jesus' grace don't you?"

"Yes, I do," she answered without a second's delay.

"Give Him your life," I began, my boldness suprising me less than her. "Turn away from sin. It's ruining your life anyway. Isn't it? Aren't you sick of sin and sinful people?"

Instead of the resistance and self-defense I expected, she just slumped and began to cry. Nodding her head without a word, the tears making tracks in her makeup, she looked fully broken. We all sort of gravitated as a group toward the altar to pray with her. I noticed as we did that she carefully removed her shoes. That touching, spontaneous, unfeigned, unlearned act of Biblical propriety touched me at the center of my heart. Would to God that all the overdressed, country club sophisticates in America could be as convinced of sin as she. How many have left fancy communion rails with sin **and** shoes unremoved?

Early in 1977, I had a dream which I sensed at the time, came from God. It was an odd dream and I could see no great meaning in it, but I am grateful now that I shared it with my wife over breakfast the next morning.

In my dream, I was waiting in a small room, hardly more than a closet. I knew that I was waiting to preach but I had no idea where I was. Several men were with me there but I did not know them. To my delight, Dr. John Brokhoff, an old friend and one of my seminary professors when I was at Candler, stuck his head in the door and spoke. "I just wanted you to know that I was here." Then, he was gone.

Seconds later, I was whisked out the door and into the strangest meeting room I have ever seen. There were several quite remarkable aspects to the architecture and decor. I entered, as it were, on the ground floor and the congregation was seated in tiers high above me. There were row upon row of unusually designed, high-back pews. Strangest of all was that they seemed stacked clear to the ceiling and arranged in the most bizarre kinds of angles as one might expect in a dream. I saw myself preaching standing on a bare floor, staring up at rows of faces, seemingly arranged impossibly up the walls.

Alison and I laughed together as I shared the dream. "Well," she said. "One thing about it. When it comes to pass, you'll **know** it was from God because I've never heard of any kind of church like that."

Nearly six years later, I was invited to speak at a Candler School of Theology Chapel program. Les Connell and I were at that time conducting a weekly devotional program for Candler students, but neither of us had been in the new Cannon Chapel built long after we had graduated. I was thrilled, of course, at the opportunity to preach to Candler's student body (at least those who attended Chapel) and I was pleased to see the brand-new building.

The morning of the Chapel service, I was met by a student who took me to a small sacristy where I waited for the service to begin. Several brother pastors and Les crowded in with me for prayer. Now as I recall the men in that room, I realize that I did not know **any** of those men in 1977. After a few moments, the student reappeared and Les and I followed him into Cannon Chapel. I sat heavily in the chair offered me and tried not to stare with my mouth open.

I realized immediately that I was staring at the unlikely sanctuary of my dream. Cannon Chapel, more than anything, resembles a surrealistic train depot. Concrete abutments and pillars support high-backed pews in odd little balconies that seemed to reach right to the ceiling. After Les sang, I preached standing in the floor and peering up at the rows of faces in high-backed pews.

I spoke with great liberty as I realized that God in His infinite grace had revealed this very room and site to me five years before it was conceived by an architect. The Lord showed me the men who would meet with me in the sacristy before I ever met them, and showed me Dr. John Brokoff's face in order to clearly identify the place as Candler. What a mighty God we serve!

I preached on "an unction from the Holy One," and seventeen Candler students came and knelt on bare, carpetless floor.

As I laid hands on them to be filled with the Holy Spirit, I was filled afresh. Seventeen seminarians at a liberal seminary weeping and seeking the Holy Spirit in a chapel without even an altar rail for kneeling.

Nothing in my future will come as a suprise to God. What a precious grace He shows when, from time to time, He lifts the curtain in order that I might know "He ordereth my footsteps."

This became increasingly wonderful to me as the trail led far away from the pristine chapels of modern America.

Chapter V
Launch Out . . .

BEYOND THE PARISH

The deafening drone of the Aztec's twin engines inhibited conversation in the tiny cabin. I took the time to meditate on the confusing events that had put me with two Baptist preachers and three laymen (only one of whom I had ever met before) in an airplane bound for Mexico.

The adventure, or misadventure, as I now began to think it was, had begun with a phone call from one Frank Philips. Frank was a wealthy Atlanta businessman with one of the most uninhibited loves for Jesus I have ever witnessed. He was big, brash, bold, and totally real. Frank Philips was a Holy Ghost will-o-the-wisp; windblown, wild, woolly, and wonderfully dedicated to seeing the last of my strict conservative Methodist shell cracked wide open.

"Brother Mark," he fairly shouted into the phone, "we're going to Mexico in two weeks."

"What in the world are you talking about, Frank?" I asked. I knew who it was by his voice, though never once did he introduce himself over the phone. He just began to talk.

"Mexico! It's just south of Texas, Preacher."

"I know that, Frank," I said. "But who is we?"

"We is us!" he laughed. "You and I and a couple of other guys are going to Mexico."

"**We** are not going," I said bluntly. "I can't just take off to Mexico. I'm pastoring a church out here whether you realize it or not. Anyway, I couldn't possibly afford it."

"Don't you worry about money," he announced. "This one's all on me. And don't worry about your church. I 'spect the Lord

59

can handle it for a week. God told me to go to Mexico and He told me to take you. Now you get a passport and I'll call back with the details. Glory to God!"

With that, he simply hung up. I tried to tell my confused wife about the trip, but I realized I knew no more than she. Where were we going in Mexico? What were we going to do there? How were we going to get there? Why me?

Somehow I felt resigned to it. I suppose I thought it was easier to go than to argue with Frank Philips. I swallowed my questions and dutifully got the passport.

Now, as we neared the Beaumont, Texas airport, I knew this was crazy. I had been informed that we were going to visit an independent missionary couple, Jim and Helen Mann, in Ciudad Victoria. I had a small suitcase, a Bible, and a passport. It was hot. I felt sick. I did not want to be in Beaumont, Texas, and I wanted to be in Mexico even less.

When we took off from Beaumont for the last leg of the flight, my stomach stayed on the runway. Within minutes of being airborne, I began to vomit. I spent the next four hours with my face in a sack. I literally vomited or dry-heaved for four hours. At first, I prayed to be healed. Then I prayed to die. The other men in the plane must have longed to throw me overboard. All conversation ceased. The only sound in the cabin was me. The only smell was utterly awful to everyone.

As soon as the wheels touched down at Victoria's tiny airfield, I stopped immediately. Yet I remained weak, sick, and embarrassed. I have seen so many others healed, but after four hours of prayer between heaves, I would frankly have welcomed a plane crash. In any confusion, however, God will still be God.

Finally, the door opened and Mexico's air invaded the Aztec with blast furnace heat. The blinding sun on the runway and desert caused us to exit like moles poking our heads above ground for a stolen and painful glance at the atmosphere. I came down the steps like a drunk. I was literally green.

There stood an American couple I took to be in their early sixties. He was bald and his limp was obvious. She was a tiny lady with a dazzling countenance and sparkle in her eyes. They were introduced as Jim and Helen Mann.

Helen looked the whole group over and turned her eyes directly on my weary, pea green face. "You," she said, pointing straight at my nose. "God has called you to missions and sent you to Mexico."

The statement seemed absolutely ludicrous. And it triggered just a little anger. "No, Ma'am," I stated rather too loudly. "I don't know who you think I am, but I am not he." I could hear a slight frantic quiver in my voice but couldn't stop. "No! I'm here to visit. Just visit!" Finally I just trailed off and the others made light of it, but Helen Mann's twinkling eyes bothered me.

Before we finally made our way to their little mission house in Victoria, I was reeling from the effects of the trip. The smell of Mexico's constant cloud of diesel exhaust and 130 degree heat combined for the knockout punch. Later as I lay on the back bed listening to muted chatter and the clink of dishes as the others ate supper, I felt utter disgust for myself. Missionaries, I reasoned, must be built of sterner stuff than I. Finally I dozed off only to be awakened by Jim Mann's gentle voice.

"All right, Mark, it's time to go," he said, sitting on the side of the bed. "Are you feeling any better?"

"Oh, yes," I lied. I liked this old man very much. The gentleness in his face and voice, the reassuring smile in his eyes, even the limp, were to become very precious to me over the years. I found in Jim Mann a depth of spirit and a supreme practicality that combined to produce a fit role model for any missionary. He knew how to pray and believe God while employing his own resources without reservation.

"Well," he said, "let's go to Laborcitas."

The village of Laborcitas, about ten miles from Victoria, was row upon row of tiny stick and mud huts with thatched roofs. They inelegantly lined the dirt roads and dotted the scrubby woods. Some could only be reached by foot paths. Children played in grassless yards defined by stick fences. Chickens, pigs, and burros roamed at will. Cook fires supported smoke pillars, and rope lines of drying clothes gaily decorated the palm and mesquite groves. The countryside seemed to take no offense at the poverty-stricken little village. The little thatched huts, though squalid enough to be sure, at least found happy friendship with their surroundings.

We drove through the village with a loudspeaker atop the van squeeling out the news that a film was to be shown on the plaza that night and that a group of Americans would speak. The announcer was Francisco Rosales, a wizened little man in his seventies who was also to be our interpreter that night.

The portable P.A. drew the eyes of all we passed. Housewives smiled broadly at the strange van. Walking campesinos on their way home from the fields warmly returned our waves, and children, in droves, ran behind us laughing and skipping. I discovered (as we followed the rocky little trails) that there were many more dwellings than were immediately visible. And each one seemed to literally belch children at the crackling sound of the van's loudspeaker.

As dark began to fall, we returned to the center of the village to find a small schoolhouse with, of all things — an outdoor basketball court. The weeds grew knee-high right to its edge. There were no goals or nets on the backboards, but I was suprised to find such an "American" sight. I later found that at one point the Mexican government, in a drive motivated partly with an eye toward public relations, had built a little school-building and a basketball court in nearly every village in Mexico. I almost never saw basketball being played on one of these, but they made wonderful spots for outdoor evangelism.

While Brother Jim and Frank Philips set up the screen and projector, I strolled down the road with Francisco. I found an immediate rapport with the old Mexican. He seemed to have a deep love for the Lord and showed endless patience with my questions.

The Mexicans were charming as we met and chatted with children and adults at each little hut. The dusty little village, the barren landscape, and the brown-eyed babies began to have an unsettling effect. I found myself not-so-gradually falling in love with Mexico.

I stood on the edge of the basketball court in those last few magic seconds of dusk before genuine darkness captured the day. I listened to the muted sounds of the village and watched little evening fires begin to come to life and I suddenly, inexplicably began to cry. I knew that God had begun a new thing in my life. Despite the knot in my stomach and the persistent wobbling in my legs still remaining from the plane ride, it was a moment of almost painful beauty. It was quite like watching one's daughter at her first piano recital. Can I, I wondered, stand on the outskirts of a Mexican village and find love at first sight?

I hadn't long to think about it. Soon the asthmatic generator was stirred from slumber and two bare light bulbs illumined the open-air "cathedral." Several hundred people had gathered by now and I returned to hear Brother Jim and Francisco greeting the crowd and introducing the Gospel film. We sang some choruses in Spanish and Jim showed the film. I stood in the darkness amidst the villagers watching the images move across the tattered screen, but not understanding a single word of Spanish. I felt very useless, unable to even greet them without an interpreter. I fervently hoped that Brother Jim would preach in English and allow Francisco to translate so that, at least, I could keep up, even if I could not contribute. The sense of a wasted week warred in my mind, with a very strong impression that regardless of circumstances, I was exactly where God wanted me that night.

The film finished and the two tiny light bulbs struggled to reclaim some real estate from the oppressive moonless night.

Jim Mann began to speak in English and Fransicisco translated sentence for sentence.

"There are some people here tonight from the United States," Jim began. "One of them is to preach. The Spirit of the Lord has shown me that he is to preach tonight in Laborcitas. He's a young Methodist pastor from Georgia."

His words were an ice bath. My God, I thought, HE'S CALLING ON ME!

"I just met him this afternoon," he went on calmly as if he couldn't see the panic in my soul. "But I just fell in love with him. He's got a real calling on his life."

"My God, help me — this crazy old man is calling on **ME** to preach. I have never used an interpreter. I have never been to Mexico before. I am half sick from the plane and I feel weak from hunger and heat."

"His name is Mark Rutland. Brother Mark, come on up here and give these people the Word of God."

Praying as I walked, I grimly made my way toward the microphone which he extended like Artaxerxes' scepter. I had never felt so ill prepared for ministry. I studied the old missionary's face for any sign of malice, but I saw only those same calm, good-humored, loving, blue eyes.

Forty-five minutes later I gave the invitation to receive Christ as Saviour. I cannot remember a word I preached and certainly do not fool myself that anyone else does. But God took hold of that little spot in the universe that night and did a miracle. Seventy-five adults took Christ as Saviour, coming forward and standing to pray the sinner's prayer before the whole village.

From that night, there arose the first Protestant church in Laborcitas. It remains active even at this writing. I returned a year later for the dedication of the church Jim Mann built there. What a joy to know that nearly every charter member was saved on that little basketball court on one night.

The remainder of the week was very much like beginning a love affair. It was a bit frightening, quite exhilarating, totally captivating, obviously temporary, yet painfully real. I simply could not get enough of Mexico. My eyes and ears proved voracious. The music in Jim's little village churches, the street scenes, the market, the barren roads, the dirt — even the poverty — I just wanted to look, touch, taste and hear everything.

A young girl in love is absolutely nauseating. She sees unparalleled comeliness in the acne-ridden face of her beau and poetic grace in his awkward, ambling gait. I was in love and I knew it. Mexico had stolen my heart.

Helen Mann turned up some Dramamine for me before we started home and the nausea of the trip down was happily avoided. I looked down and back at Victoria as we took off and doubted if I would ever be able to come back. I'm no missionary, I assured myself. This was fun but now it's back to reality.

Reality hit like a tidal wave only a few hours later. Frank's Aztec struck a solid wall of thunderstorms over Alabama and we began to toss like a cork in the North Atlantic. The small aircraft was defenseless against the power of the storm. The euphoria of Mexico seemed far away at every creak and groan of machine under phenomenal pressure. We were blown so far north of our course to Atlanta that when we finally broke out of the clouds, we were just clearing Lookout Mountain, Tennessee.

Several years later Frank Philips was killed in that same airplane. I felt a deep personal loss, of course, but more than that was the loss of him to the Army of the Lord. Not in the least of Frank's blessings to me was to introduce me to Jim Mann.

Over the years, until his death, I found Jim to be a constant source of inspiration. He was one of those rare Christian servants who had absolutely no detectable appetite for fame or public approval. He was a highly successful building contractor who had been crippled in a near-fatal tractor accident before falling into a terrible spiral of drunkenness and drugs. Finally, lying helpless and crippled in a private mental hospital, Jim Mann cried out to Jesus to save him and heal him.

The next morning when the attending psychiatrist arrived, he found the "necessary" crutches stacked in the corner and Jim Mann seated at the foot of the stairs. He was clean shaven, "clothed and in his right mind," and completely healed save for the limp. In shock, the doctor dismissed him that very morning.

Several years later, Jim and Helen sold everything, established Mountain Foreign Missions, and began their work in Mexico. Jim was an independent missionary without benefit of denominational backing, and his only ordination was a clear call to the villages of Mexico. He and Helen traveled thousands of miles, showed hundreds of Gospel films, led thousands to Christ and established more than thirty churches.

That old bald-headed layman with his "Jacob's limp" became a symbol to me of all that is good, and true and **real** in ministry. He was a plain soul winner with a good healthy contempt for artificiality, denominationalism, and the "superstar" syndrome. May his tribe increase!

As a pastor, I began trying to interest generous laymen and pastors of mission-minded churches in Jim's work. As team after team traveled with me and others to Mexico, I saw how God blessed the ministry to the Mexicans but even more how he blessed the Americans through Jim and Helen.

It was through these early attempts of mine to introduce others to his work that Jim became a mentor of sorts (and a highly unlikely one, at that) to a group of young Methodist preachers in Georgia. Among those brought under Jim's grand influence were Mark Nysewander and Randy Healan. Both later became great missionaries in Mexico themselves. When Jim died, his funeral was at Atlanta's Mt. Paran Church of God, but no small percentage of the congregation was Methodist and it touched me deeply to see tears streaming down the faces of Methodist pastors for this unsung, Church of God, lay missionary.

Mexico is one of the most "missionized" countries in the world. Much of what is done there is shallow and superficial. Some is even evil. I remember the independent missionary who falsified papers on his son, bought a grand estate in his name and raised money for it in the States as an orphanage. No less evil is the denominational missionary I know about who used his Mission Board's money to build and outfit a dental clinic which has never served a patient. Each year he turns in an embellished account of his work but does hardly more than live comfortably and take pictures. There are others, though, like Jim Mann, quietly doing the work of the Kingdom.

Chapter VI
Launch Out . . .

BEYOND THE BORDER

I arrived home from my first trip to Mexico full of bluster and protest that neither missions nor Mexico were for me. I was pastoring a full-time church and trying to see if a fledgling evangelistic work was going to sprout any wings. "I need Mexico about like I need boils," I would say. I was hardly home though, before I began planning to go back. In the next six years, I made nearly a dozen missions (most of these with Jim Mann) to Mexico. Each time I saw God move in some new and powerful way to accomplish His purpose in me or others. Some of these experiences were painful, others were powerful, but all were precious.

One blistering July afternoon, Jim and I took several Americans into the Tamilipas State Penitentiary in Victoria. The thermometer behind the Mann's little house calmly announced 130 degrees in the shade. The dingy, grey walls of the prison seemed stark white in the blinding Mexican sun.

In the outer office, we presented our pass to a fearsome looking guard with a pistol stuck in the band of his trousers. He glared at us out from under bushy eyebrows. When he spoke to our interpreter, Modesto, his teeth appeared almost the same color as his absurdly drooping mustache. After only a few words, we were passed into the prison interior.

It was horrible. Prisoners in tattered clothes straggled around in the absolute filth of the courtyard and cell blocks. One cell had blankets draped around it and from inside I heard a baby squalling. I saw pathetic dogs seeking out traces of shade. And in the open doorway of one cell block stood a ragged little girl of about five or six years. Her hair was matted and her shoes were split at the toes and sides. She never spoke, never smiled, never responded in any way. She just stared at us with her little, haunted eyes.

It was very odd and slightly unnerving to be at large in that prison without so much as a guard. A trustee escorted us but we were completely unprotected. It was like taking a leisurely stroll through hell. We talked with one American prisoner who removed his shirt and dropped his trousers to reveal huge, ugly, purple welts. He said the guards had used a cattle prod on him for hours because of fighting. He was so lonely and fearful and in a sad condition but would not repent and be saved. I could not keep from wondering how far down he would have to go.

Finally we gathered those who were interested in a barn-like building where some of the prisoners made furniture and leather goods which they sold through the bars of the main gate. It was an eerie sight to watch those pitiful prisoners hawking their wares through the bars to well-dressed tourists. Since it was Sunday, the shop was shut down and we gathered there for our service.

As Modesto sang and played his guitar, a few more straggled in until about forty had assembled. I scanned the faces. I have preached all over the world since then but I have never seen harder looking faces than those. Eyes that seemed absolutely impassive at best or burned with hate at the worst, were set in faces that were lined with sin. One brutish hulk of a man stood slightly away from the others. His sleeves were rolled to reveal gruesome tattoos on both arms. A livid scar ran across his forehead and laid hold of the corner of his left eye pulling downwards before disapearing under his left ear. It gave him a really threatening appearance. He unswervingly stared straight at my face. Every time I looked up, his cold eyes were fixed on me in an emotionless but very penetrating manner. It was quite disconcerting.

"Do you see that character with the machete scar?" I heard Jim whisper by my side.

"Are you kidding?" I answered. "How could I miss him?"

"He's a murderer. Just tell him that Jesus loves him," Jim said.

"Yeah, sure," I smiled rather wanly.

God watches over His Word and He is careful to perform it.

When I gave the invitation, the murderer stood forward, that awful purple scar catching tears like a drainpipe and guiding them down into his collar. In all, he and seventeen others took Christ as Saviour. As we prepared to leave the furniture shop, a raspy voice called out in Spanish, "Pray for us, too."

"Those are the men in the maximum security stockade behind this building," Modesto explained. "They are the really dangerous criminals."

A chair was placed against the wall and standing on it I called a prayer up to a small barred window above my head. Modesto translated phrase by phrase.

After a few seconds of silence came a simple, poignant "Gracias, Senor." I never saw any of the men behind that wall. I have no idea what can ever become of such men. But at least one of them on that day wanted a touch from God.

The man with the monstrous scar tearfully embraced me before we left and mumbled something in Spanish but Modesto was not nearby and I'll never know exactly what he said.

The way home to the U. S. on that mission was made unforgettable by some humorous circumstances. The other Americans and I rode the Oriente' bus line from Victoria to Reynosa. Due to a flat tire, we sat for an inordinate time while the bus became an oven. When we finally started North, it was at a startling speed. The packed bus rocketed toward those waiting by the road, brakes squealing and dust flying only to add more bodies into the impossibly crowded aisles.

A man standing in the aisle next to me began to munch raw shrimp from a slimy baggie. The smell was incredible. The man would crack the heads with his teeth and suck with noisy satisfaction. The lurching and swaying of the bus, the staggering heat, the tightly packed bodies, and the smells and sounds of those ripe shrimp being devoured combined for a devastating effect. I have traveled in buses and lorries all over the third world but I have **never** forgotten **that** trip.

Another Mexican bus figured in one truly touching act of the Spirit. Jim and I and another group of Americans were to be in a service in a very remote mountain village southwest of Tampico. An interpreter had agreed to come out from Tampico on the bus and meet us there. The bus broke down in transit and he never arrived. I had only a handful of Spanish words that I could string together in no more than three or four rote

69

sentences of greeting. None of those other Americans spoke any Spanish at all except Jim Mann, whose modest conversational Spanish could not possibly enable him to translate. He needed an interpreter himself! No one in the village, including the pastor, spoke a single word of English.

In a painful, stumbling conference with several Mexicans, Jim and I agreed that the pastor should preach. I would bring a few words of greeting in my two or three faltering sentences of Spanish. This would, in addition to giving the villagers a gentle laugh at the American's expense, establish a little rapport in case we ever came back.

As I stood and began to speak, the Spirit of the Lord did something marvelous. Words, phrases, whole sentences tumbled out with incredible facility. I preached in Spanish for thirty-five minutes! It was not like speaking in tongues exactly. I was thinking quite clearly in English and interpreting in my mind into Spanish. Thinking it through over the years, I have come to believe that what the Holy Spirit was doing, was to supernaturally dredge up every word of Spanish I had heard interpreted in sermon after sermon. Perhaps those words had taken root in my inner mind somehow to be drawn on by the Holy Spirit in that night. Perhaps!

Whatever happened, it was a miracle of communication. As it began to dawn on all in the church what was happening, the Mexicans and the Americans began to weep in the presence of the Lord. What a night! Seeing the power of God, many were saved and baptized in the Holy Spirit in that place.

On still another of these missions, Jim and I had arranged to take the group into the prison at Victoria. Each time the ministry there had proven fruitful. We had the pass and Lazaro Sanchez was to translate. At nearly midnight on the eve of our prison visit, Brother Jim came to my room.

"We can't go into the prison tomorrow," he coolly announced.

"Why not?" I asked. "Did the prison cancel our pass?"

"No," he said, "it's nothing to do with the prison. It's just that we have somewhere else to go."

"Where?" I asked in amazement.

"Canitas. It's a village," he said, watching my eyes. "I don't know exactly where it is. I only know it's somewhere down near Tula. The desk clerk at the hotel thinks. . . ."

70

"Tula!" I exclaimed. "That's down in the desert — over the Sierras!"

"I know where Tula is," Jim purred.

"But you don't know where the village is?" I asked.

"No."

"Then why do we have to go?" I asked in exasperation.

"Some years ago, I heard the village mentioned somewhere and it stuck in my mind. Tonight the Holy Spirit has made it clear to me that we need to go there tomorrow," he explained.

"Look, Jim," I moaned, "let's don't do this. It'll be as hot as you know what down there. The trip over the mountains is bad. We'll get lost . . . ."

"Fine," Jim said without any edge in his voice. "You don't have to go. I'll borrow a car and you can take the men in the van to the prison."

"Oh, all right," I snapped. Jim chose to ignore the edge in my voice.

The next morning at 5:00 a.m., we started up over the Sierras and down toward Tula. I thought we were on a wild goose chase. And a dangerous one. I have very little fear of demons or beasts, but Mexican truck drivers do wonders for my prayer life!

We got lost. I **knew** we would get lost. As the temperature rose on the desert floor, we all began to feel a bit jumpy. Directions at one Pemex station after another proved useless.

Finally, Jim said, "I know we're close. Let's ask again." We pulled to the side of the road where two men and a woman squatted. There was certainly no mystery in that. Half of Mexico is, at any given moment, squatting beside the road waiting for a bus. These three themselves were absolutely unremarkable.

"Do you know where the village of Canitas is?" asked Lazaro, our interpreter.

"Yes, of course," they replied, dusting themselves off. "We've been waiting to guide you in from here."

All this, of course, was in Spanish with only Lazaro speaking. When he translated their response to us, Brother Jim sensed something was happening.

"Don't tell them anything," Jim said excitedly. "Let's give the Lord room."

Indeed I did not know what there was that Lazaro might tell!

Only that until now, there had been no mention of who we were, of any reference of any kind to anything religious, and the van itself was free of any religious markings.

"Why are you waiting?" Lazaro asked as the three climbed in and settled themselves on the back seat.

One of the men told a remarkable story. "There are 750 people in our village and only two Christian families. My wife, me, and this couple here with me. We have prayed faithfully for some time now that God would give our village a church and send revival. The night before last, we were praying in my house and this brother had a Word from God.

"Day after tomorrow I will send men from another country and they will build a church in Canitas."

They had received the Word in simple faith and had been waiting there — sitting by the roadside — since dawn.

As we compared stories there in the van and watched the ends connect, we all wept and embraced at such a demonstration of God's power. I wept, as well, at my own slowness of heart to learn to live in the supernatural universe. I had fought against one of the sweetest miracles of my life because my whole life had been spent in a basic skepticism of the miracle realm. I am persuaded that spiritual power in the pulpit and not professionalism will meet the real longing of the people.

In Canitas (Little Canes) we saw the floor plan of the little church etched with shovel-edge in the sun baked earth. As we stood there amidst that pitiful little cluster of stick and adobe huts, I was humbled to be in the presence of simple men with a holy dream. Americans have sold out to a fascination with the grand until even our dreams before the Lord have too often taken on a kind of ugly gaudiness. One year later, a simple wooden church stood on that exact spot and to me it looked like a cathedral.

My Lord Jesus, where is our faith in the American Church? The New Testement church was alive in two Mexican campesinos in a desert village, while prosperous American churches fill empty lives with church bazaars and fill empty pulpits with good joke tellers. God help us!

In two villages, I had more dangerous experiences. The village of Boca de Juan Capitan (The Mouth of Captain John) is perhaps the poorest village I ever saw in Mexico. Boca's stick huts are strewn along the rim of a great volcanic stone gulch.

Steep winding trails snake down a rocky hillside to an ancient rock well shaded by a huge tree.

All day, women and children with buckets trudge their way up and down those rocky paths and an occasional young boy leads a mangy little donkey laden with sloshing gerry cans. None of this, perhaps, is very notable among Mexican villages. But the first time I saw Boca, it was quite unusual in one way.

An oppressive spirit of evil hovered over that village. Boca's wicked reputation was almost legendary among other villagers of the area. The Mexican authorities had urged Jim and Helen Mann not to even attempt a work there. Only weeks before their first day of ministry in Boca, an entire family had been slaughtered in the night by machete-wielding killers. No arrests were made. Some said the Ruralists were unwilling to come into the village to investigate.

Jim had put one of his little white frame churches in Boca and some women and children had come to the Lord. A brave young pastor had agreed to take the work on. The men of Boca hated him. They would pelt him and his family with stones in their coming and going from the village. During one service, as his wife sat at the end of a bench against the outside wall, a man urinated on her through the narrow opening between the boards.

Only weeks before I made my first visit to Boca, a thirteen-year old girl had been gang raped by a group of young men in order to discourage her new faith. She kept on going to church but her face had a haunted, shadowed look when I first met her. The whole village and the church as well, had a dark, oppressive air that was certainly atypical of the Mexican villages I had come to love.

One evening late in October, Jim and Helen and I took four other Americans to Boca for a worship service. We stopped in Victoria for old Francisco Rosales who was to interpret. In San Jose Flores, we collected a few villagers to go with us to Boca. The little van was filled with the usual laughter and bilingual banter until we turned off the main road at the sign for BOCA de JUAN CAPITAN.

Suddenly the van was silent. Jim stopped before the cattle gate and I jumped down and held it open while he drove through. Instead of driving on as usual, we stopped while Francisco prayed. It was a somber prayer binding the enemy and claiming the protection of angels. Only scattered comments broke the silence until we stopped before the little church. As darkness fell, we cranked the generator and the four bare bulbs (the only four in Boca) strung along the center of the building illuminated the interior.

The young pastor began the service and at first, save for the lack of real joy in the air, nothing seemed unusual. As the pastor's wife and several young girls struggled through a gospel number, the people began to move away from the sides of the church and toward the center aisle. Very little was said, but I soon realized that some men outside were thrusting machetes through the cracks and sliding them up and down. An occasional stone clattered on the tin roof. Fear began to grip the little congregation. The music became more ragged with each chorus.

A little boy slipped in and sat beside me during one song. He began to speak in Spanish, his eyes never leaving the front. Each time I turned my head or eyes toward him, he stopped immediately. I realized he did not want anyone to know he was speaking to me.

My Spanish had improved only slightly and I did not get everything but what I understood sent chills up and down my spine. "Bad men . . . outside . . . all around church . . . machetes . . . ropes . . . marijuana . . . very dangerous . . . very bad men."

I got up and made my way to the back of the little church where Jim and Helen sat in the lawn chairs they carried in the van. Before I could speak, Jim said, "I know. Very slowly, with as little stir as possible, get the others and bring them back here. We'll all go out together and get straight in the van."

"Jim," I said, "I believe the Lord is speaking in my heart. What I sense is that if we will all stay in the church, we'll be all right. Jim, I'd like your permission to tell the pastor that I'm ready to preach **right now**. I truly sense a great victory here. But you're the boss and I'll do what you say."

Jim hesitated only a few seconds. Then that lovely wide grin spread across his face and he said, "Oh, no, Brother Mark, Jesus is the boss. Go ahead and preach."

As I started up the center aisle to the pulpit, I noticed afresh the white lettering across its front — Dios es Amor. As if bathed in that love, I felt absolutely calm. I knew I should have been afraid. It was not courage. It was peace!

I tapped Francisco on the shoulder and he followed me to the front. The pastor stepped aside without a word. My first thought was to preach on the love of Jesus. I reasoned that "a gentle answer turneth away wrath" or that "music hath power to soothe the savage breast" or something like that. But my heart seemed to be led toward only one scripture.

"Lord," I prayed, "I believe I am hearing your voice to preach on this verse. I am trying to be obedient. Please help me not to get out on my own in this situation."

"Tonight," I shouted, "I am preaching not just for those inside but for those outside in the darkness as well. I trust you can hear my voice. I don't want you to miss any of this. Tonight, I am going to tell you about the stoning of Steven."

The words poured out of me in a torrent and Francisco never faltered in his interpretation. I preached directly to the men in the darkness, stating flatly that those who persecute Christians are the "cowards" of this world and that they will stand before the judgement of Christ for what they do to His children.

Only when I said that those who persecute Christians had "hearts of women" did Francisco hesitate. This is a dreadful insult in a Latin, macho-oriented culture. "No, Brother Mark," he said. "I won't say that."

"You **will** say it, Francisco, God is with us," I answered him.

He did. When I gave the altar call, I was as amazed as anyone when about six young men came in from outside and gave their hearts to Jesus. They left their machetes outside and knelt in tears to repent. That night was the beginning of a true revival in that village. Many others came to the Lord in the weeks to follow and as the church in Boca grew in power, the backbone of evil began to break. Today the little church in Boca is certainly tame — their pastor is a young woman!

Years later, Helen Mann confessed to me that during the sermon that night, she thought I had ruined their work in Boca — **if** we lived over it. If she had only known how sick I had felt when we got in the van to leave and I came to the realization of how close we had been to real danger.

On another night, not the Lord, but my own sinful pride brought me into another kind of danger. Jim and I had gone way out to Station Rosa, a bit larger village that sprawled out on both sides of a railroad track. Rather than actually seeing the tracks, I felt them as we bumped across them in the dark.

While Jim and Francisco prepared for the service and chatted with some early comers, I strolled in the churchyard. I had never been in this village before and having arrived after dark, I had no idea of what lay just beyond the reach of the only electric lights within many miles. Up the track about fifty yards, I saw a campfire with shadowy figures moving about it.

"Jim," I called through the open windows, "I'm going up the tracks and invite those guys to the service." Jim was used to this. Often I walked all through a village before a service.

"Be careful up there," Jim called back without looking up.

Stumbling up the tracks in the darkness, I could see more shadows around the little fire than I had thought at first. When I got there and saw the firelight playing on the faces of about six rugged-looking hombres, I wondered if I had done the wrong thing.

"Buenos Noches," I said softly.

Several answered — but if they were suprised to see an American at their campfire, they did not show it. Perhaps word had already spread through the village that I was there with Jim. The campfire, now only flickering coals, lay between the crossties. The men sat on the rails with their feet inside. As I sat and began to chat with them, I noticed a light far in the distance.

"Is that a train coming?" I asked.

"Yes," someone answered.

We sat in silence for a few more minutes with the light drawing nearer. Suddenly the whistle screamed against the night air. I shivered at the mournful sound.

"It's coming," I said.

"Yes," was the answer. No one moved.

I could tell they were watching me. I knew they were waiting to see if I'd move first and I vowed in my mind that I wouldn't. The train plunged toward us screaming like a banshee. My palms began to perspire and I waited for one of them to jump first. Whee! Whoo-eee! screeched the whistle. Now the train was so close I was terribly frightened but I watched the others trying to appear calm. Surely one of them would jump. Jump! Jump! I wanted to yell.

Just as I was about to jump, it was too late. The train was on us. With a thunderous crash, the train rocketed past us on a parallel track I had not seen before. For a second I couldn't understand what had happened. I stood to my feet and stared stupidly at the chattering boxcars shooting past me. If I had jumped the wrong way, I would have jumped in front of the speeding locomotive. My head swam as I staggered back up the tracks in the darkness.

"Are you OK?" Jim asked when I returned to the church.

"Fine. Just fine," I stammered.

The amazing thing was that all those young men came into the service. Perhaps my "courage" had won their respect, but I had to repent of a pride that very nearly got me killed.

As trip after trip saw the hand of God in dramatic demonstration, I began to be concerned that I should go to Mexico as a missionary. In prayer I seemed to find no assurance one way or the other.

I had only just begun in evangelism. A board of directors for the Trinity Foundation had been chosen and I was hard about trying to articulate my dreams. The thought of a dramatic shift at such a tender stage was less than appealing to say the least. I hated the thought of appearing (or being) wishy-washy. On the other hand, I was frightened of missing God through unwillingness for the Lord to change directions.

Mexico seemed the place to settle it. I went alone for a week to pray and preach from village to village with Jim Mann. Jim met me in McAllen and as always his calm spirit began to soothe me immediately. I did not tell him why I was there exactly but I believe he sensed the reason. As we drove South, I felt his eyes on me.

Night after night we enjoyed watching God move in great power. I saw more salvations in that week than in any previous week in Mexico. How at home I felt in Jim's little frame churches! The raftered ceiling covered by row upon row of tiny white paper doves suspended on kite string looked lovelier than stained glass. Impossibly I found the backless benches comfortable. In tiny villages with names like Rancho Nuevo, and Station Rosa, and Cinco de Febrero, I felt more at home than in many of the loveliest churches in the United States. I certainly felt a unity with Jim and Helen.

The way before me **seemed** open. But Thursday night, the Lord spoke. I knew His Word in my heart as clearly as if He had spoken aloud. "Go home. I have a use for you in missions, but you are not to move to Mexico. Go home and wait." That was it. I knew what I was to do, at least for now.

In part I was disappointed. On the whole I was relieved to feel free to get on with what seemed to lie ahead of me in home evangelism. It seemed very clear to me that God wanted me to just go on interesting others in Jim's work. Subsequent events have taught me not to interpret too liberally the word that you have.

If the Lord says "no," it does not mean "wait." And if He says "wait," it does not mean "no." "Stand still and see my salvation," never means, "plunge ahead." And **"go now"** is not a suggestion, but a command. The marching orders of the Lord will bear neither elaboration nor modification.

I returned to home evangelism with a liberated vigor. I felt literally delivered from a flirtation with missions. I jumped beyond what God had actually said. I assumed I was through with that work, and I put it behind me and plunged into the revival work in America with a fresh sense of purpose. I was determined to put all this nonsense away from me and get back to work.

My trips to Mexico became fewer and further between as the Lord blessed the preaching schedule. And bless it He did! In church after church we saw wonderful blessings from God. The Lord increased the work with blinding speed.

Staff was added, invitations came at a greater rate, meetings were full and blessed, and once a year I took a mission trip down to Mexico. I thought back to the nightmare years of backslidden, anxiety-ridden suicidal horror. How God had changed my life! It appeared that God had opened so many new doors that it hardly seemed possible He could open any more. After all, I thought, what else can change?

Chapter VII
Launch Out . . .

BEYOND THE NATURAL

I sat up in bed fully awake. The blood was pounding in my ears and adrenaline was coursing through me. Someone was in my house! There was not a sound anywhere. My wife was asleep beside me. My three children were sleeping in their rooms. Yet, I had the distinct impression that someone was in the house.

I slipped from the bed and out into the hall. I went through the house flipping on lights, opening doors, and testing locks. Finally, feeling more than a little foolish, I satisfied myself that I was mistaken. By now, sleep was impossible.

I flopped down in a living room chair to let the excitement ebb away and give drowsiness a chance to return. Instead of the sleepiness I expected, however, what happened next was to change the course of my life. It was already a life I hardly recognized. Since 1975 I had become a man I didn't know, living a life I had never dreamed of. Now God was just about to blow the lid off whatever remained.

I find it remarkably difficult to relate what happened to me that January night. Words, such as visions, had always been so alien to my staid, traditionalist vocabulary. I had always regarded those who spoke of "hearing from God" as being on a par with those who claimed close encounters with spacemen. As I sat in my living room that night, something happened to me beyond the parameters of any previous experience. Put any label on it you like — vision is as good as any — but the irreducible reality remains. That night I heard God as I never had before.

I saw (I say **saw** but it was more in my mind's eye, if you will) a map. It was a quite unusual world map. It appeared that the earth had been quartered and laid out flat in connecting ovals.

Slowly at first, then with gradually increasing rapidity, I felt myself being drawn to specific names on that map. Their names lifted right up off the map like a 3-D movie. Even more suprising than that, however, were the sensations I experienced at each name. I was absolutely overcome with loving warmth for each city and land. It was an emotion more akin to homesickness than anything else. I felt as if I had been born in each place and longed to go there again.

I had never dreamed that such names as Cuba, Peru, Colombia, Scotland, Ireland, and India could elicit such waves of love as I knew that night. I remember especially that tears sprang up in my eyes at Oslo, Norway, of all places.

I began to sense (and still do believe to this day) that God was revealing places where I would minister and see revival. The realization was electrifying to me. As the Lord moved from Latin America and Europe to India, Asia and the South Pacific, the experience became more vivid by the second, until suddenly I saw myself preaching before a strange congregation.

I will always remember how vividly they appeared to me. As each scene of ministry faded into another, I began to weep in earnest. I saw **thousands** saved, healed, and filled with the Holy Spirit. It seemed to go on for hours, though in actuality, the entire thing lasted only a matter of minutes.

The last "picture" I saw in that remarkable night was of a particular group of blacks. I saw hundreds of people in an open-air setting. They were sitting fan-shaped on the ground or on rude benches and logs and were staring intently at me. I sensed a greater hunger in them for the Word of God in that moment than I had ever known before in any congregation. Their faces were literally burned into my memory. Then, at last, as suddenly as it began, it ended.

"Oh, Lord," I prayed. "If this is from You, speak to me. I don't want to fly off the handle on something now when we've come so far. Speak to me, Lord."

He did —

"In the years ahead, I will turn your life upside down. Things will come into your life from directions you do not even know exist tonight. I will use you, change you, tax you, break you, and send as you cannot imagine. But first you must go to Ghana."

I was devastated, shocked, amazed, and totally depleted. Drained emotionally and spiritually, I fell back into bed quite exhausted. I suppose I should have been exhilarated. Probably someone more mature spiritually would have been. I was profoundly shaken.

The next morning I very tentatively shared with Alison what had happened in the night. She was affirmative and calm but expressed concern about phrases like "turn your life upside down." How sensitive she was not to ply me with questions I could not answer.

Just a few brief weeks later, I was more convinced than ever that events in my immediate future were going to change everything. The more I prayed, each time I prayed, I was convinced that the Lord was preparing me for a season of dramatic upheaval.

In April at a backyard barbecue, I told it all to my great friend, Mark Nysewander. He and his wife, Kathy, were preparing to leave for Monterrey, Mexico, as United Methodist missionaries. In the light of what I knew **they** were facing, I was reluctant to even mention my little uncertainties. Mark was great. He urged me to pray and to be obedient and relieved my embarrassment at the whole thing by confessing he had also once had a vision. In a meeting where I was preaching, to be exact! It struck me as a mildly notable event and somehow slightly humorous that two young Methodist preachers who had grown up in the very heart of traditional religion, stood swapping supernatural visions over backyard barbecue.

"I don't know what's ahead for me, Mark," I said. "The Lord just seems to have ripped away all the walls. I don't discount anything. Please pray for me about this Ghana thing. I don't know what the Lord wants me to do there. I just know He said I must go to Ghana first. I have decided to wait for God to open the door."

And wait I did. So certain was I that some invitation to Ghana would come somehow that I leaped at every call. It was a strange time in my life. I went weeks at a time as jumpy as a cat. I just **knew** that each day's mail would bring a letter from some source in Ghana. From whom, I had no idea.

In the meantime, distraction, diversion, and dead ends came from every direction. The National President of the United Methodist Men's organization asked me to lead an evangelistic mission to Guyanna in South America. Guyanna was not exactly Ghana and South America was certainly not Africa. But, I reasoned, an open door is not to be ignored. And, anyway they **sounded** a lot alike if said quickly. I had (and still have) much to learn about the specificity with which God expects to be obeyed.

On the eve of departure, the trip was cancelled from New York. All the hours of work and preparation putting the team together seemed a dreadful waste. My first inclination was to go ahead on my own. My wife, Alison, wisely urged me to take a weekend and pray first. The Lord seemed to impress on me that He had stopped the trip, not New York.

An equally disappointing collapse closed the door on a possible trip to Kenya. I had been so sure of that one. Africa **is**, after all, Africa. The door had been opened quite supernaturally. I had been invited by a Kenyan pastor at a chance meeting in Atlanta. How easy it is to be diverted by circumstances! Uneasiness about the invitation grew in Alison and me until I cancelled the trip this time.

When a major Christian university suddenly called from out of the blue, the Spirit's prophetic warning of "upheaval" was made very fresh. They flew me out to the campus. I preached and met with faculty and administrators. The possibility of a faculty position was discussed at length.

For a month Alison and I talked, prayed, and debated the pros and cons of it. Again, it proved a dead end. We had no peace about it despite the attractiveness of it in many ways. It only served to keep up the pattern of disruptions that seemed to be developing.

Throughout this whole distressing period of time, one persistent, nagging thought kept penetrating my prayers with a very worrisome regularity. I hardly dared face it squarely. For days at a time I could ignore it. The thought simply refused to be finally dismissed. In fact, the more I prayed, the more the thought took form. Go to Ghana, the inner voice insisted. Seek no more counsel. Delay no longer. Go — go now — go to Ghana.

How could such a thought be from God? To just **go** to Ghana? What was I going to do? Buy an airline ticket to a country I knew nothing about and just show up?! It was crazy! I refused to harbor such a daft notion.

However, what could reading hurt? I began to read every book and encyclopedia I could get my hands on. That same feeling of "homesickness" I had sensed faintly for such places as Oslo, Norway, now grew in my heart steadily for the little nation of Ghana.

In July an old friend mentioned quite casually that an African who had returned to his own country had been touched by my ministry while in the U. S. The mention of Africa, as always, made my ears perk up. When Jerry further described his friend as a Ghanian, my pulse began to race.

I received the address of this man, Dr. Brew Riverson, in Kumasi, Ghana, with great joy. Surely this was the contact I had been waiting for. To be sure, I could not exactly remember the man and I had no idea if he would remember me. Jerry said that I had met him at one of my "rallies" in Atlanta. Somewhere in the back of my mind, I had a vague recollection of Jerry introducing me to a foreigner. Name, face, and nationality were lost to the years. How could I possibly expect him to place my name and face from a letter after all this time.

Nonetheless, I wrote him.

> *Dear Dr. Riverson,*
> *A mutual friend, Jerry Morrow, has given me your name. He believes you will remember meeting me at a Praise Rally in Atlanta.*
> *Through circumstances that would be difficult to explain in this note, I am convinced that God has quickened my heart to come to Ghana. If this witnesses with your spirit and if you think I could be used of God in Ghana at this time, please write to me.*

I sent that letter in early July. When no response was forthcoming, I sent another copy and still another. Then I sent three similar telegrams. No answer ever came to any of them. I was dreadfully disappointed I had thought that surely **this** was the open door I had awaited. Another dead end, I moaned sulkily.

By the end of September, the thought of going to Ghana without any contact, as frightening as that seemed, was pressing me with new urgency. The idea, instead of being discouraged, was fueled by repeated possibilities turning into dead ends. The result was desperate, immature prayers that were more frantic cries for light than true reaches of faith.

I began seeking signs, confirmations, and fleeces. I do **not** recommend that kind of prayer. I stated earlier that I would never advocate the unorthodox prayers of this book. I **do** offer them as testimony to God's unfailing grace. That He would entertain such absurd prayer is a manifest witness of His great fatherly love.

Over and over again, God spoke to me with firm patience. "Go to Ghana" began to ring in my ears on a daily basis. It was said and confirmed in every supernatural way but I just wouldn't listen. It sounded so crazy!

Finally, one Thursday night in October, I knelt by my bed in true turmoil.

"Oh, God, if you want me to go to Ghana with no contact and no plan, I will. Please speak to me in a way I can **not** misunderstand. Please speak to me from Your Word. Please guide me to a passage so directly related, that it will be absolutely clear to me, if to no one else. Lord, if you will do that for me now, I'll go."

Hardly believing what I was doing, I held my New Testament in my hand. How I had laughed at those who talked of finding God's will in such bizarre ways. How gracious God is! The little Testament flopped open in my hand. Closing my eyes, I thrust in my hand. Oh, how silly I felt! (I still **do not** advocate this "**racing** form" prayer.) On the other hand, I had the queerest sense that God was willing to honor it that night.

I jabbed my finger in like Little Jack Horner. My forefinger and thumb rested on Galatians 1:15, 16.

"But when it pleased God, who separated me from my mother's womb, and called me by his grace, To reveal his Son in me, that I might preach him among the heathen; immediately I conferred not with flesh and blood."

As I read the words, my heart began pounding in my chest. God had done just what I had asked. What grace! What infinite grace. Not beholden to answer **any** prayer with such direct power, God had condescended to answer such a childish one as I had prayed.

Now I knew I must go. Perhaps I had really known it for months. Now it was sealed. I went, Bible-in-hand, to my wife.

84

She listened quietly and thoughtfully and without protest. The affirmation of her smile and the confirmation of her spirit was worth more to me than Fort Knox.

The humbling and breaking process began in earnest the very next morning in the travel agency. The room was full of smiling agents, tourists, and computers all competing for the available space.

"May I help you?" chirped a young lady, wearing too much makeup and her little sister's sweater.

"Yes," I answered easing into the chair by her desk. "I want a round trip ticket to Ghana in West Africa. I want to leave in two weeks and return on Christmas Eve."

"All right," she said. "Now let's just see."

She spun with flair to her computer friend.

While she pecked brightly at the keys, she said with obvious delight, "I've never sold a ticket to Ghana before. Are you a hunter?"

"No," I answered flatly, hoping to discourage this whole line of questioning. She was impervious to the hint.

"Well, I didn't think so," she continued blithely. "All the hunters go to Kenya. You're not in business, are you?"

"No!" I said a bit more sharply.

She leaned over the desk conspiratorially, "Are you with the CIA?"

I realized there was no avoiding it. Women are simply amazing. They will **not** be moved. No, no — they **never** drop a subject. Why we even **have** male detectives in this world, I will never know. Once she sets her mind to it, a woman is **going** to get the answer.

Leaning toward her as she propped on her desk, we must have **looked** like confederates in some CIA ploy. I said, hardly above a whisper, "The Lord has told me to go. I am not certain why. I am just obeying."

Suddenly I felt as if I were in an E. F. Hutton ad. The whole room fell silent at once. Every computer stopped and every head turned toward us. The room seemed frozen to motionlessness. I sat staring straight into her eyes. I felt like a naked man in a subway trying to look natural by reading his newspaper.

"Oh," she replied primly, and the room whirred back in action.

Round-trip ticket in hand, I left that agency with the clear knowledge that I had made a complete donkey of myself. I can only guess what transpired inside after I left. My feet were to the fire. God had seen to that. In my car I prayed, "Lord, I want to go where you want me to go. But please don't ever ask me to go back in **there**."

The two weeks before I left were filled with packing, praying with friends and family, and pursuing a visa. Into this hectic air floated the Job's friends who are so dreadfully helpful. "Are you **absolutely sure** you're doing the right thing?" Of course, I was not **absolutely sure**. I was filled with doubt and turmoil.

"It doesn't seem like the Lord would ask you just to leave your wife and children. What if something happens to them?"

"I believe the Lord can plan better than this, Brother Mark."

"I'm not saying you're doing the wrong thing. But are you **certain** of the timing?"

"I just don't feel good about this."

And so on, and so on, and so on. How unnerving they were! Despite all their good intentions, they made the obvious craziness of the whole thing just that much harder for Alison and me. I determined then to try to be more careful not to go tramping about on other folk's dreams and visions.

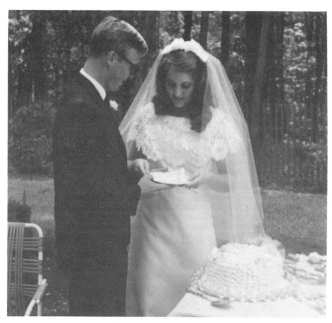

Our Wedding Day (1967). Only a few years later disaster struck.

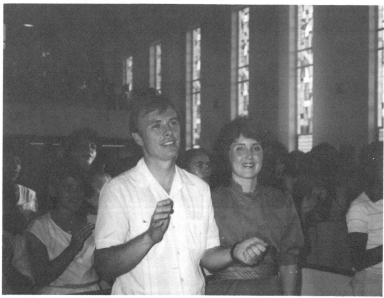

The joy of ministry together — a Youth Convention, Monterrey, Mexico.

A seemingly happy scene (1975). The day this was taken I tried to shoot myself.

The Mercies of God — with Alison and my three children today.

With Jim and Helen Mann in Mexico — my introduction to missions (1976)

A Healing Service near Ciudad Victoria

An open-air crusade in Monterrey, Mexico

Street Gang Members, among others, accept Christ.

A vision explicitly fulfilled — The Cocoa Grove; Santasi, Ghana

Praying with seekers Accra, Ghana

Evangelist Crusade (1985) Kumasi, Ghana. Translator, Trinity Evangelist Sammy Odarno

Kumasi Training Institute (1986)

Full Gospel Businessmen's Fellowship Meetings, Ghana (above),
Georgia Men's Advance (below).

Tremendous response to Invitations in Nigeria (above), Ghana (below).

Preaching at a school, Pueblo Neuavo, Peru (students stand at attention for sermon)

Esperanza means HOPE!

95

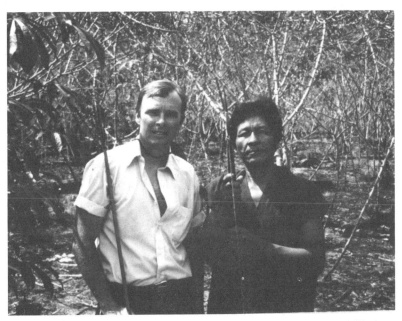

With a Campa Indian in Peruvian Jungle — this man accepted Christ.

Crossing a mud-slick log, the only entrance to this village.

Tamil Nadu, India (1984). Trinity's India Director S.E.A. Jesudason Translates.

Teaching Christian Workers

Instructions to new Hindu converts

Baptism service for converts near Salem, India

98

Chapter VIII
Launch Out . . .

AT HIS WORD

London was much colder than I had prepared for. In fact, I had not prepared for it at all. A three-hour plane change became a three-day delay in a flash of gunfire thousands of miles away. While I was in the air over the Atlantic, an abortive coup in Ghana had ended in the execution of the rebels and the imposition at martial law.

A British Caledonian service representative greeted me with the news that Ghana's airport was closed. She also informed me very graciously that my return flight to New York was free. "Or," she said as an afterthought, "You may have two nights in a hotel and use your return coupon which you already have. You have an hour to decide."

In the stall of the men's room I prayed, "Lord, what shall I do? Is this Your way of keeping me from doing something stupid? Or is this just a discouragement from the enemy?" How I wanted to go home! That did not seem to be God's answer.

"I'll stay in London," I told her when I returned. "I believe the Lord will open the airport before the two days are up."

"Very well," she said with no trace of reaction.

Each day I took the train into London and did a little sightseeing, but my heart was not in it. The cold, the preoccupation with Africa, and the nagging fear that this might just be a sign from God to go home combined to rob the two days in London of much satisfaction. I prayed for hours and called Alison for advice. She said "stay."

I found the British amazingly stereotypical in many ways and a great suprise in others. A cockney cab driver proved a fount of information as well as being splendidly humorous. At times I felt he was doing his impersonation of a cockney cabdriver. He was straight out of **My Fair Lady**. The major suprise was the warmth of the British. I had expected Byron's "Chilly England with its chilly women." Instead, I found folks talkative, interesting, and interested in me. The headmaster of a high school spent an hour talking about local politics and an elderly doctor's wife unhurriedly asked and answered questions over tea in the breakfast room at the Hilton.

Longing for a bit of refreshment in the Spirit, I stayed in London until evening the second night. I planned to find an evangelical worship service and encourage myself in the Lord. Easier said than done! I am sure there must be such midweek services somewhere in London, but I never found one. I finally went to mass at Westminster Abbey but the "beauty" of it was hollow to me in my need. I wanted a touch from God in an atmosphere of lively worship. Instead I found a ponderous display of pomp and circumstance. Afterward, an Irish priest that smelled of liquor directed me to a Methodist church where he thought there **might** be a midweek study.

In the basement of the church I found a musty little group in tweeds and turtlenecks munching biscuits and taking tea. I was welcomed warmly, but the "Bible Study" was a pathetic discussion of Isaiah and prophecy in general. The pastor said that it was obvious to everyone that Isaiah could not possibly have meant Jesus since it was impossible to look ahead to an event hundreds of years in the future. The coup de grace, however, was the suggestion that perhaps ESP was the modern corollary of prophecy. No help here, I thought. I quietly excused myself, took the train back to Gatwick and determined to find encouragement in the Lord alone in my room.

When I checked in with British Caledonian the next afternoon, I found the airport in Accra opened for daylight landings. The nation was under curfew from 5:00 p.m. until 5:00 a.m. In a mattter of hours I was in the air again. The long flight was interrupted only by a brief stop in Lagos, Nigeria, where most of the passengers deplaned. In the air again I realized there were no other whites on the plane.

A young man came and sat beside me. He was filled with questions. He was frankly suprised to see an American going into Ghana, but he was friendly and gave me his address. I later discovered this hospitality and warmth almost a universal good trait of the Ghanians. Frequently, after only a casual conversation, I was invited home by a Ghanian — even to spend the night. Furthermore, their positive optimism seems to be utterly indefatigable, even in the worst circumstances. This buoyancy of national spirit is the greatest plus in Ghana today.

Just after dawn we left Lagos for Ghana. The sun called forth rich morning shadows on the ground as we swooped in for a landing. It was about what I had expected. Lush undergrowth crowded right to the edge of the runway. Palm trees waved in a soft morning breeze. A small black girl with a bucket on her head waved at the plane as it taxied down the runway. However, as we taxied toward the little terminal, I looked out into the very business-like stare of a tank cannon. Along the tarmac were Russian-made tanks, armored personnel carriers, and heavily armed soldiers everywhere. On either side of the terminal building were sandbagged machine gun nests. Lounging soldiers gazed somberly at the British Caledonian jet.

At the sight of the tanks and soldiers, I shrank inwardly. Satan, buckled into the seat beside me, whispered in my ear.

"You've gotten yourself in a real mess now — fool! Look out there. What do you think you're doing here? You've plunged way out ahead of your God. Furthermore, you're in dangerous waters and you do not have God's protection."

While the plane rolled to a full stop I quickly pulled out my pocket Testament. I found my verse again from Galatians 1:15, 16. I tried to sop up all the comfort I could, but I remained shaky in my faith, to say the least, as I stepped on African soil for the first time.

Gripping my carry-on bag in one hand as if it were a wayward child, and with my passport and visa held like diamonds in the other, I entered the customs hall. Inside was a seething mass of confused, shouting, pushing humanity. In almost total darkness (I later discovered Ghana was suffering from a dramatic shortage of light bulbs.), rag-tag "customs agents" with no uniforms dispensed pink and white cards with a passion. I took mine and filled in the blanks.

Suddenly one of the agents said, "Come with me. Come." When I hesitated, he grabbed my arm firmly, "Yes, come with me." He spoke English with that lilting West African accent that has become so familiar to me now.

101

He took my passport and all my documents and started away quickly. I followed hard on, fearful that he would disappear with my passport. I had no idea whether he had any authority whatsoever, but I certainly had no idea what else to do. Perhaps, I thought, he is an angel. "Wait a moment," I said, "what is your name?"

His smile spanned his broad face and he looked back. "I am Peter. Come with me."

I have been in many airports in the world and seen some that were badly in need of organization. I have **never** in all my life experienced anything quite like the airport in Accra, Ghana. Every landing and takeoff is a riot of sound and movement. Porters shouting in multiple languages clutch at the bags of struggling passengers who doggedly refuse to give them up. Soldiers with submachine guns scowl at everyone that comes within range. When the baggage comes into the main terminal, there is yet another human explosion as greedy porters, tired passengers, armed soldiers, and frustrated B-Cal employees vie for control of the suitcases and boxes dumped unceremoniously in a heap in the middle of the floor.

I nervously watched all the madness about me while I stood in line with Peter. It was the Mad Hatter's tea party! I knew that trusting this Peter was my best bet. We presented my documents, the visa was stamped, and we moved to a bare table behind which stood two or three soldiers in uniform. I opened my carry-on bag for one, while another peered at my documents as if they were printed backwards in Cyrillic alphabet.

"You are with the CIA," he finally announced. "Your visa is not in order."

"I am certainly **not** with the CIA. I am a Methodist preacher and my documents **are** in order," I said.

The man at my elbow whispered, "Give this man $4.00 American."

I dutifully peeled off four ones and slipped them to the scowling soldier. Others may flinch at this but I was frightened and intimidated. I tried to think of it as "creative diplomacy."

"You are an Osofu! You can pass," he said handing me the documents with a wry smile. I had no idea what the word Osofu meant but I hoped it was something good.

Next came the unbelievable scramble for my luggage. Peter cleared the way ahead of me and I felt like a runner following his interference. At the customs desk there was more shouting, more charges, more explanations, but no more money. Peter kept saying, "This man is a Methodist Osofu. Don't you understand — Osofu!" He shouted at the guards with the guns seemingly without fear. Finally the bags were marked wildly with chalk and reclosed. Peter grabbed them up and we burst through the doors into the blinding African sunshine. By comparison, the darkness of the terminal seemed even more like a loud, dreary mine shaft. How glad I was to be out of it! One question remained, however. Where to now?

"Shall I get a taxi, Osofu?" Peter asked.

"Yes, Peter," I answered confidently."We shall certainly need a taxi. And Peter —"

"Yes, Osofu?"

"If I pay you, say $10.00 in American cash, will you stay with me to help all day?" I asked.

By way of an answer, he said, "I will collect a taxi."

Peter put my suitcases in the boot and we slid into the backseat of an ancient Mercedes Benz taxi that reminded me of an old movie star whose memory of glory days had long outlived her beauty. The handsome young driver in a brightly flowered shirt smiled as he turned to face me.

"Where shall I take you, Osofu?" he asked.

I stared back into his warm black face as if I might find an answer. "I don't know," I finally answered.

Now **they** stared at me.

"Why are you here?" the driver asked.

"I don't . . . I don't really know," I stammered. "All I know is that I believe God has sent me to Ghana." How ridiculous I must have appeared to them. How utterly absurd I felt! They could not quite manage to veil the astonishment in their eyes. In the gentle eyes of the driver I also saw something else.

"You are a Spirit-filled Christian, aren't you?" I asked.

"Hallelujah!" he said. "I am."

"What is your name?" I asked.

"Moses," he said.

Suddenly it hit me and I laughed aloud. "Well," I said, "I have come nearly 8,000 miles to find myself in a taxicab with Peter and Moses!" Whether or not they understood the slight edge of desperation in my laughter, I'll never know, but in that lovely hospitality of Ghana, they laughed with me.

"I suppose I should go to a hotel," I said. "Where do the B-Cal flight crews spend the night?"

"Please, Sir, they do not stay in Ghana any more," said Moses, the driver, a bit apologetically. "But before they stayed at the Continental Hotel. Shall I take you there?"

Later while I unpacked in my room, Peter and Moses waited in the lobby. The Continental epitomized Ghana's cracking veneer. The hotel had once been a lively center of sin where Europeans, Asians, and Africans drank and gambled in the casino bar or danced to the throbbing melodies of "high life" bands. Now the once luxurious hotel was an empty shell with a machine-gun-toting soldier in the lobby and an armored personnel carrier parked in the front drive. The room itself was as barren as a prison cell and cost $90.00 American a night.

Taking only my camera, I returned to the lobby. I had the address of the Ghanian Methodist headquarters. Being a Methodist, I thought perhaps that might be the place to start. Frankly, I was grasping at straws. I told Peter and Moses where I wanted to go and we started back to the taxi. Then I saw a scene that I just had to photograph. The soldiers clustered about the armored vehicle seemed such a striking and ominous picture that I instinctively raised the camera.

Suddenly Peter and Moses were all over me! The camera was firmly pulled away from my face and one on each arm, they ushered me briskly into the taxi and we sped away. I felt rather like Jimmy Hoffa on his last date. Looking back on it now, I see that my naivete must have been amazing to them. Glancing out the back window, Peter smiled and exchanged a brief but knowing look with Moses, but neither said a word. They did not have to. I got the point. Discretion was going to prove a necessary virtue on this trip.

What happened at the Methodist building was no less than absolutely predictable. The President of Ghana's Methodist Church was a diminutive man with a heart of a lion, a jolly little face that laughed easily, and the caution born of nearly half a century of ministerial experience. He listened patiently to my story and responded as lovingly as he could, but as firmly as a stern father.

"There was shooting in the streets here two days ago," he said gently. "You just couldn't have come at a worse time. I cannot arrange meetings for you or tell my preachers to take you in. I simply don't know you." I knew that he was perfectly correct in not just taking in some stranger. I was disappointed, to say the least, but I could not fault him. I knew I would have done the same. I suppose I had gone there hoping the heavens would open. I am not sure what I hoped. It was simply my only lead. I **do** know it seemed like the handwriting on the wall to me.

"What are you going to do?" he asked.

"Well, Sir," I said, "I have the name of a man in Kumasi. Brew Riverson. I guess I will try to go there."

"Does he know you?" he asked.

"I believe we met once in the States. I hope he remembers me," I said, trying to sound confident and reassuring. It sounded hollow, even to me.

"Does he know you are coming?" he asked.

"Well, actually, I don't exactly know," I stammered.

"Did he invite you?" he asked.

"No, Sir. But I think —" I just let it drop.

He smiled a patient, warm, fatherly smile. "Go home, Rev. Rutland. That's my very best counsel. Stay in your hotel as much as possible. Then catch the B-Cal flight on Thursday. It would **not** be wise for you to make the trip to Kumasi alone and for such uncertain reasons. It is a dangerous journey. Go home."

Back in my room at the Continental Hotel, I was near collapse. I stepped out onto the little balcony and stared at the traffic jouncing by on the main road in front of the hotel. People jammed into decrepit lorries and ancient taxies while women with impossible burdens balanced on their heads filled the roadway. Autos and pedestrians competed for space on pavement that looked as if it had been bombed for a week.

I looked at the armored vehicle in the parking lot just at the exact moment that one of the soldiers looked up at me. He said something to a young officer who in turn stepped forward and stared up at me shielding his eyes from the sun. At that very moment, a great green lizard chinned himself up onto the balcony with me. His orange head and yellow and red tail gave him a grotesque appearance.

The lizard, like the soldier, stared straight into my eyes. His tongue darted about and it seemed to me that his stare became a mocking sneer. An involuntary shiver went down my spine and I yielded the balcony to the prehistoric-looking creature.

Back in the room, I absolutely caved in. All spiritual, physical, and emotional strength fled away. I could not even pray! It seemed as if Satan came right into the room with me. Frankly, in that moment his voice seemed clearer to me than God's. It was the voice I had heard on the plane. Now it refused to be silenced.

"Fool! Look at the mess you're in now. Tuck your tail between your legs and run. You have disgraced yourself, embarrassed Christians everywhere, and heaped derision on God. Fool! Go home before something horrible happens. You are out of the will of God."

How real that voice was to me. And how devastating! Satan's being suddenly concerned with God's reputation eluded me then. I was completely shattered. Fear, embarrassment, and confusion closed in on me. Fatigue also played a part, I'm sure. Whatever the causes, they worked in tandem to combine for a near knockout punch.

The utterly absurd situation into which I had placed myself pressed me heavily. Futhermore, the nagging fear that I really **was** outside God's will hounded me. The heat, the loneliness, the sense of dead end failure all liberally laced with self-pity, brought down a cold steel curtain on what should have been a joyful first day in Africa. I fell back on my bed in the stifling, little room listening to the strange African sounds from the street. They only seemed to increase my sense of separation. A more oppressive spirit of "aloneness" than I had ever known before filled the room. I was shocked at my inability to fight back spiritually. What a spiritual weakling I was. I literally cried out to God, not for help in the mission, but for help in prayer.

"Oh, God," I cried, "please help me to pray. Just help me to pray."

He did! About 4:00 in the afternoon I began to be able to pray. I learned something that afternoon in that sweltering, African hotel room. No matter what you **think** you know about grace, God can bring you into a theater of experience where you will learn a greater level of dependence on God than ever before. It is a veritable seismic disorder in the stratified layers of our self-sufficiency and pride to realize that when we need it the most, we cannot even pray, apart from His grace.

The grace to pray slowly began to flood my heart. It began to bring feeling, a bit painfully at first, back into my spiritual extremities. The "blood" of prayer began to flow back into areas that had nearly been lost to spiritual gangrene. The momentum of prayer informed by my desperate need combined for the necessary thrust.

From 4:00 p.m. until 4:00 a.m. I prayed as I had never prayed before. Not leaving the room, not eating, not sleeping, I prayed. I walked, I crawled, I wept, I harangued, I pleaded, I bled, I shouted, I praised, I sang, I rolled on the floor, and I lay prostrate on my face. What an unforgettable twelve hours of crying out to God. I was alone, afraid, and totally confused in a foreign country, on another continent, in a hotel room in a city under night-hours military curfew. I did not know whether to go home or to stay. My hopes for making any contact anywhere were pretty dim. I did not know how in the world I would get from Accra to the city called Kumasi; and if I did, what would I find there? The only thing I knew about Kumasi was its name on the map. You bet I prayed!

At 4:00 a.m. I knew the peace of God. Suddenly — in response to what particular prayer I don't know, I was flooded with a magnificent sense of rest. I had no "Word from God" other than that with which I had left Atlanta. It was not a new direction or fresh marching orders. It was the infusion of peace. I did not know how, or when, or where, or who, or anything else. I only knew, suddenly, marvelously, that it was all right.

I slept until 6:00 a.m. when I showered and dressed. I opened the drapes and sunlight flooded the room. I stepped out onto the balcony again and just as I did a small boy on the pavement below saw me.

"Obruni! Obruni!" he shouted gaily, waving madly.

I had no idea what he was saying or even in what language he spoke, but his smile was comforting and his wave enthusiastic so I returned them both, to his obvious delight. This little incident did nothing but enhance the morning's new hope. Leaving the balcony door ajar, I returned to the room and sat on the bed. I was filled with a sense of expectancy. I had no idea what to expect. Nothing had really changed. But, thank God, all the fear and confusion of the afternoon and night before were gone! I had no specific Word from God as to what would happen but I knew things were very near a great shift.

At precisely 7:00 a.m. a loud, confident knock sounded at the door. I opened it and there stood a pleasant-looking black man in his forties. He smiled warmly but looked me up and down before he spoke. Whatever he had expected or hoped for, I was evidently not it.

"Are you Rev. Mark?" he asked doubtfully.

"Yes, I suppose I am. I am Mark Rutland from the United States," I answered. "Are you looking for me?"

He spread his arms out wide and his tentative smile became dazzling. How his eyes twinkled! He had the jolliest countenance I have ever seen. He was a slim, handsome, black Santa Claus. He was merriment personified. It would have been impossible not to respond to this man.

"Ha, ha!" he cried out loud, and throwing his head back, burst into spontaneous laughter. "Welcome to Ghana, Brother. I am Godfrey Bamfo. I have come to find you to preach tonight. It's a miracle!"

His laughter, his smile, the bare fact of his presence were all the miracle I needed right at that moment. My heart catapulted into aerobic exercises and I began to laugh also, not knowing exactly why we were laughing! It is nearly impossible to imagine mere words being able to express how glad I was to see him. We embraced like long-lost friends.

"But how did you find me?" I asked. "Why are you here? What I mean is, how did you know I was here?" The questions refused to wait for the answers.

Over breakfast in the hotel restaurant the story unfolded. In my estimation, it was, in fact, nothing short of a "miracle" as Godfrey had said. It turned out that the letter which I had written to Brew Riverson on July 1st arrived at his house in Kumasi (150 miles in the interior) on the very day that I had arrived in Accra, December 2nd! The letter had said,

> Dear Dr. Riverson,
>
> I do not know if you will remember me or not. Along with our mutual friend, Jerry Morrow, you attended an evangelistic rally where I preached. This was in Atlanta, Georgia. I hope you have good memories of my ministry there.
>
> I have been sensing for some months that the Holy Spirit is directing me to come to Ghana. If this agrees with your spirit, please write to me as soon as possible.

108

Pray about this, if you will, and let me know how you feel. I only want God's will in this as I believe you do.
Yours truly,
Mark Rutland

Dr. Riverson, the principal of a small Methodist college in Kumasi, had taken the letter with him to a faculty prayer meeting even as I prayed in my room at the Continental Hotel in Accra. After having read the letter, several professors joined him in praying for guidance. Should they, they asked the Lord, invite this American to Ghana at such a desperate time in her history?

Suddenly one of the professors had cried out, "Stop! We must not pray anymore! I sense in my spirit that the Lord is saying that this man is already in the country, even now!"

Finding a telephone, they managed to get through to Godfrey Bamfo in Accra. After he heard how sketchy the whole story was, Bamfo told me later, he went back to sleep. He was awakened the next morning with the compelling sense that the American **was** indeed in Ghana. Between 5:00 a.m. and 7:00 a.m., in a city of 1.75 million, he found me!

From that morning until I left on December 22nd, I never went another day, save one, without preaching. Often I preached more than once. On one occasion I preached eight times in one day. I preached in almost every setting imaginable and some I could never have dreamed of. God had moved miraculously to confirm His Word to me. Through those in Kumasi, through Bamfo, even through the coup attempt and the delay in London, God was majestically at work seeing that the letter written six months earlier, the faculty prayer service, and my own arrival coincided perfectly. What grand timing God has. A million "what ifs" immediately arise.

What if the letter had not arrived when I did? What if I had been late? Or early? What if that faculty prayer service had been less faithful? What if Bamfo had been disobedient to the Lord? What if I had gone home from London?

The simple fact remains that He who spoke it, brought it to pass. It was the Lord's doing and it was marvelous in my eyes. At the same time I knew that far from being "over," it was only beginning. Where I would speak, go, or stay was still to be learned, but the Lord had brought me this far.

I checked out immediately and accompanied Godfrey Bamfo

to his home in Accra. As we drove along the old beach highway I saw the ancient castles that had been built by European slave traders and they made me shiver. What an unbelievable evil the slave traffic was. I wondered what demons must **still** be in those castles.

My first speaking engagement in Ghana was at the Accra chapter of the FGBMFI. Due to my past happy relationship with Full Gospel, I felt this was an auspicious launching pad.

The Accra Chapter met for breakfast in a night spot called **Black Caesar's**. A couple of hundred jammed the small dining area. For that breakfast meeting each month, the night club became a restaurant and served a modest breakfast. I sat at the head table with Godfrey Bamfo, the chapter officers, and Issac Ababio, a prominent Ghanian evangelist.

The lights were dim, of course, due to the nature of the establishment and a room full of blacks reflects so little light anyway that I found myself squinting toward the back of the room trying to see individual faces. The humorous thought crossed my mind that they would not have the same trouble picking out my face at the head table.

It was my first opportunity to inspect a really dressed up Ghanian crowd and I found it quite impressive and joyful, and a bit paradoxical. First of all, Ghanians are among the handsomest of Africans, and their traditional garments are very beautiful. The Kente' cloth draped toga-style around the men is often rich purple or maroon. Women in long skirts with hip-length tops are a flower garden of brilliant yellows, reds, and greens. The natural ebullience and gaiety of Ghanians, the lilting music, and the beautiful smiling faces add a delightfully festive spirit to religious gatherings.

At the same time I found an undertone of almost exaggerated dignity. The Ghanians are great orators and at times have a tendency to be verbose. They will seldom use fifty words if one hundred will do. In churches in Ghana I often found the parish notices to be excruciatingly lengthy and repetitive followed immediately by singing of uninhibited and spontaneous joy. It makes for an odd mixture.

All in all, the people of Ghana are a delightful and disarming combination of wit and wisdom, pomp and informality, disorganization and classical British discipline. In the days ahead, I was to see this enigma in many ways.

At the Full Gospel Chapter, I wondered if my testimony would be relevant. How meaningful would the personal testimony of a white, American preacher be to a congregation of black, African businessmen and women? As He had done so many times in the U. S., God anointed it and used it. At the invitation, many responded for salvation, Spirit baptism, and healing. I was blessed beyond measure at the eagerness and joy of their response.

Following the Full Gospel Chapter, Godfrey Bamfo delivered me to a home in Medina, not far from Accra. There I was received warmly but I hated to see Bamfo leave. From his dancing eyes to his ready baritone laugh, he is one of the most infectiously joyous Christians I have ever met. **And** he played such a key role in my arrival.

I found my hosts to be gracious and I soon felt a part of the household. The man was widely traveled in Africa, Europe, and America and is, among Ghanians, a comparative cosmopolite. He is energetic, hard driving, determined, outspoken, and opinionated. He was a fount of information on Ghanian politics, culture, and religion.

We shared until late into the night, but when we retired I found sleeplessness haunted me. This insomnia has been a matter of much prayer for me on subsequent mission journeys. The next morning I was up and dressed at dawn, while in the States, I am usually a morning deadhead. In the courtyard I found Steven, a young man who lives in the home. He was washing the car. Due to the pervasive dust, this is a daily ritual. In fact, Ghana always seems to be sweeping itself off. This is especially true during the Hamatan, a slightly cooler desert wind that carries dust and sand straight off the Sahara and deposits it in Ghana. I arrived in Ghana with the Hamatan and found even the plants coated with a fine, red-brown dust.

The early morning coolness was refreshing and the walled courtyard and garden were quiet and peaceful. The young teenage girl who also lives in the house, came out to feed the animals and I watched as the goats and chickens took their breakfast eagerly.

Suddenly children's voices split the post-dawn calm with cries of "Obruni! Obruni!" Five or six little grinning faces peered through slots in the wall. I waved and called "Hello!" but when I stepped toward them they disappeared like so many puffs of smoke. Moments later, the cry came again, "Obruni!" with much laughing and jostling outside the fence. The faces were so filled with smiles and their tone was so obviously friendly that I knew no offense was meant. I remembered the youngster at the hotel calling out this same word to me.

"Steven," I called softly across the courtyard, "what does that mean? That word they are yelling?"

"It is Obruni, Sir," he replied.

"Yes," I said, "but what does it mean?"

Steven indulged in a quick grin before he said, "Please, Sir, it means 'white man.' "

I was seeing the beginning of an unfolding future reality for my life. How strange it is to be a novelty! The nice cozy domesticity of my life seemed to somehow have been transformed into little black faces peering through fences. Was I, I wondered, born to be shouted at by the children of the continents? My future seemed more real to me than my past in that Ghanian garden dawn. And I sensed my future to be in curious little eyes peeking through the fences of the world.

Chapter IX
Launch Out . . .

TO HIS GLORY

A black star on a field of green and yellow whips in the breeze above the parliament house in Accra. The flag of Ghana seems somehow unrepresentative and somber for a nation with such a dancing heart. In the time I spent in Ghana, I fell in love with Ghanians just as I had with the Mexicans. Ghana is a troubled nation. Drought, food shortages, governmental instability, curfews, martial law, and unimaginable inflation are abiding realities. Many there speak of even worsening conditions, perhaps even of mass starvation, revolution, and civil war. Yet, I found many of the people of Ghana to be not only hopeful about the future, but remarkably good-humored in the face of this winter of their discontent.

Perhaps the positive by-product of cataclysm in Ghana, however, is an atmosphere of such openness and even hunger for the Word of God, that doors of utterance spring open at the slightest nudge. In the month of that first trip to Ghana, with absolutely no advance notice of my arrival and with no set itinerary, I preached every single night save one and often more than once. By the most conservative count, denying **all** evangelistic hyperbole, I saw about 1,500 public salvations in twenty-eight days of ministry.

The first Ghanian church I preached in was the Methodist church in Medina. The service was the perfect expression of the contrast I had already observed in Ghana. The first part of the service seemed hardly more than the fatigued vestiges of Colonial British religion. The choristers processed a bit pompously to some stately hymn of the church while the organ wheezed out its strains. At each step they swayed slightly from side to side. How quaint they were in flowing black robes and mortarboard hats. They looked rather like an American graduation class having had a serious celebration **before** the proceedings.

The prayers and the responses were read phonetically from British prayer books. The utter lifelessness of it all was depressing. The old pastor in his black robe and white collar lacked only a powdered wig to be a tired Caribbean magistrate gazing with ennui at his usual Monday morning caseload of drunken sailors.

Just when I had given up hope of life, the whole mood of the service shifted dramatically into high gear. Suprisingly enough, the turning point was the offering. As the choristers finished, the group called the "singing band" took over. Instead of the sedate tones of an English hymn, tall drums throbbed and the swaying singers, dressed not in robes and hats but in traditional Ghanian garments, began to bring the church to life.

The melody and rhythm were catchy and soon the entire congregation was on its feet, clapping and singing in Twi (the language of the Ashanti tribe). It was as if the past and tradition had been paid off early on and now they could be themselves. After a few praise songs and a couple of specials, a blue plastic basin was placed on a table before the altar. Row by row they danced, not walked, forward to put in their offering. How gracefully they moved in a kind of soft shuffle! Their joy in the music, the dance, each other, and the moment was obvious. I wished that more American congregations could give with such joyful abandon.

Soon it was my turn to move toward the offering bowl. A quick glance assured me that every eye in the house was watching me. I decided to make the plunge. I had come too far to turn back now. Imitating the step the best I could, I danced toward the front. An immediate and spontaneous burst of applause mixed with laughter filled the church house. I could feel the color in my face and I knew that I must look to them about as graceful as Quasimoto in flight. Their obvious appreciation for my willing attempt took the sting out of the embarrassment.

Unlike the Full Gospel Chapter, it was necessary for my

sermon to be interpreted. The response, as at the Full Gospel meeting in Accra, was fabulous. More than twenty-five persons, **including the pastor,** came forward to receive the assurance of salvation.

Someone later explained to me that much of the denominational religion in Ghana, though lively in appearance, is in actuality quite Spiritless. The music and the dancing, though certainly more uplifting than the tired, rote remnants of British Methodism, may at times be more Ghanian culture than true joy of the Lord. I know this is true. Frequently, I saw people who danced with great liberty in the course of the service come to the altar for salvation at its conclusion.

Where salvation by faith is not preached and holiness is not taught, cultural religion, regardless of its vivacious character, will be the insufficient answer of an insufficient church. I have seen this in socially oriented,country-club churches in the U. S. I have also seen it in the singing and gaiety of denominational churches in the third world where culture, **not** the true joy of the Lord, strummed guitars.

I preached twice more in the Accra area before making an attempt to get to Kumasi. That city had always been my goal and I began to feel strongly that I should be there. Bamfo and I had never been able to get a call back to Dr. Riverson to tell him I was, in fact, in Ghana. Perhaps, reason said, I should just stay in Accra. The Spirit, however, seemed clear that I should go on to Kumasi.

On Tuesday morning, Godfrey and I managed to get a ticket (miracle of miracles) on Air Ghana to Kumasi. By several hours of traipsing from office to office and wrangling with official after official, we finally found a duty officer who heard our appeal and promised to add my name to the manifest. Bamfo labored to try to explain the rationale for this tedious exercise. I finally understood that Air Ghana sells as many tickets as it wishes for a given flight, irrespective of the actual number of seats on the plane. Though helpful, not even one's name on the manifest is a guarantee of a seat.

"Now listen, Obruni," Bamfo said with a good-natured chuckle, "If you stand back and act with dignity, you will not go on this flight. When I say run, you run to that security station."

The twin props on the Air Ghana plane from Monrovia had

not even stopped when the double doors at the rear of the terminal swung open. I ran out across the runway with the others. So desperate was I to make that flight, that with two bags I was still third in line at the security station. On that mad, little dash, I did not, I think, "act with dignity."

At the airport in Kumasi, I hired a taxi to Wesley College. I was shocked to find the roads in Kumasi even worse than those in Accra. The driver pontificated on the petty vengeance of the government in Accra, claiming that the roads in the Ashanti district were neglected because of Kumasi's fierce independence.

Whatever the reason, they were awful. The decrepit taxi bounced and pounded its way along dust choked roads until I thought I would suffer permanent back injury. Despite the roads, however, I found myself immediately attracted to Kumasi. The city had the character and personality that teeming Accra seemed to lack.

The taxi finally turned in and stopped at the President's home at historic Wesley College. I was instantly in a swirl of excitement. No sooner had I stepped out of the taxi than a bubbling, shouting, laughing woman embraced me as if I were her long lost son. She was Victoria Riverson, absolutely the merriest lady I have ever met. Her excitement that I **was** indeed in Ghana and at **her** house was a spark to the tinder of her short-fused emotions. As her children tumbled out of the house after her, I was completely engulfed in a shouting, laughing, kissing sea of questions, embraces, and exclamation.

Victoria and her children made me immediately and totally a part of the household. Ebenezer, the eldest, is a strikingly handsome young man. He carried my bags upstairs while little David dashed across the campus to the administration building to collect his father. Dr. Riverson arrived moments later to join in the festivities.

Brew Riverson is a tall, slim, profoundly intelligent, professorial type presiding with great dignity over a small Methodist college in deep difficulty. He, like his school built by the British in the 1920's, is a bit anachronistic. In his long Sunday robe and collar he is a striking and quaint incongruity with the jet age. Yet a more precious Christian brother I do not have in all the world. In another time he would have been a Fanti Warrior. In this day, he is a prince of the church.

His scholarship has failed miserably to make him the least bit stuffy. He seems completely devoid of conceit. His humility and grace charmed me immediately and his sense of humor is typically Ghanian in its readiness for laughter.

At times, however, in unguarded moments, I caught a trace of sadness in his eyes. Perhaps the cracking walls of Wesco's (as Wesley College is called) buildings have become a symbol to him of a seriously eroding nation, government, and society. I have hardly ever met a more fiercely loyal Ghanian than Riverson, yet his sensitive heart refuses to be completely stilled by his government's false hopes and patchwork programs.

I remember watching his face growing more and more weary with the passing moments as we listened together to Ghana's Head of State, Jerry Rawlings, in a one hour and forty-five minute tirade. I love to hear Riverson, himself speak of mystic symbolism in the ancient Golden Stool of the Ashanti.

I spent the balance of my stay in Ghana in Kumasi. The Lord opened doors of utterance there that were absolutely amazing. Through Brew's invitation, (and I found he commanded tremendous respect in Ghana), I spoke at several Methodist churches in and around Kumasi. At each church I was welcomed with love and the Gospel was received with an eagerness beyond my dreams.

The Sunday morning service at Wesley Chapel (the nation's largest Methodist Church) was a remarkable example of the contrast I had seen in Medina. The building itself is a veritable cathedral with a fine organ, huge vaulted ceilings, and a U-shaped balcony. The congregation was obviously of a higher class and station than Medina's. The early part of the service was formal and stylized but the singing band brought a livelier touch. As before, the 750 to 900 or so in the congregation showed greater vitality in the offering than anything else.

As I preached, perched high in a raised "crow's nest" pulpit, with the interpreter, I felt a great movement in my spirit. I sensed something was about to happen. But it was beyond what I dreamed. Using Acts 16:31, I preached on salvation by faith.

"All those who want to receive Christ as Saviour by faith, please stand up," I said at the close of my sermon.

More than half the congregation stood!

Oh no, I thought, they have misunderstood the invitation. I wondered if the interpreter had made some dreadful mistake. I just knew that 350 to 400 people there were not going to receive the Lord in one morning. I instructed them all to be seated and gave the invitation again.

"**Please**," I said, "if you are already assured of your salvation by faith **do not stand**. Only those that are not sure and want to accept Christ as Saviour and Lord by faith should stand." This time even more stood! More than half the choir stood in their mortarboard hats.

I was belligerent in my attempt to limit God. I asked them all to be seated yet again. I explained in careful detail that no saved Christians, born again of the Spirit by faith should stand. "Only those who want to receive assurance this very morning should stand."

Absolutely determined to receive God's gift of eternal life, they stood for the third time. They refused to be discouraged even by my strange, faithless antics. There were far too many to call them forward. Their voices filled the air as they repeated the sinner's prayer after the interpreter. I wondered if any other evangelist ever in history had been so reluctant to receive such a harvest.

At church after church, the Word of God was mighty and the harvest was great. Grace, Calvary, Asawasi, Grace Bible, Calvary Assembly, Old Tafo — precious names, precious nights of revival power. Methodists, Presbyterians, Assemblies of God, and independents of stripe. What a harvest!

It was exciting to see how the Lord opened new doors each day. In the United States I had become accustomed to following a detailed itinerary planned out months and even years in advance. It was new and actually fun to watch the Lord bring the opportunities in His own way.

One morning a small delegation from a church on the outskirts of Kumasi appeared at the Riversons while Brew and I breakfasted. It was arranged for me to preach there the next night. A physician from Old Tafo came around one afternoon to invite me to teach a men's fellowship in his church and a young professor at the college took me to preach at the Assembly of God where he attended. Soon there were more doors open than I could go through.

The perfect example of this "Holy Ghost Scheduling" occurred during an afternoon service at an independent church just outside town. During the congregational singing I noticed a car pull to the side of the church and stopped. The driver leaped from the car and motioned for the pastor. Through the window I watched the two men talking earnestly. I wondered what was wrong. In a few moments, the pastor turned to the open window and motioned for me to come out.

"Brother Mark," he said, "this man has come from the seminary in Kumasi. They have heard how God is using you. They invite you to be their graduation speaker. Will you accept?"

"Why, yes, of course," I said, shaking the visitor's hand. "When is your graduation service?"

"Oh," he said, realizing my misunderstanding. "It is **now**. We hope that you will come now. You see, I have my car. The students and faculty have heard what you are doing here and they are waiting now for you to come."

"But what about your people?" I asked the pastor. "Aren't they expecting me to preach here? I don't want to just go off and leave them."

The pastor smiled one of those smiles usually reserved for the mentally retarded. "I will explain it to them. They will wait if I tell them you are coming back. Go. It will be fine."

We bounced and jounced our way across Kumasi and into a long dirt lane to the small, independent seminary. As I entered the students stood beside their desks. Later, after the sermon, they stood again as I left through a side door to return to the other church. I fully expected no one to be there but instead, a few more had been added through extra singing and praise. They had waited nearly two hours! I wondered how many U. S. congregations would be willing to do that.

At a prayer meeting on the eve of my departure from the U. S., some special friends and I had prayed fervently for, among other things, "doors of utterance." Since I was so completely "without portfolio," as it were, this was a major burden of all our prayers. Before that month in Ghana was over, I was nearly to the point of asking God to ease up. One particular day I preached eight times!

The Kumasi Industrial Chaplain, an energetic and dedicated brother, set up an ambitious preaching program that took me from a biscuit (cookie) bakery, to a brewery, to a shoe factory, to the district offices of the board of education in the same day. It was thrilling to witness the power of the Gospel to such diverse groups in the same day. Secretaries and office workers at the brewery sat riveted by the words of love and holiness. Illiterate laborers at a shoe factory blinked back tears and the leaders of education for the Ashanti District asked questions for more than half an hour after I spoke.

At a fertilizer formulation plant the manager brought both shifts together to hear the Word. They stood in hip boots and work clothes, listening intently to the strange white man from America. God had promised me in January that He would take me to many unusual places, but I could hardly have imagined such a day.

The last stop of the day was Darko Farms. Mr. Darko is an extremely astute businessman who has parleyed his poultry business into a formidable and prosperous enterprise. In a land of such disorganization and disruption in business and government, Darko Farms is an island of peace and prosperity. It is well ordered by Biblical guidelines. Darko is a quiet, peaceful, and truly dedicated Christian man. His business is an extension of himself. In an uncanny way, one senses Darko's personality and spirit almost immediately upon entrance to the grounds of Darko Farms.

Mr. Darko had agreed to bus the workers in from all of his farms if I would come preach at the central warehouse. Four hundred workers (mostly men) gathered in the huge metal building. They were seated on bales, drums, and boxes nearly to the ceiling. This was easily the most illiterate group to which I had spoken on the whole mission. There were tribal marks on a greater percentage of the faces than in any other congregation. Four hundred men stared down darkly from the banks of drums and bales at their employer, a Ghanian Chaplain, and an unfamiliar white man.

Mr. Darko suprised us all with a rousing baritone solo and a testimony. His testimony was in Twi, but I could tell from the men's faces that he had their attention **and** that he commanded their respect. I watched carefully to pick up any signs that they considered him a hypocrite. I saw none.

He called on the Chaplain who introduced me and I stepped to the middle of the floor. I sensed an uncomfortable air of suspicion and doubt. The faces were somber and the eyes piercing.

I had only begun to bring greetings when looking far into the rear of the huge warehouse, seated high among the topmost rows of workers, I spied two delicate young white girls in their late teens or early twenties. It had been weeks since I had seen a white face except for one British missionary, and their flowing blonde hair and pale skin was in shocking contrast with the rows of black men in the dark warehouse. I must have been comical indeed, as I stopped, mid-sentence, mouth open to stare up at them. It flashed across my mind that they were angels. They giggled down at me and waved gaily, realizing the effect their presence had had on me. I thought they looked quite satisfied with themselves. Those two little blondes looked almost bizarre perched high among hundreds of African poultry workers. **But, I thought, why not? Everything else on this trip has certainly been bizarre.**

I recovered in a few seconds and began to preach. My topic was from Daniel; the "Handwriting on the Wall."

The interpreter had liberty and the Spirit of God began to work the miracle of faith. I closed like this:

"You can know beyond a shadow of doubt that you are born again of the Spirit and that in death you will go to heaven and not judgement and hell.

"Belshazzar was a king, but he suffered God's judgement because of sin. Hell will be full of rich men (that got a slight stir) and generals, and kings, and presidents — and poultry workers who do not have Christ in their hearts by faith. God does not care if you are white or black, Ghanian or American, rich or poor. Are you born again?

"You **can** have the assurance of salvation right now by faith. If you will give your life to Jesus Christ and turn away from sin, Stand up! If you want to put your faith **only** in the blood of Jesus, stand up right now. If you are not truly saved and you want Jesus Christ to come into your heart right now and take away your sins, stand up and I will pray with you."

I have given thousands of altar calls, yet I never fail to find immensely exciting, that one slightly breathless moment of waiting to see who will respond in faith to the great promise of the Gospel. I knew God was moving. I bowed my head and began to pray softly in the Spirit as I frequently do in such moments. I could hear movement. When I looked up, more than half were standing with heads bowed and eyes closed. They repeated the sinner's prayer with gusto but I felt strangely led to do something extra that day.

After they were seated again, I said, "Now your names are written in Jesus' great Book of Life. This means your name is now very important. You are born again! You must never be ashamed of that or of your name. Now if you just received Christ as your Saviour, I want you to stand up again and call out your name very loudly."

The seconds were ponderous. I waited staring up into the rafters, looking for some movement to signal a response. Suddenly a man near the very top stood abruptly. Arms stiff to his sides, he shouted out his own name. He was immediately followed by dozens, then by more than two hundred as those who had accepted Christ stood again and began to shout their names. Tears glistened on many of the faces. It was a soul-stirring scene indeed. For many of those men it was perhaps the first time their names had mattered for much of anything. Later in Mr. Darko's office we rejoiced at the harvest. I urged Mr. Darko to nurture the new converts and he committed himself to exactly that. When I returned to Ghana a year later, I found that he had hired a full-time chaplain just for Darko Farms. A Bible study had been started on each farm and many of those men had been baptized and added to churches.

The two blondes, by the way, I discovered to be Swedish foreign exchange students. They did **not** answer the altar call and I never saw them again. Someday, perhaps, I **will** see a real angel, but those two, I was told, were **not**.

Some of the most precious memories I have of that journey are of Wesley College. The fading, decaying beauty of the old buildings became almost alluring to me. The road in front of the college is bad; to call it rutted is to say that the Grand Canyon is a good-sized hole in the ground. I could never get used to the bone-shattering jolts of riding on it. Somehow, though, I found a kind of tropical gentility and peacefulness that made the campus into a sanctuary.

I sat writing at my desk upstairs at the Riverson's home late one evening, when drums and music from across town became quite loud and frenzied. I went downstairs to the family room and inquired about them. Dr. Riverson cocked his head slightly, listening for just a moment.

"Someone has died," he said, "those are Ewe drums; though, not Ashanti."

That contrast again. It seemed very strange to me to be

standing in the family room of an erudite and cosmopolitan college president who could interpret the primitive throbs of funeral drums. What a country!

I enjoyed long walks alone and as I became more familiar with the area, these strolls took me further and further from the Wesco Campus and into more and more isolated and out-of-the-way areas. In these places I caused a mild stir. I suppose white men strolling nonchalantly through such streets are simply not seen. Everyone waved and I enjoyed addressing them in Twi. How they smiled when I called out a cheery "Maachi" (Good Morning), or "Wo huntisen?" (How are you?). Sometimes I drew quite a crowd, especially children. Each one wanted a pat on the head — I think to be honest, this had something to do with luck — or a handshake. I must have looked like the Pied Piper in some of those streets with a literal host of children trailing along behind. The abject poverty and filth hardly seemed to dampen their spirits. We were a laughing, happy band.

Once I turned a corner and directly before me sat an elderly chap in shorts and a tattered British army blouse. He was reclining on the roadside, his back against a tree, waving softly at flies without any trace of energy. When our eyes met, his were suddenly ablaze. He scrambled to his feet, brushing off the seat of his khaki shorts, and struggling to fasten the one remaining button on the old blouse. All set, he forced his old body to "attention" and gave a snappy British salute, palm forward. For just a moment there was such a flicker of life and joy in his eyes that I thought perhaps I could read his mind. **My God!** He seemed to be thinking, **It's the young captain! He's back! After all these years, he's back!**

I was not sure what to do. After only a split-second of hesitation, however, I halted, snapped to attention, and gave my best imitation of the palm-frontward British salutes I had seen. When we dropped our hands, I extended mine for a handshake and he grasped it firmly and rewarded me with a totally toothless grin that spread across his face like a valley in black hills.

The worship services at Wesco were remarkable experiences. The students are bright and attractive, and those true believers on the faculty are extremely serious about the spiritual well-being of their charges. As the Lord would have it, the student

Christian Association had arranged for a campus-wide preaching mission in December, but they had no speaker. When I suddenly arrived on campus from "out of nowhere," they were certain God had sent me to Ghana just for their religious emphasis week at Wesco. Several of the leaders came round to "look me over" and I felt a bit like a quail in the camp of the Hebrews.

Each night God gave us fruit among the student body. Numbers were saved or baptized in the Holy Spirit. One night all the lights in that whole area of Kumasi went out. This was not an unusual occurrence in the least, but it left the old auditorium in total darkness. Not a student left. The spirit of praise in the place became even sweeter. The Holy Spirit seemed to come upon one young girl in particular who refused to yield to the darkness. Her beautiful soprano voice led out on one chorus after another until she became an obvious rallying point holding the whole situation together.

God honored her faith by reminding Dr. Riverson of a generator in a nearby church. The thing was collected and, miracle of miracles, it had fuel in it. When the lights came on, a rousing spontaneous cheer burst from the throats of the students. It was perceived as a victory for the Christians on campus. I felt it was a message from God for us all to stand fast in the darkness and praise Him. Soon the light will come again.

The Wesco students became very precious to me and within days of my arrival on campus I was having a constant parade of visitors for counselling. I was constantly amazed at their innocence and lack of sophistication. What a contrast they were to the suburban jades I had become used to in the United States. Many of their problems were universal and were shared by American youth. In some cases I knew that only the Holy Spirit could enable me. Nothing in my background, culture, or education had prepared me to deal with a young boy whose parents had forced him to take part in pagan worship rites including drinking some concoction composed mostly of chicken blood. Seminary classes in pastoral care seemed far away when dealing with a college girl who believed her aunt had put a curse on her.

The constant difficulties and obstructions to ministry met so gallantly by those in the third world are manifestly evident in Ghana. The shortages in every commodity from light bulbs to gasoline are extreme and the results range from inconvenient to shocking. Night meetings are dimly lighted, transportation is complicated and communication is frequently impossible!

Poor Dr. Riverson's administration at Wesco is constantly struggling with the basic problems of how to feed his student body and how to put one more band-aid on a campus plumbing system showing its age. His efforts to educate and inspire his students while feeding them and keeping some semblance of a roof on their buildings is nothing short of heroic. A man of less character would either yield to discouragement or become brittle. Riverson has done neither.

It was not all grim. The Lord constantly filled our mouths with laughter. The battery in Riverson's antiquated Peugeot had fairly given up the ghost. Replacement was impossible. The shelves of every auto parts store in Ghana were utterly barren. The black market offered its precious few batteries at a mere $800-$1,000 U. S. currency.

If necessity is the mother of invention, she is the aunt of perspiration. Dr. Riverson would always try to park on a grade for a rolling start. What a picture! Bespectacled, intelligent Dr. Riverson with his clerical collar on, seated behind the wheel of his ancient Peugeot, powered by a sweating, straining white man, and both of us laughing at the sight we presented to those who watched. Help was often handy and the old car started each time.

Very early one morning I stood on the little balcony outside my room, watching the post-dawn activity in the street below. The road through the campus was a pedestrian thoroughfare. The traffic was constant from 5:00 a.m. until dark. A woman was patiently casting a heavy stick into a tree and collecting into a heap the long flat dried pods that fell out. Two little boys manipulated, with no small difficulty, a two-wheeled cart supporting long bamboo poles. Women with huge basins of Kenke balls, or rice wrapped in banana leaves made their way toward some favorite street corner for a long day of peddling to passersby. Their babies snuggled peacefully against their backs in the wide band of Kente cloth where they would spend virtually the whole day.

A tiny blackheaded finch and a large cockatoo-like bird with a beak nearly as large as its body, gossiped in the top of a palm. I imagined how my mother, an inveterate bird watcher, would

125

enjoy making her "African checklist." Lizards of multiple varieties had begun to scurry about their lizard work and buzzing insects shouted warnings to their neighbors.

Suddenly it seemed as if I could hear the entire third world waking at once. How different from the blatant noise of the U. S. America awakes like a hungry child — fussy and cranky. Her cacophonous morning sounds blur into one great honk and the corporate squeal of every brake drum in the world. One does not hear sounds in America's morning streets, but **noise**. Dawn is a symphony in Ghana. It is played with only minor variations all across the whole third world every morning. It is the poor ear that has not heard it.

As I listened, it seemed that God was reminding me by His Spirit that I was to hear such sounds in many places before I rested. The memory of the experience in my house that had spawned this trip in the first place flitted across my mind. I sensed a gentle reminder from the Lord that this was not **the** trip to Africa. I had not finished with the third world on this journey any more than I had finished with missions when God had sent me home from Mexico.

The Wesco students began to make their way, in softly chatting clusters, toward the chapel for morning prayers. Several spotted me on the balcony and waved. It troubled me just a bit to feel so very "right" there.

Later that afternoon I stood on the same balcony and watched several of the college yard workers kill a snake in the brown grass below. It was accomplished with a great deal of shouting and noise and when it was complete, one of them lifted the lifeless creature up on a stick for me to see it.

"What kind is it?" I called down.

A flurry of discussion in Twi produced the answer. One that spoke English shouted, "A green mamba. Very dangerous!"

"Will it kill a man?" I asked.

His deep laughter was soft. "Kill a man quick, Sir," he said. "Kill him sure." He lifted the snake a little higher, enjoying my obvious willingness to remain on the balcony. I determined to be a bit more careful in the future. I later found that the green mamba is perhaps the most dangerous snake in the world.

The loneliness for my family grew the longer I stayed. One night, I went to sleep with a special burden in my heart for my middle daughter, Rosemary, who at age three, was beginning to twine her father about her fingers. I wanted to see her so badly that tears came in my eyes. I began to imagine all sorts of terrible things had happened. Sleep finally came, but it was restless and unsatisfying.

Just before morning I dreamed that I awakened to see Rosemary standing beside my bed. In my dream I sat up in bed, startled, of course, to see her there.

"Rosemary!" I said. "Are you all right?"

"Yes, Daddy," she answered soberly. "I'm all right. I love you."

"I love you too," I said, but when I reached to embrace her, she was gone and I was awake. I received it as a word of assurance from the Lord and took great comfort from the dream. I thank God for the miracles, but those moments when He reveals His concern for our hurts and fears are so special. Sometimes I **need** to know Him as Jehovah-Jireh. Sometimes I need a **Father** who will "kiss it and make it well."

In the later part of that time in Ghana, I grew increasingly fond of a young man named Samuel Odarno. He became my driver, companion, tour guide, interpreter, and advisor. Dr. Riverson's busy schedule at Wesco dictated that he put me frequently in Sammy's hands, and Odarno and I grew very close.

His intensity and certain personal mannerisms made me think of my own pastor and friend, Lawrence Lockett. Odarno is perhaps the most intent soul-winner I have ever met. He seems to be absolutely without personal ambition. His eyes are so fixed on the goal that the petrol shortages and the curfew and the transportation problems are simply minor irritations, hardly to be considered. I have seen him listen as other Ghanians listed the difficulties surrounding a certain task. It became obvious to me that they were inviting him to draw the conclusion that it was impossible. Instead, he sat patiently until they finished. Then, without commenting on the difficulties, he proceeded as if he had not heard a word. I believe the Spirit of Caleb is upon Sammy in a double portion. He simply refuses to be sidetracked or discourged.

Among the places I went with Sammy Odarno, one is forever embossed on my memory. Santasi is actually a suburb of Kumasi, but due to such severe traffic difficulties, it appears quite separate. It is poorer than some other areas; but the little church, quaint in appearance and idyllic in setting, is pleasant enough. The structure itself is a bit rude and the interior is in dreadful condition. The wide veranda about its entire circumference looks out at a large yard with a good number of trees.

When we arrived the first day, the building was empty and only a few children were playing in the yard.

"Look, Sammy," I said, "no one has come."

"There are too many, Brother Mark," Sammy answered. "The building would not contain them. They are meeting in a cocoa grove."

We wound down a hillside along a narrow trail. Cocoa foliage grows much closer to the ground than most trees and in rolling hill country, visibility is very poor. Suddenly we were in a large flat area filled with people. There, under the cocoa trees, several hundred men and women sat in groups of about a dozen each where they studied the Bible. I learned that they had been thus assembled for three hours when Sammy and I arrived at noon.

Sammy and Scripture Union worked together with an independent evangelist named Francis Amoaka. This Brother Francis called the groups together and they assembled at the foot of a huge mahogany tree. As they drifted in from the groups, I realized that there were many more than I had thought at first.

After a few choruses, Sammy introduced me and I stood to greet them. I preached from between the waist-high exposed roots of the massive mahogany. With Sammy at my side to interpret, I began.

Suddenly — I **SAW** them. I mean to say that I **saw** as it were, with my eyes unveiled. They were seated fan-shaped before me on the ground and on rude bamboo benches. Their black faces and traditional garments were a riot of color under the green tent of the cocoa grove. They stared at me with naked curiosity. A more obvious hunger for the Word could hardly be imagined. Straining forward, eyes fixed, attention unwavering, their tattered Bibles open on their laps, they were a poignant picture. Much more than that, I suddenly realized that this was the **very scene** that had confronted me in that remarkable midnight visitation in my house.

Tears filled my eyes and the lump in my throat threatened to shut down my speaking altogether. I struggled to explain to them why I was so touched, but it was as impossible as it is here in print to articulate the marvel of seeing in actuality an **exact** scene that had been revealed to me ten months previous and thousands of miles away.

The sense of fulfillment and affirmation that the entire mission had given me was almost beyond words.

That one scene was a blazing confirmation of God's faithfulness. I have hardly ever known such a gripping personal awareness of Him in a worship setting. It was as if the Lord put His arm about me and said, "Mark, you see these people? These **very** people in this **very** place were revealed to you in your living room in January that you might see and believe."

Hallelujah! What a wonderment! Now I knew for sure. The night of doubt and fear in the Continental Hotel in Accra seemed far away now. The layover in London was completely gone. The months of agonizing over His will in the U. S. now seemed so silly. There in that cocoa grove, the whole experience of that mission suddenly was once and for all confirmed for me. It was lifted fully and without a doubt, beyond and past adventure or a happy guess that it ended well. It was, at least to my satisfaction, **settled**. It was the clearly commissioned, divinely executed will of a sovereign and utterly faithful God.

At the invitation that day, God moved on the hearts of many. I especially remember a pitiful young witch. She confessed to having practiced witchcraft since her early childhood. Among the evil she had done, she listed cursing several unto death. To her way of thinking, it was "spiritual murder." Prostitution was among her credits and her stories of levitation, evil voices and "snakes" (that is, spirits) within her were more than a little unnerving.

In the name of Jesus, though, she found peace and deliverance. She prayed deep and sincere prayers of repentance. Tears coursed down her face and her body trembled as if she were standing in a cold wind. When she prayed for her deliverance, she shuddered softly and slumped to her knees.

Finally, she stood with assistance and received Christ as her Saviour. Later she was filled with the Holy Spirit. The following Saturday she returned to the meeting at Santasi with all her witchcraft paraphernalia, which Francis and Sammy promptly burned. She was known in that area as "queen" of the witches and her deliverance and conversion caused quite a local stir.

129

For long stretches, there was no pavement at all and, periodically, we saw vehicles broken down or overturned. Several times I saw men standing by the road offering some kind of small animals for sale by holding them aloft for us to see. The long tails of the little creatures were threaded through huge black fists, the animals lifelessly suspended beneath like a clump of grapes.

"What are those men selling?" I asked. "What are those animals?"

"Rats," answered someone in the back.

"To eat?" I asked.

"Yes, Brother Mark," the answer came. "Do they eat rats in the U. S.?"

"Uh — no," I answered. "At least, I never heard of it."

At the military checkpoint on the outskirts of Accra, we had an unsettling experience. These checkpoints are on all Ghanian roads and usually they are no problem. In fact, I have been waved through most of them. However, on this particular day, there was an occurrence that reminded me how tenuous peace is in many countries.

A heavily loaded lorry was in line just ahead of us. We were not close enough to hear the exchange between those in the lorry and the guards, but whatever was said or done, it thoroughly enraged the soldiers. A big sergeant became so suddenly violent that I feared the situation was on the verge of really exploding.

The soldier seized a yam pole (a hard wood pole about six feet long and four inches in diameter) at the end like a huge baseball bat. Screaming at the top of his lungs and ranting like a madman, he began swinging the pole in wide lethal arcs, ending with a shuddering crash against the sides of the lorry.

I watched as the passengers began to climb over the tailgate. They were so shaken, so totally cowed, that I saw what an affront to a man's dignity that kind of abuse of authority really is. I was very sorry for them and felt as if I ought to avert my eyes. At the same time I was in touch again with that hollow place in the pit of my **own** stomach.

I was so wrapped up in the moment of violence just in front of us, that I failed to notice another guard approaching my own window. When I did see him, I could not get the window rolled down before he was right beside the van. Suddenly, he smashed the barrel of his automatic weapon against the window right at my temple. Miraculously it didn't even crack. With shaking hands, I finished bringing the window down.

When he snarled at me in Twi, I said, "I'm sorry, I speak only English."

"Why don't you learn our language?" he shouted. "You come to our country. Why don't you learn to speak our language? We want to speak Twi in Ghana, not English!" His face was contorted in rage.

"I can understand that," I answered, trying to sound calm. "I am an ignorant American and you **must** excuse me. I have not been in your country for even a month. Please forgive me."

The answer seemed to mollify him a bit and after a brief exchange with Dr. Riverson, he waved us through. I was relieved, to say the least, and spoke out of a month of trying to use the few phrases of Twi I knew.

"Medawasee Paa," I said in Twi (thank you, very much).

Suddenly we all froze. He steadied his gaze straight at me. Speaking in all innocence, I appeared to have lied. Worse, he might think I had tried to make him look foolish.

Instead, he seemed to think it a great joke and burst into raucous laughter. Dr. Riverson drove around the empty lorry and back into the road. It was only when we all started to laugh that I realized how silent and tense the little company had been.

We stopped by a pastor's house on our way to the airport. Dr. Riverson and I took tea with the couple and told them about the wonderful ways the Lord had blessed the time in Kumasi. Later, John drew me aside and made an astonishing suggestion.

"Why don't you send me a missionary?" he asked. He went on to outline a special program of youth evangelism and discipleship training that he had devised. It **was** a provocative plan.

"It sounds great, Brother" I said. "And I think it is a wonderful possibility for a work for a missionary. But why ask me?" I don't send missionaries out. I am an evangelist. You need to ask WGM or some big organization."

"But," he protested, "I prayed and the Lord seemed to tell me to ask you. That is all I know. I have been obedient."

The implication was obvious and it rankled. Who did he

131

think he was? Who did he think **I** was? I was not a missionary sending agency. That was someone else's work. I was called to be a preacher — and that's **all**.

Compliments of British Caledonian, I nursed a cup of tea 35,000 feet over the Sahara Desert and meditated over the whole journey. I knew the trip wanted months to sink in and find satisfactory expression. Some things were clear immediately. I had gone out weeping and now I was going home bringing my sheaves with me. I had seen an "absoluteness" to the faithfulness of God. I could say with Paul —

"I know whom I have believed and am persuaded that he is able."

Chapter X
Launch Out . . .

BY HIS WILL

It was like a grain of sand in my shoe. No matter what I did, I could not seem to shake that pastor's disturbing request that I send him a missionary. No matter how I tried to dismiss them, those words were there and simply refused to go away.

Yet they were so totally unreasonable. I found it difficult to believe that I was to begin sending missionaries. I knew nothing about all that. I had never been a missionary. I had no great organization behind me to throw into action. Wonderful blessings had been mine, but my entire paid staff was my father, my mother, and one part-time secretary. How was I supposed to start in a whole new direction? Was the Trinity Foundation to become a sending agency?

I felt clear on the call to preach an uncompromised Gospel message in all of the world that God chose to open for me. I was determined in my heart not to be disobedient to the heavenly vision. My confusion concerned the "hows." At times, we must wait on God to open a door — nay, even a ray of light. At other times, the doors before us open so rapidly that the challenge is more a matter of going through the **right** one. I had a real fear of being in the right church and the wrong pew.

I began to sense the leading of the Spirit to forget the **plan** and take the steps at hand. It seemed that the more I prayed for a sight of the "big picture," the less light I had. On the other hand, the more I sought the Lord about the specific question of sending a missionary to Ghana, the more confirmation I felt.

I am beginning to discover that there is a basic principle that lies very near the heart of God's whole plan of obedience. When the Spirit issues marching orders, He expects the soldiers of the King to cease seeking explanations and simply — march. How often by waiting on some grand blueprint that never materialized, I have missed the opportunity to do something **real** in the Kingdom. Perhaps if God gave us the plan, we might begin to trust it instead of Him.

I determined that my goal in ministry was to be as faithful as I could in each step. Instead of setting out to accomplish some set of long-term goals, I would try to allow the Lord to set the course. I remembered that with the great challenge of Egypt before him, Moses heard God say, "What is that in your hand?"

This was not to say I would never entertain a dream. Quite the contrary. I would not want to live or preach without a vision. The point is, rather, that I would never want to pursue a dream, no matter how precious, at the risk of ignoring or even challenging orders I cannot understand. The general and the private soldier may share a common dream of liberating the next town. At his sergeant's command to "dig in," the private must limit **his** horizon to the excavation at hand. The general does not expect or even care that a soldier see the big picture, only that he obey. "I am the Lord's — the future is His," became a very real prayer to me. I have not always lived by it. When I have, it has not always been without storm and struggle, but it has been my abiding prayer.

It is easy for the men and women God has chosen to use, to miss His will in specifics by trying to build up a "ministry." I can hardly believe that anyone in ministry wants that to happen. It is rather, I think, that it simply becomes too expensive to hear God. Yet, throughout Scripture, the Lord reveals Himself as calling His people into unknown waters.

It was only after Abram had become Abraham and received the child of promise, that God laid out a new step of sacrificial action. It was in his affluence **and** the security of a promise already received that Abraham faced his greatest challenge. Years before, Abram had obeyed, "get thee up into a land that I will show thee." Surely, he thought he had settled in. He could hardly have expected **now**, as an old man with the reward of that obedience living before him in his tent, to face an even stranger command.

Jesus' words to Simon Peter at the Lake of Tiberias put into focus the constant call of the Holy Spirit. He said, "Launch out into the deep and let down your nets for draught." It is in "launching out" that we find our dependence of Him truly quickened. In Kingdom living, we are not to lust for the luxury of learning yesterday's lessons again and again. It is cowardly to do so. We had best not drive our stakes too deep. We are leaving in the morning.

Within two years of returning from Ghana that first time, I found myself with a staff of fifteen men in full-time ministry stretched from India to Africa to South America. In one twelve-month period, the associates of the Trinity Foundation preached twenty-five overseas missions in thirteen different countries. We were supporting indigenous evangelists on three continents and overseas missionaries in three countries.

Yet my dream was not to be a great sending agency like OMS or WGM. In one year, if God wanted us to send five missionaries, I wanted to be willing. If it became thirty or one hundred, then by His grace, I wanted to "launch out."

By the same token, if, in the next year, He said call them all home, I did not want my "ministry of sending missionaries" to keep on a course not pleasing to the Lord.

My goal became to pack light and just try to be the Lord's man as He saw fit. I thought of the 7-Up commercial and prayed, **Lord, let me find an "unministry" that is pleasing to You.**

It has been a strange course. It has not been without its hurdles. I have seen the providence of God, however, and I would not trade with any man I know. I am in the embarrassing predicament of really being happy doing what I feel God is leading me to do. Not the least of my blessings is the sense of being educated by the Holy Spirit in the realm of miracles. I grew up with such a fuddy-duddy religion that it has not been easy even for the God who made heaven and earth. My suspicion is that creation ex nihilo is far easier and done more rapidly than uprooting a stuffy preacher from his superficial, inconsequential, faithless churchianity.

Constitutientes is a poverty stricken colonia (suburb) of Monterrey, Mexico. Something over fifty-thousand people live jammed in an area of a few acres. With no Protestant churches in the colonia, Florencio Guzman began a little house mission. Florencio and I ran the first evangelistic crusade ever conducted in Constitutientes.

We met in the back courtyard of the tiny home where Florencio's house church had been meeting. Students from the Juan Wesley Seminario, a Methodist seminary where Florencio served as Dean, went door-to-door through the early evening. By the time we began, the little courtyard was packed. Several students worked with the children on the front steps. The Spirit seemed present in power, the crowd assembled was better than we had hoped, and the evening promised much fruit for the Kingdom.

When the rain began, it dampened our hopes along with our clothes. It began to drizzle but soon became a steady pour. Several ladies brought bed sheets, which they draped over the clotheslines stretched above our heads. It was a fruitless gesture. In moments, the sheets were soggy sieves, hardly impeding the rain at all. Florencio and some of the seminaristas gamely went on with the service, but it began to look discouraging.

Across the courtyard from me, I could see Mark Nysewander, the missionary, praying. I knew the rain was his concern as well. We were **all** praying. I saw bowed heads and closed eyes all through the courtyard. The rain showed no sign of letting up. In fact, it seemed the harder we prayed, the more it rained.

"Lord," I prayed, "I don't want to sound rebellious, but I don't understand. This crowd is not full of Christians. They won't sit here in the rain much longer. This is our one chance to reach some of these. Everyone is praying, Lord. Why won't You stop the rain?"

It seemed that the Lord spoke to me in my heart. *"Mark, if I answer these silent prayers, I will get no glory. When you pray **aloud**, then the unbelievers will know that I stopped the rain."*

Praying for the rain to stop before a crowd of unbelievers was more than a bit scary. There would be no "claiming anything by faith." One hundred and fifty Mexican unbelievers jammed into an open courtyard were not going to understand any prissy Charismatic lessons on positive cofession. That all sounds good on the radio but people **know** if they are being rained on.

With something less than bold faith, I told Florencio that I felt led to pray about the rain. I asked him to interpret for all the people to hear. Within three minutes, the rain halted dramatically. We could see the rain in three directions, but in the courtyard, it was dry. It was just as if God held His hand over us there. It was a miracle not wasted on the crowd. That night, about forty people were saved.

Two other times during the little campaign at Constitutientes, we saw God's hand clearly. The third night, some of the seminaristas managed to bring in a street gang. They ranged in age from about 8 to 26. The older ones, including the leader, stood against the back wall. The younger ones were scattered through the seats. They were a grim-looking lot, but at the invitation, they came forward with broken hearts. One after the other, they made their way toward the front. There they clasped arms in a circle like an American football team huddling before the play. Their sniffs and sobs betrayed them for what they were, children seeking a loving Father.

The one "holdout" was the leader himself. He was a hard-looking young tough in his early twenties. He lounged against the back wall with his muscled arms folded over his chest. In a tight-fitting soccer jersey, he was an excellent physical specimen. His face was deep brown granite and his flashing black eyes were hard as coal.

The next night while his "gang" was at the front praising the Lord and claiming his salvation, the young leader again stood at the back. His eyes were brooding and a slight sneer was on his lips. At the invitation, however, he pushed his way through the crowd to join his friends **and** his new Saviour. How they all wept and embraced!

Two nights later, after the last service in Constitutientes, Florencio, Mark, and I were in the house with some of the students from Juan Wesley. A surprise cake was brought out as a going-away present for me and soon guitar music and praise choruses filled the little house with joy. After less than half an hour of singing, we began to pray. I have, perhaps, never experienced a sweeter spirit of praise in prayer than we knew in that tiny living room. Sounds of weeping mingled softly with prayers in Spanish, English, and tongues. I was so moved by the sense of what was happening that I opened my eyes just to look at the faces of the others. How precious they were! Their faces looked like angels.

Out of the corner of my eye, I caught sight of a more provocative scene. Faces filled each window. Men and women with wide eyes stared in wonder at the prayer meeting. I realized that many of them, having grown up on the rote prayers of priests, had probably never heard a layman pray spontaneously in Spanish — let alone in tongues.

I took one of the students who could interpret with me and went out the front door. On the way out, I tapped another young man named Lorenzo and signalled for him to follow me. I had been watching Lorenzo and thought I had perceived that he had the gift of an evangelist.

Out in the front of the little house, Lorenzo analyzed the situation quickly and plunged in. Lorenzo, working quickly, and I laboring slowly with an interpreter, went from one small group to the next answering questions and witnessing for Christ. Before we left that night, twelve more had accepted Christ.

Oddly enough, it was not until several days later, thinking back on it, that I realized some of the significance of what I had seen. It was the second chapter of Acts in a small way. Outsiders, unbelievers if you will, drawn by a demonstration of the Holy Spirit in power found in Christ. **That** is the Bible way of church growth.

A year later, I returned to preach at the Jerusalem Church in Constitutientes. It was a formidable block structure with a solid congregation. More importantly, it was a church deeply mindful of its roots in a courtyard revival. Too many American churches have spiritual amnesia. If they ever knew a God-wrought, supernatural revival in the past, they have forgotten it. A church with no memory of the revival it once knew is a pathetic betrayal of its own heritage.

The deadly legacy of forgotten revivals is by no means confined to the United States. There are dead and dying churches on every continent. Even in a country like Korea where the fires of true and enduring revival are obvious to all, there are those stupefied by self and the world even to the tragic extent of missing a true move of God. The further away from revival a church or denomination is in time or attitude, the more apt it is to become institutionally petrified.

When revival winds begin to blow, the response of the church structure will be directly related to its memory. There is no more nauseating classicist than the child of sharecroppers who has married well. Perhaps the petulant response of so many "mainline" churchmen to any full-bodied proclamation of the

Gospel may, in part, be a subconscious effort to drown re-minders of embarrassing roots well planted in historical revival fire!

I recall a United Methodist District Superintendent who told me that revivalism was outdated. He went on loud and long that "those methods are no good in this day and time." He bore down hard on the oft-repeated charge that converts in revivals seldom last. I was certainly shocked when he admitted to me near the end of our conversation that he himself had found Christ at a Billy Graham crusade.

I was even more amazed to discover that one of the most ardent liberal voices in my entire denomination was a graduate of Asbury Theological Seminary. Here was a man trained by and with some of the great spirits of that fine holiness school who now pathetically wandered the hinterlands of theological absurdity, handing down inane statements of confused mis-siology and penning venomous works on liberation theology.

I was hopelessly naive. I need not have been suprised at all. There is no opponent of evangelical theology more rancorous than a former evangelical. There is no tongue more acid in its mockery of a soul winner than that of he who vaguely remembers such "misguided" work in his own youth. And there is no one who hates a visionary as bitterly as the compromised company man who has drubbed his own dream into silence to satisfy his lust to be bishop.

The more bound a man is to the system, the more apt he is to perceive threat in renewal. Rightly so! God is no respecter of persons and the church politician senses instinctively that in the hurricane of true revival, such tidy little kingdoms as his own might be gone with the wind.

It was the Pharisees and the Chief Priests who crucified the Lord of Life. The publican and the prostitute had no ecclesias-tical turf to defend. Bartimaeus squatted in darkness and saw a great light. Caiaphas stood in the floodlight of public recog-nition and was struck stone-blind by it. At the judgement, Bartimaeus exchanged his beggar's rags for a robe of glory. Caiaphas' priestly robes were torn away and the shame of his murderous heart was shown in stark nakedness. "The common people heard him gladly."

From the beginning of the Gospel, it has been so. The tavern owners and the tax collectors would never have gotten Jesus killed. It was priests! The people rose up to greet Luther with open arms. Rome rose up to excommunicate him. Britain's most depraved sinners received Wesley into their grogshops and coal mines. Anglican priests refused him access to their pulpits. Billy Sunday railed at bars and brothels and the most renowned preachers of his day railed at him.

There is a longing for God in all the world and those who are willing to be crucified to reputation and advancement are going to see miracles in ministry. In our day!

The open door of utterance for the Gospel in our day was made clear to me one hot August afternoon through the strangest invitation I ever received. I was chatting with the students at a Trinity Foundation Missions Institute when I was told there was someone to see me in my office. There I found a short, stocky, bull-like black man wearing a hopelessly wrinkled blue suit and a pair of outrageously warped, horn-rim spectacles.

"Hello," I said, as we shook hands. "I am Mark Rutland. Did you want to see me?"

"I have come from Nigeria," he said. "Can you come there and help us?"

It has often been with just such Macedonian dramatics that God has opened new doors for utterance. I did, in fact, go to Benin City, Nigeria with him and have returned frequently since.

Once one opens up to third world ministry, invitations are the least of the problems. God is so faithful and the world is so hungry, that appeals for evangelism and discipleship come from third world bishops, individual missionaries, indigenous agencies, and native denominational structures at every level.

Following the first mission to Ghana, I was suddenly in an absolute hurricane of action on five continents. The vision God had given me of a ministry in many lands began to move from faith to sight even as I watched. And each new trip — each country, each little village and native church became a staging ground for miracles!

The behind-the-scenes hassles of any ministry are not the stuff of which soul-stirring testimonies are made. They are, I believe, the "hindrances" through which God allows us to move so that we can stay in touch with the realities of work, discipline, and integrity. Amid five rooms full of equipment, luggage, and crates of food, strewn everywhere, with adhesive tape like carnivorous vine; visas pending; tickets and travel arrangements being juggled and all the collecting of passports, money, and pictures; with the meetings and instruction to prepare a team for an African mission and get supplies in to missionaries; with the rubble of it all around one's ears — it is quite impossible to be too captivated with one's own hyper-spirituality.

It is hardly ever in the great crises and issues that ministries suffer most. It is more often the tedium of administration and preparation that dulls the cutting edge of many ministries. Yet, without faithfulness in the administration, ministries often become slovenly and ineffective in the long run. It sometimes taxes the spirit, however, to just get a team in position to preach.

That moment — oh, glorious moment! — when planning, preparation and tedium finally give way to the actual event. When revival begins to break open in a church, or a crusade realizes its first converts, or when an overseas mission finally begins, all the birth pangs are forgotten in the joy of the child.

Seated near the rear of the huge KLM 747, I mentally checked over the team, luggage, and the equipment one last time. Too late now, I reasoned, dismissing those thoughts. With only a brief stopover in Amsterdam between us and West Africa, it had begun again. Soon I would see again the teeming, rutted streets, the waving, shouting children, and the crumbling relics of British Colonialism that are West Africa. Eagerness and excitement were laced with just enough healthy apprehension to keep my adrenalin flow in check.

Our arrival scene at Accra airport was absolute lunacy, of course, as always. In recent visits, I have found the situation there notably improved organizationally. In the early 80's, however, bringing in five whites with twenty-five boxes was like tossing a fox in the window of a hen house. Total bedlam broke out. The scene became a madhouse of fighting of unwanted porters who descended like swarms of locusts and arguing with gun-toting soldiers while simultaneously trying to ascertain that none of the luggage disappeared.

The press of bodies was actually crushing us against the side of the truck. Suddenly in all the tug-of-war, the tailgate on the truck was ripped loose. A storm of shouting, arm-waving

141

accusations and counter suits erupted among literally dozens of would-be porters. The tidal wave of bodies and boxes jolted and jerked its way from terminal to parking lot and some kind of final disposition of personnel and gear.

At the height of all the madness, I happened to look straight into the face of an American pastor making his first trip with me. He was the color of a blanched peanut! His eyes darted wildly across the faces of the sea of porters until they met mine. They were a touching recipe of terror, confusion, and game faith.

"Praise the Lord," he squeaked. "We're here."

It was just the medicine I needed. I burst out laughing. Not at him! God forbid! I laughed at myself, at the moment, at the madness, at the useless anxiety that would help nothing, at the ludicrous scene itself, at **nothing**. I laughed because it was —well — Africa! And it was even a little bit good to be back.

Chapter XI
Launch Out . . .

THROUGH HIS POWER

The years following that first "sans portfolio" mission have been filled with miles and countries and memories. The pace has, at times, been nothing short of phenomenal. During one six-week period, I traveled solo completely around the world, preaching well over one hundred sermons in six countries on four continents. The fruit has been lucious as well. That mission alone registered more than three thousand decisions for Christ including many Moslems and Hindus. My wife once remarked that I could hardly write this book for living it. Some of the experiences have been harrowing, others breathtakingly miraculous, others have been tedious. Yet, in each I saw the Hand of God.

The only Biblical goal and purpose of missions is evangelism and discipleship. Even charitable and philanthropic works must serve the end or they remain merely unanointed and temporary adventures in sentimental humanism. The ministry of the full counsel of God in Word and Power is the Biblical model. God is pouring out His Power again today! Unheralded, low-profile, truehearted little ministries all over the world are being used mightily by God in this hour. The big television ministries serve their purpose, but God is also at work in a vast multiplicity of ministries which will probably never hit the front page.

Rawlings Park is the common name for an open marketplace in Accra, Ghana. It is so named in "honor" of Flt. Lt. Jerry Rawlings, Ghana's head of state, who ordered it demolished because of black marketeering, only to see it reopen full scale in less than a week. We backed the truck onto its outer perimeter and set up shop for an impromptu evangelistic crusade.

Three American pastors and Gee Sprague and I watched as the crew ran extension cords, wired in loudspeakers and set up musical instruments for the band. With the sun in a fury overhead, the band finally began. The blasts of the coronet and the bouncing high-life melodies soon drew a crowd. The five white faces were no less a draw and soon we were literally surrounded by hundreds of people. The dust swirled in a cloud and the traffic and the band competed hotly for the airwaves.

We were not at all sure how such a crowd of rough, largely uneducated, market folks would respond to Gee's **profoundly** American music, but they were obviously thrilled. I preached with a Ga Interpreter who did an excellent job. The anointing was heavier than the heat and at the invitation to "come stand right here in front of me if you want to give your whole life to Jesus Christ," no fewer than 250 stepped forward!

The Lord seemed to direct my eyes to one man in particular and I called on the crowd to let him pass through. As they complied, he suddenly began to cry out and then to scream.

"Why? Why? Why?" he wailed pitiably, then added, "oh, my God, how long? How long?"

What, I wondered, have I gotten into this time. I hadn't long to wonder anything. He came straight to me looking wilder with each step. I responded more in desperate instinct, I think, than in great faith.

I lifted up my Bible and called out at the top of my lungs, "Whether there is one of you, or one thousand, all evil, foul spirits in this man — in the Name of Jesus, I command you to loose him and come out!"

He crumpled in the dust at my feet as if shot. He moaned horribly, rolling at my feet until the pastors with me knelt beside him and prayed. Momentarily he fell silent and finally stood up completely delivered. We prayed and counseled with him and then led him to the Saviour. His testimony was bizarre.

He had gotten involved with a secret order of para-Mohammedan wizards who, having sucked him in, abandoned him to a dreadful life of horrifying demon possession. Finally, evil spirits took such complete control of him that he would wander in a living nightmare in the forest hills around Accra. Wearing no clothes for weeks at a time, living like an animal, eating anything he could find, he became hardly more than a beast. At times, he would enjoy brief respites when he would come to himself sufficiently to find some rags to cover himself, wander down into Accra and scavenge in the marketplaces. Even so, he had come that very day to Rawlings Park — and to Jesus Christ, the mighty deliverer.

One other case of true and dramatic deliverance occurred in India in the state of Tamil Nadu. I had been invited to preach that Sunday in a very cold, stiff, oppressively formal Anglican church in a small town. The Lord led me to take John 3:1-3 as my text. S. E. A. Jesudason, a Trinity Foundation indigenous evangelist in India, interpreted, as he always does, with great clarity and power. The sermon could hardly have been more simple or, for that matter, have made a more direct frontal assault on formal religion.

At the invitation, more than sixty men and perhaps as many as forty-five women stood for salvation. Afterwards we prayed with the sick. An elderly couple brought a young woman whom I judged to be in her twenties. Her furtive eyes refused to meet mine. A sneer curled her lips and in answer to questions, she would often chuckle wickedly and wave her arms wildly about her head as if warding off bees. Indeed, she kept saying, "Things are buzzing in my head."

Jesudason and I raised our Bibles and began to take authority over the demons in Jesus' name. Her reaction was immediate and dramatic. She flailed her arms like a drunken windmill and screamed, "Ile, ile" (no! no!).

As we continued to pray, she dropped to the floor and her body contorted in an awful fashion while she pulled her hair and cried out. We began to sing, "Power in the Blood" and the contortions became truly wild. I honestly thought she would surely break a bone. We battled about ten more minutes until suddenly she went as limp as a rag doll. We sang again and after a few moments she awoke.

How stirring it was to see her calm face and peaceful eyes! "Clothed and in her right mind."

It is a frequent and not easily avoided danger of Christian testimonies to leave out the unhappy parts — the times when prayer simply did not seem to penetrate. Of course, our God is a God of victory, not defeat. But how in touch with reality can a man be who has no memory of faith in the crisis of a momentary setback?

Two particular memories in the area of deliverance are still painful to recall. In a Monterrey, Mexico slum, I went to a little, walkup flat with some seminary students. We had been called there to pray with a young woman who was reportedly demon possessed. As we started up the filthy little stairwell, any doubts I may have had concerning the veracity of the report began to fade. Such ungodly (I use the term advisedly) sounds emanated from inside the apartment, that an involuntary shiver went through my body.

Screeches that can only be described as "demonic" greeted our approach. The voice was the raspy croak of an old man but with an animal quality and unnatural volume that echoed eerily down the staircase. We had been told that all the neighbors lived in fear of her. Small wonder!

I have never seen anything before or since to compare with the sheer horror that met my eyes. The demonic proved to be a frail, bird-like creature of about 25. Her face, a horrid revelation of the demons behind it, was a masque that defied the imagination. Her features were contorted as if in constant pain. The eyes had waxy-looking circles of rainbow hue that covered a third of her countenance. It was difficult to believe, in fact, that they were not enameled on. The "whites" of her eyes were a lurid vermillion in which not one trace of actual white remained. She appeared as if she had been struck with a baseball bat wielded with incredible accuracy and strength. We were informed instead that it was a symptom of a life of near sleeplessness — often as little as ten to fifteen hours a week, week upon week.

She lived her life **only** in the family bathroom. There she even ate the few morsels of food she would receive, mostly just crouching on the floor, screaming curses hour after hour. When we arrived, her family finally forced her out into the room with us and restrained her in a chair.

Pleading the blood of Jesus, singing, praying, taking authority in the Name of Jesus, we began to claim her liberty. Sometime later, we quietly left without one single trace of any progress that I could detect. I felt as if all my knuckles, knees, and forehead were raw and broken open from a tragically futile assault on a stone wall.

I was shaken, beaten, and downcast. That poor wretch! My, how I had wanted to see her free. Yet, as far as I could perceive — **nothing**. Satan mocked at me. My own flesh cringed. The seminarians were silent.

I had to preach in a matter of minutes and I had seldom, if ever, in my life felt less prepared to do so. All strength seemed gone. Faith lay badly wounded. How could I preach in such shattered form?

"Young brothers," I said to the seminarians, "we must pray **right** now."

"Yes, Brother Mark," one agreed quietly.

"I don't understand why we fail when we do," I said. "But we do. I don't really trust preachers that never have a failure. Tonight we lost. As far as I can tell, we just got whipped and I am hurting pretty badly right at this moment."

A female student named Lily Gonzalez opened her Bible and read, "But we have this treasure in earthen vessels, that the excellency of the power may be of God, not of us. We are troubled on every side, yet not distressed; we are perplexed but not in despair; persecuted but not forsaken; cast down but not destroyed. . . ."

We fell to our knees and prayed a prayer of brokenhearted sorrow at our powerlessness. I am not ashamed to admit that I have had to pray like this since. Would to God for a life of prayer and fasting rich enough to win such hell's prizes as that poor wretched girl. When reality proves otherwise, I refuse to hide from it.

I preached less than an hour later with shaking hands and a shaken heart. More people responded to the invitation that night than any other night of that particular campaign. The Lord seemed to be reminding me that all ministry is by His grace. Sweet grace, sweet holy grace that soothes my battered soul and dispels my deepest gloom!

Several years later in Africa, I was helping in a deliverance prayer with another young woman. We were praying earnestly, I with my eyes closed, when the girl suddenly slapped me. Instantly, without hestitation, instinct and unsanctified SELF lashed out as I soundly slapped her back. It was the kind of immediate and unthinking action that so devastatingly betrays the **real** state of one's soul behind the careful, public mask of spirituality.

147

My face flamed with a blush of humiliation and shattering embarrassment. Gee Sprague, my associate, was thunderstruck. The African ministers stared at me in unveiled shock. What could I say? The deed spoke for itself.

The girl was dismissed and Gee and the Africans listened graciously to my apology. Their genuine words of comfort and encouragement helped, but that miserable, naked kinship with the sons of Sceva remained.

In the interest of honesty, such "failures" must be made note of. To refuse to acknowledge them is hypocrisy. However, wallowing in the poison of defeat will deny one's ministry any possible good that might be had in it. We can find grace in Jesus to refuse to be immobilized by such ignominious moments and in faith believing, to stretch out our hands to the next one in need of prayer. Anyone who cannot stand to lose, daren't stand for office. Anyone who must have every prayer met with a miracle should never offer to pray with the sick. I should also say that I learned one really practical lesson that day about ministry in the field of deliverance. Now I stand back —**and** keep my eyes open!

Thanks be to God, however, that the miracles **do** come. In a rural camp meeting deep in the hills of Virginia, God showed me one of the sweetest deliverances I ever witnessed. One night after the service, a young man in his late teens or early twenties came seeking prayer for healing. His poverty was on his sleeve and his ignorance was painfully obvious, but my heart was strangely touched by his humility.

"Brother Mark," he drawled, "I want you to pray that I won't never have to take this here medicine no more."

"What kind of medicine is it?" I asked. "What is your illness?"

"Well," he hesitated, "I ain't fer sure I understand it. The doctors say I have schizophrenia. I can't sleep and I have them God-awful nightmares most every night."

In that precious way of His, the Spirit of Jesus began to speak deep in my heart. I felt I was sensing even minute details about the boy.

"You hear voices, don't you?" I asked.

"Yes, Sir," he said in surprise.

"They whisper in your ear, don't they?" I went on.

"Yes, Sir," he said hesitantly.

"What sorts of things do they say?" I asked.

"Uh — I don't exactly know," he lied, dropping his eyes.

"You don't have to be embarrassed," I said, trying to comfort him. "I already know. They whisper obscenities — dark, dirty words. Evil things that you hate to hear."

"Oh, Lord, Brother Mark, I do hate it. I swear I do!" he said with passion in his eyes.

"I know you do," I said softly, not wanting him to bolt. "And these voices also talk about you. They tell you that you are stupid and ugly and worthless. They say you are just garbage with no rights of your own."

"That's true," he whispered, shivering as if he were standing in a cold rain.

"In fact," I went on, "you can hear them right now at this moment. Isn't that right?"

He looked confused and a little panic-stricken. "I can hear you talking," he said. "I can't hardly, though, because they're talking too. Please help me. I can't even sleep. They talk all night. The medicine really don't help none."

A young Baptist preacher from the area stood listening at my elbow and I turned to him. "Do you understand what this is?" I asked.

"Yes," he said soberly, "I think I do."

"Are you ready?" I asked.

His back went straight as a ramrod and his Baptist jaw jutted like granite. He was pale of face and owl-eyed, but steady as a rock. He clutched his big Bible in front of him like a shield, his knuckles white on its black leather binding.

"I don't know anything about this," he said shaking his Bible like a kid with a mysterious Christmas box. "But I know it's in here. I'm ready!"

He braced himself as if to receive a blow. I feared for any demon that attempted to resist such humble faith. I was deeply touched by the young preacher's childlike determination to be unwavering, but the moment of deliverance came in majestic softness.

"I command, in the Name of Jesus," I said quietly in the boy's ear, "that every evil spirit, every agent of Satan, and every lying devil be silent and come out — right now. In the Name of Jesus, you must leave this boy and never come back and never speak to him again. Now!"

If the lad moved or made any perceptible reaction to the

149

words, I did not see it. He just stood quietly with his head bowed for several moments. When he looked up, his eyes were filled with cautious light.

"I — I think they're gone," he said. "I don't hear nothing. Thank God, I think they're gone."

I led him in more prayer and counseled with him briefly before he left. I watched the boy's retreating back move down through the trees. I had forgotten the young preacher until he suddenly breathed out with such a gush of air that I wondered how long he had been holding his breath.

"Whew," he said, staring after the boy.

"Amen," I said. "Amen, Brother."

Without another word, he shook my hand and walked away to his car. He had that slightly too straight posture and heavy, measured stride of a grateful man who has had a sobering brush with near catastrophe. Bless him, Lord, I thought, he **was** ready. I hope his congregation is! The final night of the camp meeting, that young boy gave a sweet, unaffected testimony. I stole a glance at the young preacher who solemnly nodded his head.

Over the years, I have seen miracles of many kinds, including healings. I have never believed that healing was the central gift of my ministry. I am a preacher, an evangelist. I have found some anointing as a teacher of the Word. I have prayed with the sick and will continue to do so. Some have been healed. Many have not. I do not want my ministry to be based on the miracles of God, but on the God of miracles. By His grace, I will preach **and** pray with the sick. Miracles are **His work**. My passion is to be a soul winner.

One of the most supernatural moments of my life had nothing at all to do with healing. I was with two associates, Gee Sprague and Sammy Odarno, at a National Christian Workers Conference in Kumasi, Ghana, when I learned something new about the Wind of the Spirit.

The conference was being housed at old Wesley College, the school of my friend, Dr. Brew Riverson. Due to a leaky roof in the main auditorium, the lectures were being held in the dining hall. One entire wall of that building is bifold doors that may be opened to snare any evening coolness. Due to the number of bodies in the place and the stifling weather, all the doors were wide open but no detectable breeze offered us any relief.

My appointed topic that night was to be evangelism, but as Gee led in praise choruses, the Lord seemed to be directing me to drop that and speak on the Holy Spirit. I read a few verses from Acts 2 and began. After only ten or fifteen minutes, the room began to experience a dramatic change in the air. Some kind of atmospheric shift began not too slowly, and then suddenly broke into a full wind. It shocked us all. Bible pages began to turn in the strong breeze. Then, as it gathered strength, students clutched futilely as notes and loose paper took flight in the gathering wind. The bifold doors began to bang against the side of the dining hall and the wind inside gained force by the second.

People began to fall on the floor in weeping and prayer. The Comforter Himself had come. The next morning, more than 150 testified that they had been spontaneously baptized in the Holy Spirit.

The testimony of one elderly man especially touched us all. He spoke to the group through an interpreter. Being much older than the others and less educated, he found himself the only one there unable to speak English. Since we thought there was no need with this more educated group, none of the lectures were being translated. In pride he had stayed through the first two days of lectures unwilling to admit his need, but understanding nothing. He had finally determined to leave the conference after the second night.

"But last night," he said, "when the wind blew in the house, I fell on my face and prayed to God. 'Lord, I have not understood a word of these foreigners, but this is Your power here tonight.' I asked the Lord to fill me with His Spirit and He did."

Then he sang a beautiful chanting song in his own language (which I have on tape) and danced gracefully before the Lord. He stayed for the duration of the conference with several students taking turns interpreting quietly at his side. God had blown away his pride and hurt feelings with the Wind of the Spirit.

All too often we miss seeing God's miraculous hand in very beautiful ways because of our obsession with miracles of healing. There are many kinds of miracles. Financial miracles, relational miracles, and miracles of protection are just a few. All are miracles and none is less or greater than the other.

On a lonely Nigerian highway one Saturday afternoon, I

witnessed a great miracle of protection. Leaving Benin City with a team of national pastors and one missionary, we were heading for the city of Obiaruku for outdoor meeting there. I was riding in the lead car with the driver and two pastors. Young Eric Owen, a Trinity Foundation missionary, came behind me with their driver and another pastor.

At 120 kpm (70 mph) the rear tire on the second car exploded like a cannon shot. The auto careened madly, flipped over on its top and crashed into the jungle like a comet. As we turned our own car around and saw Eric's crumpled twisted car, I just knew all were dead. I was sick at the thought of the death of the precious young missionary and those fine pastors. Visions of arriving in Atlanta with that casket filled my mind. Instead of death and disaster, we saw the Hand of God.

Miraculously they escaped unhurt! Each one crawled out of the mangled VW through the one open window. Not a scratch on anyone! Not one bruise! The Lord has triumphed gloriously. The horse and rider were thrown into the sea. We fell on our knees there beside that jungle road and thanked God. How we praised Him!

Two Trinity Foundation missionaries in Nigeria, related a stirring account of God's protection. Passing through a small town near the Niger River, they were forced to drive slowly due to some congestion. Just ahead of them on the shoulder of the road stood a madman. He was typical of those mud-encrusted, half-naked wretches one sees on a daily basis in Africa. They sleep on the street corners and eat what they can scavenge. Their hair and beard will stand out wildly because of filth. As the Kailings drew near, they saw that he held a machete by his side, but they were not in the least concerned. In Nigeria, machetes are as ordinary as neckties in the U. S.

As the madman stared into their car, the devils inside of him went berserk at the sight of two whites. Just as they drew alongside him, he raised the machete over his head with both hands. Staring into the wife's horrified eyes, he hurled the massive blade with savage force straight at her open window. He was not more than five feet away. At that distance, he could not miss and they had no time to react defensively.

The crash of metal upon metal was heard, for instead of hitting its mark, miraculously the machete struck the car body, leaving a sizeable dent. It seemed as if injury or death must result but God turned the blade aside with His power. What a beautiful manifestation of Isaiah 54:17!

At the height of a severe petrol crisis in Ghana, we saw the Lord turn defeat to victory in small but precious ways. The queues at the petrol station were often three to five days' long. Block after block they stretched out in lines of frustrated, angry men spending days and nights in line just for a few precious gallons of gasoline.

The stations became knots of shouting, shoving, cursing patrons and soldiers jockeying madly for position at the pumps. Often they became so snarled that no cars could move. Fistfights and even shootings were not uncommon as tempers ran at fever pitch.

A group of several pastors from the U. S. had gone to Ghana with me for evangelistic meetings, only to find our efforts extremely hampered by this transportation crisis. However, we watched the Lord open doors, provide gasoline, and bless us in ways we would not have known otherwise.

At one station in Kumasi, Sammy Odarno left me with the car and went to make an appeal to the station manager for preferential treatment based on our ministry. The area around the pumps was as volatile as I had ever seen. A drunken soldier on a motorcycle was demanding more than his ration card allowed and the manager was holding fast. Dozens of angry men and soldiers threatened to explode at any moment. I doubted if Sammy could even reach the manager to make an appeal. To be honest, given the angry mood around the pumps, I was not very excited about breaking the line anyway. I was not sure how men who had been camping at the station for days might react to such blatant favoritism.

Momentarily Sammy returned downcast. It did not look good, he said. With only a few days left in Ghana, I could not afford to spend them waiting in a petrol queue. Sammy suggested that he wait with the car while I stood in sight of the station manager. Perhaps, he reasoned, my white face amidst a sea of angry blacks might keep our request in the manager's mind.

After half an hour, I realized it was hope against hope. The manager studiously avoided my eyes and the crowd grew more threatening by the moment. I bowed my head and putting my hands over my eyes, I began to pray silently for God to help us.

I do not know how long I prayed but when I looked up, the station manager was staring straight into my eyes over the heads of dozens of shouting men.

Suddenly his voice boomed like a howitzer, "Clear a way! Clear a way!" He spun and waved Sammy, who was still standing by the car, toward the head of the line. An armed soldier offered protest but the manager was a brick wall. In two minutes Sammy's car was hungrily drinking while the battle in the parking lot raged around us. An unknown face in the crowd caught my eyes. I did not recognize him. He mouthed quite plainly, "Praise the Lord!" Speaking aloud would have been useless in such a din, but his words were unmistakable. "Hallelujah!" I shaped carefully with my own mouth and Sammy and I were off.

In a similar setting in a station in Accra, the Lord moved in a strange and humorous way to provide petrol. An African had gone into the station to make an appeal when one of the American pastors naively stepped from the car with a camera. Photographing the unbelievable snarls at the petrol stations was expressly forbidden by the government. Such pictures might become "anti-revolutionary propaganda" in the Western press.

The pastor boldly stood, camera to forehead, adjusting his lenses when soldiers with guns drawn descended from everywhere. The moment threatened real disaster. The manager, not wanting any problems in his domain, reacted swiftly, rushing to intercede for the hapless American. No one seemed to be giving until the word missionary was used. At that, the station manager took the bull by the horns.

"Oh!" he shouted. "So you're missionaries! Well, that's different," he crooned buoyantly to the soldiers. "They're **missionaries**." He said the word in the way one might introduce royalty. It fairly dripped with unspoken significance.

"Pull through," he said effusively. "Pull through. Let them pass!" The now enfeebled protests of the soldiers were totally ignored as petrol was pumped and we sped away.

Later we laughed at the innocence of the pastor, the anger of the guards, and the verbal resourcefulness of the manager. It was a tense moment at the time, but the subject of much praise in retrospect. Not perhaps, the resurrection of Lazarus, but a welcome miracle when it was needed.

I am only beginning to learn the ability of God to turn our obedience in the least of matters into miracles for the lives of others. Many, many times I have missed or disobeyed His voice and the ministry has gone lame. When, by His grace, I **have** obeyed, I have seen His power at work.

This has not frequently been matters of earth-shattering significance, I suppose. In fact, such miracles have often mattered only to a few or even to one person. God forbid that we should measure the preciousness of the miracles of God by the number of spectators. The Kingdom of God is not meat nor drink — nor is it a percentage of the gate.

Once at the World Convention of Full Gospel Businessmen's Fellowship in New Orleans, I struggled desperately for obedience and nearly missed the hand of the Lord. Seated in a convention hall with several thousand others, I noticed a young couple several rows ahead of me. The Spirit seemed to quicken my heart for them in a tender way. I had never seen them before, yet suddenly the Lord was giving me a deep awareness of them. The strangest thought intruded. At first, I rejected it with a shake of my head and self-rebuke. Then it came again and yet again. It seemed as though I sensed the Holy Spirit kissing the young woman on the cheek.

This was too much! It seemed almost blasphemous, let alone utterly daft. What could such a thing mean? I put it away but it returned with urgency. Then it seemed that the Holy Spirit spoke more clearly in my heart.

"These young people have been comforted in a great crisis. Go and tell them what you have seen. Tell them that now I will open up for them a ministry of comforting others."

The thought was clear and truthfully I had very little doubt it was from the Lord. I lacked the heart for it. It was so absurd. Also it seemed just a bit chancy. I had no longing to walk up to a strange man in a convention hall in New Orleans and calmly inform him that I just saw the Holy Ghost kiss his wife.

I became so agitated that I could not hear the sermon. When it was over, I grabbed the arm of the businessman friend with whom I had attended, and we plunged out a side exit plainly marked for emergencies only. The young couple moved on up the aisle with the crowd.

"What's the matter with you?" my friend asked. "What's the hurry?"

"I had to get out of there," I answered lamely. "I didn't feel so great."

We walked quickly up the sidewalk toward the crosswalk until at the corner of the great convention hall we were suddenly face to face with that same young couple. My heart leaped into my throat.

"Now," the Lord seemed to say, "do as you are told. Immediately!"

To my companion's shock and to my own dismay, I found myself blurting out the whole thing to the amazed young couple. Their response was a blessing. The husband gave this account of their story.

In the early years of their marriage in Texas, they had little concern for the things of the Lord. Then tragedy struck. In a freak accident, their two-year old daughter had been killed. As is so often the case, the young wife had turned to God for help. At first, in a Baptist church, then through a women's prayer group, she had grown closer to God — and to the power of the Holy Spirit. One night she awakened her husband in tears of joy. While he slept, she had been filled by the Holy Spirit while praying alone in their den.

"She described it," he said to me, "as seeming like the Spirit had kissed her and comforted her! Those were her exact words."

I talked with them again on the last day of that convention and the prophecy of ministry was already being fulfilled. God had opened several doors for them to minister to couples in crises in those few days.

Tommy Tyson, a precious Spirit-filled and Spirit-led United Methodist evangelist was a great help to me in this area of hearing and obeying the voice of the Spirit. It was he who encouraged me to "listen with more boldness" to the inner voice and cease to dismiss the guidance of the Spirit as "Christian hunches."

I have often missed. I have missed horribly. It is as easy for me to get in the flesh as it is for anyone else. I have also seen God honor His Word with Spirit-led direction. My prayer is to grow in sensitivity **and** obedience to the Spirit, especially in the small things.

Once while praying with a woman for healing, I saw in my mind's eye a large stone church. It was as if I could hear bells ringing and then a line of silent nuns moving into the church. This seemed very strange to me since we were in a United Methodist church.

"Are you a Roman Catholic?" I asked her.

"Yes," she said, "I am a visitor here tonight."

Then I saw her as a child. A clear picture presented itself to me of a little girl standing and watching those same nuns. It seemed that I was able to hear the girl speak. "I promise, God. I promise I will be a nun when I grow up. I promise."

"I believe," I said to the woman, "that lasting physical healing will elude you until you allow the Lord to help you deal with the guilt you bear over that broken childhood vow."

"What vow?" she asked.

"Your vow to become a nun," I answered.

She absolutely dissolved into a floodtide of tearful remorse over a half-forgotten childhood vow. Perhaps on the surface it may seem insignificant — even silly. However, the Holy Spirit had pulled back the veil far enough for me to see the connection between the tortuous guilt in that buried memory and the abiding illnesses of many years.

On yet another occasion, in a youth camp, the Holy Spirit showed how His gifts, honored with obedience and use, bring healing in the body. The daughter of a United Methodist pastor came for healing prayer in the matter of migraine headaches. As I began to pray for her, an unusual scene came before me. I described it to her as carefully as possible.

"I can see a girl — not even a teenager yet," I began. "She is on a stage before a large crowd. Her mouth is smiling but her eyes look fearful to me. Her hands are tense at her side. I sense great anxiety in her."

"That's me," she gasped. "I know it is. I have been in one beauty pageant after another since I was a little girl. Now I direct them for a living."

I asked her to see the same scene in her mind as clearly as the Lord would allow it. Then I said, "Now I want you to see the Lord standing behind that little girl. His arms are out-stretched. Listen! He says, 'Turn around. Come to Me. Turn around and come here'."

"No!" the young lady said spontaneously, her eyes tightly shut. "No! Don't! Never turn your back on the audience!"

Sensing the direction the Spirit was taking us, we prayed

157

further, until a word from God seemed to come through for her like a bolt. "I believe," I said, "that the Lord wants me to tell you that He will set you free — to fail. He can take away the bondage of success and set you free to turn your back on any audience any time."

A sob rippled through her and she cried, "Oh, God, please. Yes, Lord," she said, "I will turn to **You** now."

From that very decision of hers to turn her back on the audience and turn to Christ, she was healed. I prayed for her, but I believe **that** was the key, not my prayer. Years later she and her parents testified that she had never had another migraine headache.

Obedience in the Gifts does not always come easy. Once in a meeting near Tokyo, I felt led, in the middle of a prayer, to switch from English to Spanish. Over the years, I had learned enough Spanish for basic conservation and very simple prayer. The question remained — why in Japan?! The urging of the Spirit was so strong, however, that I reluctantly complied. I felt like a complete donkey standing before a congregation of Japanese and four American missionaries praying in Spanish. Only after the meeting I learned what that little prayer had meant to a Chilean woman seated on the back row but unknown to me.

It was painful to me when a friend reported the comment of another Methodist preacher and a mutual acquaintance that he was "concerned about this clairvoyance" in my ministry. It hurt to be so misunderstood by a friend, of course. It hurt even more to realize how ignorant we are, in much of the Body of Christ, about the Spirit's greatest gifts. I include myself in that as well. Oh, for the faith to really trust the promise of 1 Corinthians 2:16 that, "we who are Spiritual think the thoughts of Jesus" (Phillips). I long for a fuller balanced understanding **and** greater fluency in **all** that 1 Corinthians 12 means.

The Gifts of the Spirit, including the so-called "intuitive gifts" of the **Word of Knowledge, Word of Wisdom,** and **Discernment of Spirits,** should not seem weird to the ministers of God. We should walk and minister in them as the Apostlic body that we are. These ministrations of the Spirit are not "clairvoyance" or ESP, but valid, **Biblical** gifts that belong to the Church today.

Chapter XII
Launch Out . . .

FOR HIS DRAUGHT

I fear that many Charismatics have accepted the mind-set that if, in the pursuit of miracles, some souls happen to get saved, that is icing on the cake. I am equally convinced that many classical denominational ministries have come to believe that "saving souls" is passe and gauche at best, and at worst, actually counter-productive to the great work of building larger congregations. At the same time the "old-line" holiness groups have all too often squandered their evangelistic fire in a sequestered camp meeting mentality that, far from saving the lost, slams the door on their fingers. It is so easy to fall into a kind of musty monasticism that safeguards "the good old days" instead of going on the offense to rescue the perishing. All three are tragic!

To lay aside soul-winning is blatant dereliction of duty. This can happen in the euphoria of charismatic experience, or in prissy, uptown evangelism that loves to talk of being Christ-centered but blushes at an altar call. It may also happen in barnacled Wesleyan dogma wholly sanctified but pathetically sterile. The **kind** of evangelistic failure hardly matters to the sinner. All he knows is that he is dying in darkness and no one seems to care enough to throw a light.

The pastor at "First Church" is busy playing dress up with robes and candles on Sunday and is preoccupied with running for Bishop Monday through Saturday. The folks at the Spirit-filled prayer cell down the block meet three nights a week for Charismatic parlor games. The "holy club" is happily conducting a clinic for pastors on the history of the Wesleyan movement. And the lost remain lost in the shuffle.

The fields are white. The laborers are few. But, glory to God, the Holy Spirit is ready to pour Himself out in power wherever the church is willing to put in the sickle. We must rekindle a passion to "win the lost at any cost." Jesus' call to Peter was **not** "launch out in the deep and enjoy the view." We are commanded to be "fishers of men." When we do, we can know that we do not have to approach the task in our own power, but in His who "came into the world to save sinners."

At one large Methodist church in Atlanta in a Sunday morning service, I gave such an invitation and one young woman came forward. She knelt at the altar in deep remorse, not even trying to hide her tears. She confessed that she was living with a man, that sin had taken over in her life, even though she taught a Sunday School class in that very church. As Christ came into her heart her tears of guilt turned to tears of joy. Spontaneously she lifted her hands and said aloud, "Oh, thank You God! Thank You."

I looked over her head at the stony stares of many in that congregation and wondered how long it had been since anyone had been saved at that altar. Indeed, at the door, one man even refused to shake my hand. His face approached the color of a turnip. His fists were clenched.

"I never thought I would see such a display of emotionalism in our church," he fumed. "Personally, I was outraged!"

Laughter, involuntary laughter, sprang up. Before I could stop myself, even if I had wanted to, I found myself laughing. "Why, Brother," I told him, "you are the most emotional Methodist I've met in some time."

I heard of one "evangelical" pastor who based his entire doctoral thesis on the premise that revivals are the poorest means of church growth. I had to wonder if he would know a true revival if he saw one. I also had to ask myself what he meant by "church growth." The faculty of a liberal seminary might do cartwheels over such a document. Paul the Apostle, Charles Finney, Francis Asbury, Dwight Moody and Len Ravenhill might be a tougher jury.

I am also bored with the charge that the fruit of preaching evangelism does not endure. Wherein does the fault lie there? Perhaps with the local agencies to whom new converts are committed for care and discipleship. If a fisherman surrendering his catch to his lazy wife, returns later to find them uncleaned and unrefrigerated, should he fall to breast-beating and self-condemnation because his work is spoiled?

The Wesleyan revival sprang from preaching evangelism. The public proclamation of the Word with the clear expectation of response was Wesley's "secret." His "genius" was his plan of follow-up and cultivation.

When Wesley undertook the task of evangelism, at which the lazy, self-indulgent pastors and churches of his day failed so wretchedly, he was charged with "enthusiasm" (fanaticism). When he organized for the task of discipleship, a task equally refused by the "church" of his day, he was branded a demagogue. Before anyone undertakes evangelism in the face of a barren church and a backslidden clergy, he had best be ready for such treatment himself.

When the local church accepts its task of caring for the fruit of evangelistic efforts, great good for the Kingdom can be realized. In Nigeria, we conducted a small open-air campaign for five nights registering about eight hundred decisions for Christ. In one nearby local church, we held follow-up classes daily for those who came forward the night before. Despite the fact that these were weekdays at midmorning, the attendance grew daily. On the Sunday following one campaign, sixty-five new converts in one church registered for discipleship classes. Now, that is sixty-five people who had never been to that church (or probably any other church) before and were seeking encouragement in the salvation experience they had found in an open-air meeting some distance away.

In an American high school we also saw the lasting quality of revival matured by the local church. The principal of the Adairsville, (Georgia) high school invited me for a four-day campaign in his school. Since it was a public school, the principal was taking a great risk. God honored it marvelously.

Each night students crowded the front of the auditorium. One hundred teenagers registered for decisions for Christ. That is, one in every nine students in the little high school was saved in four nights. A very sincere young Methodist pastor in Adairsville agreed to handle follow-up. Each Wednesday at noon, a group of students met with him for teaching and prayer.

I will always treasure the principal's testimony that the very atmosphere of the school was altered by what happened at that crusade. Revival is not just seeing the lost saved. When the conduct in the halls and classrooms of a public high school is changed by a sudden change in the students — **that's** revival. Evangelism and discipleship must work together for lasting fruit. It works. It still works **today.**

In a county crusade in McRae, Georgia, I received an insight into what it means that the "wind blows where it will." It is difficult to program true revival. At the same time, it is difficult for the devil to stop it.

I had been asked to come preach at the local public high school on the Monday of the crusade. On the Friday before, there was a considerable racial disturbance. Fighting and serious property damage had brought out the Georgia Highway Patrol, and the Georgia Bureau of Investigation came to quell the storm. When we arrived for the assembly, the air was full of anger and tension.

I preached standing in the gym floor with the students in the bleachers. It was an unruly audience to say the least. The cat-calls and heckling threatened to turn the assembly into a mockery at any moment. Periodically my message was interrupted by sarcastic calls of "Praise the Lord" or "Hallelujah, Brother," punctuated by waves of laughter.

At the invitation, no one budged. I knew it would take a supernatural miracle for anyone to walk out on that gym floor to the hoots and jeers of hundreds of teenagers already on the brink of riot. God moved in a way that no one could have predicted.

The special education students (educable mentally retarded) sat in a group at the opposite end of the gymnasium from where I stood. A young white boy among them stood and started down the steps to the gym floor. At first the ripples of laughter and sarcastic remarks continued. Then a black girl from the same group stood to follow him. They joined hands and walked together straight toward me. It could only have been orchestrated by the Holy Ghost. The gym gradually fell utterly silent as they came toward my extended arms. They walked in that awkward gait of the retarded and the sight of them — a black girl and a white boy holding hands in that atmosphere of racial tension — tears streaming down their faces, fearlessly braving the jeers of the "normal" kids, absolutely silenced the entire student body. Then the dam broke. The next thing I knew I was surrounded by weeping high school students. That day and the next we prayed with more than seventy-five students to accept salvation by faith. "A little child shall lead them."

On the second day the principal and school superintendent from the adjoining county came to the assembly. They tendered an invitation for me to come there and hold an evangelistic assembly in **that** school. I gladly accepted, of course, and preached there the next day.

As if to demonstrate His rich variety in means of operation, the Lord opened it in a different way. At the invitation, no one moved. Hundreds of teenagers just stared down from the bleachers. No catcalls or hoots broke the air. They stared at me as if I were some extra-terrestrial being, suddenly deposited in their midst. There was something else too — suspense. "Who will be first?" they seemed to be thinking as with one mind.

On the very back row, a tall, black teenager stood, abruptly. He did not take a step at first. He just stared straight into my eyes. His sleeveless black T-shirt boasted a single word in vivid purple written across his chest — **Violence.** As he started down the steps, movement swept across the gym. When the last student came to stand there, I led more than fifty in the "sinner's prayer."

I offer these examples as testimony of God's willingness to honor the foolishness of **preaching evangelism** in our day. No amount of ivy-covered whining from half-baked seminary professors who have never seen a true move of God can ever convince me that the fruit born at altars is less enduring than any other. Having said **that,** I pray that nothing in the following will be misconstrued as "hedging my bets."

I would not, for all the world, be numbered for one second among that dingy host that slights preaching evangelism. I do, however, hasten to add that there is plenty of work for all. Not everyone is equipped or called to preach marketplace crusades in Ghana or even in the wilds of an American high school. Yet, not one Christian is exempt from the work of evangelism.

There will always be a place for mass evangelism, regardless of the cutsie-pie doctoral theses of ambitious pastors. The most precious work of evangelism, however, will always be done by individuals with fire in their bones and with quickened hearts for the souls of men.

Not all preaching of all the evangelists in the world will ever substitute for one businesman inviting another to take Jesus. Soul-winning is not merely a duty — though it certainly is that — it is a grand and glorious privilege, and an adventure to stir the blood! I have come to love the very offense of the old words "soul-winning." They seem to deliciously blister the hide of accommodated modern religion in a way that "witnessing" or "personal evangelism" never will.

Soul-winning is not a concept. It is a task, an action, an intentional work for the one prize worthy of the concerted efforts of the children of God. It is a war, a fire fight. Soul-winning is not buttons pushed by generals miles behind the lines. It is hand-to-hand combat. It is down-in-the-mud, bare knuckles, no-holds-barred "rassling." It is not a struggle for a few yards of real estate, or a frontier or national pride. The prize is the eternal soul of one person.

Returning home to Atlanta from revival services in another city, I found myself on a very lonely stretch of highway at 2:00 a.m. on a Saturday night. On the shoulder of the road rested an old Chevy wagon with the hood raised. Two black men stood, hands on hips, staring dully at a steaming engine. As I passed, one of them feebly waved as though he really did not expect me to stop and I did not.

Not a hundred yards later, however, I began to sense the Spirit telling me to go back and help them. "Oh, God, I prayed. You must speak clearly. I could get killed here. Those two big men on this deserted stretch at this hour? Do You **really** want me to go back there?"

It seemed He did! "Go back," said the voice of the Spirit in my heart, and tell them, "The Lord has sent me to you."

I slowly turned the car around and returned hoping that someone else would have already stopped. They were still alone. Heading my car into theirs so that they stood in my headlights, I stopped and stepped out. I remained beside my own car with the door open in case of the least sign of danger. I proceeded to ask perhaps the most stupid question one man has ever asked another.

"Are you having trouble?" I shouted.

What did I expect? That they **enjoyed** standing on a lonely highway in the wee hours of the morning. Did I suppose that the hood was up collecting dew?

"The radiator's out of water," one of the men called back. "We ain't got nothing to get water in and don't see a house."

He sounded nice enough. Squaring my shoulders I called out what the Lord had directed, "The Lord has sent me to you!"

The same man took an involuntary step forward and leaned toward me as if into a stiff wind, "Say what?" he shouted.

"I said, the Lord has sent me to you," I answered. "Come on and we will find some water."

I could see them discussing the matter briefly before the talker ambled my way. I could not help thinking with a chuckle that such a line had perhaps made him more leary of me than I was of him.

"It's only about a mile to a little town up here," I said, once he was in the car.

"Yeah," he replied, "But I doubt we gonna find anything to bring water out here in."

"Do you believe," I asked him, "that God would send you a strange white man out here at 2:00 in the morning and not supply something to get water in?"

"Yeah!" he said in sheer amazement at the revelation. "Yeah! I hadn't thought of **that.**"

At a gas station which was closed we found six empty milk jugs in a trash can. In less than a half hour we had their car in the gas station parking lot where they fixed the leak and refilled the radiator. It was only there that I realized that one of them had his pregnant wife in the car.

"Now," I said, "I want to ask you a question. It is a very serious one. Suppose that instead of my coming to help you, you had been struck from the rear by a semi and killed. Are you 100% certain that you would be in heaven?"

For the first time the girl spoke, "I'm sure," she said. "I'm born again. I been saved."

"What about you?" I asked the men.

Neither of them had been saved.

"Would you let me share some scriptures with you?" I asked.

I showed them 1 John 1:9 and Revelation 3:20. A few words of explanation and even fewer words of testimony were all the narrative I offered. I then turned to Acts 16:31.

"Don't you want to ask the Lord Jesus into your hearts right now?" I asked. "Wouldn't you like to be born again into His kingdom?"

165

"Yes," said the quieter of the two. "Yes, I would."

"Me too," agreed the other. "I been knowing this was what I needed. I guess I'm tired of putting it off."

Kneeling there at that pre-dawn hour in the driveway of a closed service station we must have made quite a picture. As I led them both in the salvation prayer, I wondered what a Georgia highway patrolman would think if he saw a white man and two blacks kneeling and holding hands at 3:00 a.m. Such thoughts could not really detract from the joy of their salvation. When the men promised to go to church the next morning and testify about their strange conversion, the young wife actually wept in happiness.

As I started to drive away, the "talker" came running toward my car. "Wait," he said. "I want to know something. Please tell me the truth."

"I will," I said.

"Did, you know — well — did the Lord really send you?" he asked with his eyes boring into mine.

"God is my witness," I answered him. "The Lord sent me to **you.**"

"You know," he said with a touch of awe in his voice and obvious mist in his eyes, "They ain't nobody never done nothing for me."

Later I thought that there are absolutely millions who believe that, not realizing that Jesus has already done a wonderful thing for them. How shall they hear without a preacher?

I have found that in soul-winning, formulas are useless but there are certain verbal skills and patterns that can be helpful in many settings. Not the least of these is a simple question.

I have asked it of the rich and the ragged, the poor and the powerful, the independent and the indigent. I have had better results with it than any other question. I do not always use it. But I use it more than all other approaches combined.

The question is, "If you died right now, are you 100% certain that you would go to heaven?"

That question cuts through all the baloney and gets right to the heart of the matter. It discards all theological debate and safely avoids the mine field of red herrings and side tracks. It is a question that frequently gets a response when nothing else will. Often the responses it does get are unforgettable.

On a flight out of Philadelphia I sat next to a very prosperous-looking, late middle-aged executive type. He began to order cocktails and showed no sign of letting up. I found out he was a Roman Catholic lawyer from Pittsburg with a lucrative practice. He admitted that he hated and dreaded air travel.

"What if this plane crashed?" I asked. "What if it exploded right now in mid-air and we were all killed?"

He visibly paled. "Oh my God, man!" he gasped. "Don't talk that way! What's the matter with you?" He looked hurriedly out the window, presumably to check our altitude. "Please, don't talk like that."

"I'm sorry," I said. "What I mean to say is are you ready to stand before God if you had to? If you died now, of whatever reason, are you 100% sure you would go to heaven?"

He was not ready that day to receive the Lord and there is no way to rush it. I do know this; he left that plane thinking about it with a new urgency. If the fruit is ripe it will fall in your hands at just a tap. If it isn't ripe, forcing things may only bruise it.

God ripens the fruit and if we are open to the Holy Spirit, He will move us into the right orchard at just the right moment. When we move in the Spirit, soul-winning, far from being tedious and difficult, becomes more a matter of cooperating with His supernatural power to bring the lost sheep home.

On many other occasions I have seen sweet proof of God's follow-up abilities. Driving through a north Georgia rainstorm I passed a man and two children huddling under an overpass. I felt the impulse of the Spirit to pick them up but I was driving a brand new little Chevrolet of which I was very proud. "Lord," I thought, "they are so wet and dirty they will ruin my new interior." "Mark," He said, "I can arrange for you to drive a car they will not harm." I pulled off at the next exit and went back for them.

They were easily the most wretched, filthy, dirty Americans I have ever seen. Their ignorance was pathetic and their story was tragic. The wife and mother had deserted them in St. Louis from whence they had walked, living in the woods, eating berries and begging at doorsteps for scraps.

"While we ride," I said to the man, "let me tell your children a story."

"Okay," he said dully.

I began to tell a very simple, obvious version of the prodigal son. They listened enraptured. When I finished, the little girl, about eleven, spoke.

"That's wonderful," she sighed. "Ain't that wonnerful, Daddy?"

"It is," he answered looking sideways at me. "Did you just make 'at story up?"

"Why no," I confessed, fearful of such flagrant plagiarism. "That's from the Bible. Jesus told it. Didn't you ever read the Bible?"

"Didn't ever read nothing," he mumbled. "Cain't read."

"We ain't never had no Bible," said the young boy, about ten.

Over the next 100 miles I explained to them the story of the Gospel, starting with Adam, trying to tie it all to the prodigal son. At the end all three accepted Christ. When I let them out, my impulse was to give them some money. It seemed like practical love. The Spirit checked me, saying "Don't do that. That will confuse the moment for them." I gave the man my card and I never saw them again. Several months later, however, he called my office and told my secretary that he had gotten a job and a place to live. He said that he and his children had been baptized and joined an Assemblies of God Church and that their lives would never be the same because of Jesus. Sometimes we simply **must** trust the follow-up to God. This is not an invitation to slovenliness. We should follow-up when we can. When we cannot, we can trust that He still knows how. How refreshing it is to remember that there are still a few things for which God Almighty does not need our help.

I am painfully aware of the need for follow-up on this business of soul-winning. Every effort should be lent, when possible, to integrate new converts into the life of a Spirit-filled, Bible-believing congregation. The simple fact remains that quite frequently **no** effort is possible.

In Acts 8 when Philip won Queen Candace's CPA to Christ, He baptized him on the spot (no membership class) and did absolutely no follow-up. How this would scandalize the contemporary sages! Yet I believe with my whole heart that there were Christians in Africa when David Livingstone arrived.

Coming out of an American grocery store one day I suddenly found myself in the embrace of an unfamiliar black man. He hugged me like an old friend and clapped me on the back so

168

energetically that I racked my brain for a name.

"Don't you know me, Reverend Mark?" he asked.

"No," I confessed, "I'm sorry I cannot quite place you."

"I am Charles Butler (not his real name)," he said. "You led me to Jesus on the last night before I was released from Alpharetta (a state prison farm)."

I had conducted a prison ministry there for nearly two years while pastoring in my last church. Among all the prisoners I had met and prayed with his face looked only vaguely familiar.

"Well, Charles," I asked, "how are you? Are you walking with the Lord?"

"Oh, yes," he beamed. "I am married. I have a good job now. And I am the youth director at the Union Baptist Church."

My wife, Alison, was at the heart of one of the most soul-winning victories I ever witnessed. She began to feel that God was leading her to start a door-to-door evangelism effort in our home community. On her heart were the housewives who, home alone in the day, might be ripe for the Gospel. This was not to be calling on prospects and visitors to the church. Her vision was for cold contact evangelism — women to women.

At first God raised up only a partner for her. Those two began alone. Then gradually others were added and as women began to be saved some of them joined in as well. They called themselves the Midwives. Their concept was simple and effective. Calling on women home alone in the day, they offered them Christ. Those women responded in a way that surprised everyone except Alison.

By the end of their second year the Midwives were sending out an average of a dozen teams a week. In that year alone, nearly 250 women accepted Christ, and that became an annual pattern. The women of the Midwives are not pastors, nor some handpicked group of especially talented women of great ability. They are simply housewives who accepted for themselves the commission of Christ.

It must be remembered in soul-winning that God has undertaken the task in His own mighty power and we are only invited to act as His agents. Before the soul-winner ever comes on the scene, the Holy Spirit has been long at work. I saw marvelous proof of this prevenient grace in a hotel lobby in Africa.

While waiting there for a pastor, I was approached by a

friendly, well-dressed young man with that excellent but slightly stilted English of many educated Africans.

"Are you a Canadian?" he asked.

"No, I'm an American," I answered. "My name is Mark Rutland. I'm a missionary evangelist."

Even as we shook hands I noticed his obvious reaction to this introduction. I discovered that he was a young tuna firm executive who was waiting in the lobby, just as I was, for an associate to arrive. I did not even have time to turn the conversation to the Lord before he did.

"I'm so glad to find you here," he said. "I have some very serious questions I have wanted to ask a priest."

"Are you then a Catholic?" I asked him.

"Yes," he answered absently.

"I'm not actually a priest, you see. I'm a Protestant minister," I explained. "But I would like to hear your questions. I hope it doesn't matter to you."

"No," he said vaguely, "It doesn't matter." I realized that he was uncertain of any distinction involved.

"My questions," he said, leaning close, "are about dreams. I've been having the same dreams two or three nights a week for months."

"Are they frightening?" I asked.

"No, not exactly," he explained. "I think they are more troubling than anything else. But that's mostly because I don't understand them. One of them starts bad. I dream I am being chased by a snake. It strikes at my feet, never quite hitting me. I run and run. I cry out for help but no one comes to help me at first. Then my friends and family try to help. They hit the snake. Sometimes they even cut off its head. But it grows another and keeps coming after me."

"Then a man comes. I can never see his face. He steps on the snake's head and kills it. Then he lifts me up. He sets me in a chair above the ground — high up above the earth. Then he sits beside me. There I feel very safe."

I couldn't believe what I was hearing. Could it be I wondered that he really did not know what he was saying? Or was I being had? No, I decided, his face seemed completely guileless. It was amazing!

"Have you ever read the Bible?" I asked him.

"I am really embarrassed to say this," he admitted, "but I

have never read the Bible very much. I haven't even been to Mass since I was a little boy."

When I showed him the promise of Genesis that the Seed of the Woman would bruise the serpent's head, he was obviously surprised. When we turned to Ephesians 2:6 he was even more surprised.

"But wait," he said, "there is another dream which I have very often. I dream that I am in a grove of trees beside a beautiful wide river. There is such lush fruit that the limbs are bowed down. In the river there are fishermen with nets. They are catching so many fish that they can barely haul them in. In the dream I am so happy and so filled with the beauty of the trees and the peaceful river, that when I awake it makes me depressed and sad. Could it be that, that dream is in the Bible?"

"Why, yes!" I exclaimed. "It is! And it is in more than one place. Let me show you."

I showed him Ezekiel 47, then turned to Zechariah 14. He was shocked, to say the least. Then we read Revelation 22:1-2. At this third clear picture of his own dream he was utterly flabbergasted.

"But I don't understand!" he protested. "What can it mean? How can I have been dreaming of passages of scriptures that I have never read or heard of in my life?"

"Don't you see?" I began. "The Lord has been supernaturally preparing your heart for this very moment. It is no accident that we met. The Holy Spirit has been revealing these things to you, to show you God's love. God has been speaking to you through the Spirit. Give your life to Jesus Christ. You must be born again by the power of this same Spirit that has granted you these dreams and has brought us together here. How God must love you! Out of all the men on earth He showed **you** these things — not once but many times!"

Tears sprang into his eyes as he said, "I don't know what to do."

"Take my hand," I said.

Right there we prayed together and Jesus Christ came into his heart. The Holy Spirit had been miraculously preparing his heart with absolutely no help from me. The Holy Spirit does the supernatural "work" of soul-winning. **We** just pick up the nuggets and put them in the wheelbarrow.

This is not to suggest that we will have 100% success. The

171

rich young ruler looked Jesus Christ Himself right in the eye and turned away!

One evangelism paper said that on the average it takes 25 meaningful contacts for Christ for each conversion. Someone made the very valid point that no one can expect to make that 25th contact all the time. Obviously! At the same time, however, I cannot understand a Christian without a longing to be number 25 **some** of the time!

The driving passion of every Christian ought to be to rob hell blind. Right doctrine and a good devotional life hardly excuse anyone from Christ's command to "go into all the world and preach the gospel to every creature." What kind of Christianity is content to constantly study holiness in laboratory sterility and never get in the battle? Kibitzing in the name of mysticism is nothing more than overdressed negligence. The war is on. Spectators are superfluous.

As in any desperate conflict some desperate measure must be employed. On one trans-Atlantic flight I found myself seated next to two Hungarian girls who spoke absolutely no English, while I was without one word of Hungarian. As soon as we all pointed to ourselves and said our names and nationalities, it appeared that communication had run aground. I had a real sense that the Lord wanted me to reach out to them with the Gospel.

I wrote all three of our names on the back of a cocktail napkin pointing to each one as I did. They laughed and corrected my pitiful effort at spelling their Hungarian names. Taking out my New Testament I printed B-I-B-L-E and drew a reasonable facsimile. After a brief conference one of them wrote the Hungarian word undernearth. It was amazingly similar. I pantomimed reading my Bible, then pointed to their names with a questioning look. They vigorously shook their heads.

At my rendering of a church there was considerable confusion. This may very well have been the result of the dubious quality of the artwork. When they finally deciphered the meaning of the mystery, I pretended it was a yellow pages ad to give the impression of walking into my picture of a church. Again I pointed to them. This got an even more vigorous denial.

Finally I drew three valentine shaped hearts under each of our names. In the middle of the page I drew a big cross. From that cross I drew a line to my valentine and bowed my head as if in prayer. I pointed to each of them and made as if to question. They both very solemnly shook their heads. Perhaps they understood none of it. At any rate it seemed to be over with at that point so I grabbed their hands, closed my eyes and began to pray aloud. It was useless to try to seek permission. I prayed that the Spirit would touch their hearts.

When I looked up one of them jerked her hand away and turned coldly to the window. The other stared at me so intently that I thought she would bore a hole in me. She wistfully ran her finger over the gold words on the cover of my Bible and leaned her head back and went to sleep.

We never said another word throughout the duration of the flight and I have no idea of that brief encounter's effect. Yet I have often thought that just when the devil thinks he has someone completely insulated to the Gospel, the Lord may just send another someone to draw stick pictures on the back of a cocktail napkin.

I am convinced that no one is absolutely "safe" from the Gospel. The Holy Spirit can penetrate iron curtains, barroom doors, and walls of hatred and prejudice.

On the front porch of a house in Legon, Ghana, I met a neighbor of the family I was staying with. I have found most Ghanians to be very pro-American. There are some few very vitriolic, radical, anti-American, anti-white, anti-West, communists. He was one of **those.**

He was obviously shocked to see a white man there at all. When he found that I was an American he lit into me with a vengeance. He poured out every Marxist cliche' ever uttered, heaping invectives on my country, my president, my government and all its agencies as well as every white man that had ever lived. My long-buried and long-neglected roots in conservative Young Republicans were pricked and awakened. Roused thus, my chauvinism ached to respond to every word. But the Holy Spirit checked me.

"Don't!" the Lord seemed to say. "Hush, now! Have I brought you here to defend Ronald Reagan? Wait and see My victory."

Finally, like an inflated balloon released by careless fingers, he sputtered madly to a deflated finish and dropped into the chair across from me completely wrung out.

"Well," he said disgustedly, "aren't you going to say **anything?"**

"Yes," I said, as calmly as I could, "I am. I invite you to give your life to Jesus Christ. Only He loves you perfectly. He can take out all the hate and bitterness that sinful white men and greedy governments have put in your heart. I want to say only this. Jesus loves you so much that He died for you to be able to go to heaven. When I die I will go there and I would like to know that I will see you there also."

He stared at me as if he were seeing a ghost. His silence gave me courage. "I want to ask you a question," I said. "If you died right now are you 100% certain that you would go to heaven?"

"No," he said softly, "I am not."

"Won't you take my hand," I asked him, "and pray with me to ask Jesus Christ to come into your heart? You need to be born again."

Without the slightest trace of hesitation he put his black hand in my white one and opened his heart to Christ. The next few mornings, as long as I stayed there, he came each morning at 5 a.m. to sit with me on that porch and discuss his new Saviour. When I left there he carried my suitcases and paid for the bus ticket. When he embraced me at the bus station, I thought how only days before there had been bitter hate where now hearts entwined. Jesus breaks every barrier down!

I am constantly bedazzled by the splendor of His work in preparing hearts to hear the Gospel. Frequently this is without any apparent vehicle.

At one soul-winning conference in Atlanta I saw this more poignantly than ever before. After a day of teaching on various aspects of soul-winning the participants went out in two's for a door-to-door evangelism laboratory experience. Bill Edwards from Moultrie, Georgia, was my partner. With our time exhausted, we needed to return to the conference center to meet the other teams, but I was discouraged. It was my partner's first try and we had enjoyed no success. I had hoped each team would win one and now I, the teacher, had failed to land one single fish.

Not far from the conference grounds we passed a shabby white frame house slightly hidden in the trees. Its yard was littered with that array of rusty auto parts, discarded bicycles and broken toys that so often serve for shrubbery in such "lawns."

Just as we drove past, the Spirit seemed to speak with

urgency. "Go in that house," I felt He said, "and I will give you a soul." I failed to heed the voice and let Bill drive on. How sad to be in too big a hurry to obey the Lord! But the Spirit was determined that morning and continued to speak so strongly that I finally obeyed.

"Bill, we have to go back," I said. "Turn around. I believe that if we go back to that white house on the corner the Lord will give us a soul."

Bill turned the car around and parked at the side of the house. Getting no response at the front we went around to the rear of the house. Walking up the driveway we found ourselves in the midst of quite a bizarre group. Seated on, or around, a half-dozen huge Harley-Davidsons, were that many or more very rugged-looking young men. Long hair, beards, dirt and a fierce countenance appeared to be the uniform of the day. One "boy" just in front of us was tatooed in blue, **BORN TO KILL.** I thought, "Lord, I hope it's not me." With the men were several wild looking young girls and, oddly enough, four or five elderly folks. These I assumed to be their humiliated grandparents.

It took no genius to see that Bill and I had walked into a slightly dicey situation. My instinct was to quietly excuse ourselves and walk backward to the car. The Holy Spirit seemed to be firm that I should plunge on.

I felt that my best chance was to go on the offensive with a show of boldness. The problem was that I could feel my reservoir of boldness hemorrhaging badly. I took my Testament in hand and striding into their midst, I began to preach. I knew that any hesitation would afford them the necessary latitude for interruption. I suspect that the plan of salvation has never been more violently erupted. Waving the little Testament, I bounded along the "Roman Road" at speed worthy of Ben Hur.

The element of surprise evidently took the day. The Neanderthal bikers and their female confederates stared with unmasked astonishment at this strange herald. Open mouths and wide eyes liberally decorated the gang. They were not enraptured by the content. They were stunned to silence by a presence and a situation so totally unexpected that it avoided being easily classified as threatening. Hence, response waited upon further data.

"Now," I said, finishing with a brief exposition of the

invitation of Revelation 3:20, "I want to know who would like to ask the Lord Jesus into his heart **right now**. Who is ready to let Jesus take away his sins and be born again?"

There was not a sound. Not even the shake of a head. I decided to go to each one individually. The Lord had told me that He had prepared a soul there and I was determined to ferret him out. I began with an elderly woman seated on the steps, proceeded through the handful of young girls and men, ending with a shirtless biker in whose acne-scarred face the light of civilization seemed to have gone out. Each time the invitation was rejected, sometimes with a grunt or a sneer, but more often with a bovine head shake. The total unanimity of the refusal, however, was undeniable.

Had I missed the Lord? Perhaps in my inner fear and trembling I had botched the presentation so thoroughly that they had no idea of **what** they were rejecting. At any rate the fish had evidently slipped through the net.

"Well," I said, suddenly very eager to be away from there, "I thank you for listening. The Lord loves you and I urge you not to wait too long."

Just as Bill and I turned toward the car we heard a voice. It was that of a child.

"Wait a minute, Mister," said the voice.

Behind the big choppers, well out of our view was a table covered with a filthy sheet of canvas that draped to the floor forming a tent-like structure. From his den there, a lad of about 10 or 11 had listened to the whole thing, undetected by Bill and me and ignored by the "adults." He crawled out wearing only a pair of khaki cutoffs.

"Wait a minute," he repeated as I turned back to him. "I want Jesus to come into **my** heart." His scrawny, nearly naked little body gave him the look of a Dickens pickpocket, but his dirty face was as guileless as Billy Budd.

"Did you hear all that I said?" I asked.

"Yes," he said. "What you said about being saved. I want to be saved."

"All right, Son." I began, "Come here and kneel down with me and we'll pray. Jesus will come into your heart right now."

"No!" shrilled one of the young women. "He don't even know what he's doing. He ain't. . . . "

"Shut up!" barked a bearded man sitting on a gleaming

176

black motorcycle. One booted foot rested on the handlebar and a yellow-brown home-rolled cigarette of dubious character dangled from his lips. He never moved a muscle but he squinted through the smoke at the girl and spoke with a tone that offered no room for debate. "At least give the kid a chance," he said. No one said another word.

I waited only a second for any possible fall-out before praying with the boy. We knelt on the concrete carport and I led him in a prayer of faith for salvation. How strange it was to know that those around stared down from their motorcycles while the lad was born again.

Before we left, I talked with the boy about prayer and gave him a Gideon New Testament. He sought and obtained permission to walk to a nearby church the next morning. I left him and only a few weeks later they vacated the house and I never saw any of them again.

It would be easy to scorn such a conversion as temporary and even useless in the light of the odds he faces. I have a great confidence in the power of the Holy Spirit to raise up a Gypsy Smith or a Buddy Robinson right under the enemy's nose. Regardless of any moot debates about the endurance of the lad's conversion, the greater point remains. **God** knew that little boy was hiding under that table. God, who knows the thoughts of every heart, knew that child had some raw, unformed longing, some inner desire to be better than anything he had seen. Something in that boy's soul protested to the power of darkness that **he** was not born to be an animal. And God honored that.

What the church must ask itself is this. How many others are hiding under tables, or in shabby hotel rooms or trailer parks or in idolatrous Indian Villages, or in godless Long Island condominiums screaming in the darkness for someone to shine a light? God told Moses, "I have heard the cry of Israel in their bondage." Oh, that was well and good. But then the Lord continued, "I have decided to **send you** to them."

Chapter XIII
Launch Out . . .

TRUSTING HIS GRACE

An ancient Tartar curse says, "May you spend your entire life in one place."

One cold winter night God awakened me and gave a "tour" on a world map and turned my world upside down. In that moment any hope of being thus "cursed" was shattered. Many of the exact cities and countries I saw that night in the Spirit I have already seen with my natural eyes. I have confidence that the others will be fulfilled in God's time.

This is not even an attempt at a complete autobiography, even if such a thing **were** possible. Only Moses recorded his own death. I simply felt led to chronicle the faithfulness of God as I have seen it so far. Perhaps I should have subtitled this, "My first million miles."

They have not been miles totally without bumps. There have been some great burdens of my wife and children. The care and feeding of an absentee husband and father requires a very special family. However, wives and children of many traveling salesmen pay a much higher price with less enduring rewards.

The miles have also taught me more than ten years of seminary could have done. This "living laboratory" has had its pain and loss but it has also had its miracles — and its humor.

In order to journey from Southeastern Nigeria to Amsterdam, I flew Okada airline (a Nigerian line) to Lagos and connected with KLM there. This caused a ten and one-half hour layover in the Murtala Muhammed airport in Lagos. I was totally exhausted already and fully intended to do nothing but vegetate during that stretch. A Nigerian carrying a suitcase approached with a young white girl in tow.

"Please, Master," he began, "This girl must wait for an Air France flight tonight. I need to leave. Will you watch over her?"

She was a dumpy little teenager with dishwater blond hair and an acne problem. I spoke to her in English and found she understood very little.

"Master," the man said, "she is French."

"All right," I said, remembering that it had been nearly fifteen years since I had spoken French, "You may leave. I will make sure she gets on her plane."

We sat for some time trying to converse in my smattering of French and her even slimmer English. I discovered that she was the child of a French planter from Togo on her way back to Marseilles for a holiday. The man with whom she had arrived was driver for one of her father's friends in Lagos. I tried translating a **Paris Match** she had but soon wearied of that. Perhaps due to my own exhaustion or the language barrier, but for whatever reason, any attempt at witnessing seemed useless and finally the conversation fell silent.

I sat nodding and watching Moslem men spreading their prayer rugs and beginning their ritual of standing, kneeling, bowing, and sitting in strict order. An Arab family settled in nearby us, several men sprawling on the floor. The veiled women chattering among themselves.

Suddenly the French girl blurted out what sounded like, "You won play bottle sheeps?"

"Bottle sheeps?" I asked.

"Oui," she said excitedly, "This game I know. You won play?"

She began hurriedly to scratch out some kind of drawing on a pad of paper. Triumphantly she handed it to me. I immediately recognized its grid of squares with numbers across the top and letters down the side.

"Oh," I said, "Battleship!"

"Mais, oui! You won play?" she repeated.

I shrugged, and began to draw my own board figuring playing battleship would at least help me stay awake. We sat there calling out the letters and numbers trying seriously to sink each other's armadas, when suddenly I burst out laughing. I could not crack the language barrier enough to explain the cause of my mirth. In fact, I am not at all sure I can explain it yet.

It was the utter absurdity of the situation that broke me up. It just suddenly dawned on me that we were an American missionary evangelist and a French teenager (living in Togo) playing battleship in the Murtala Muhammed airport in Lagos, Nigeria, surrounded by veiled Arab women and praying Moslems. It seemed like a scene from Monty Python.

I have always tried to establish rapport with the indigenous people wherever I traveled. Once in a village in rural Nigeria I was taking lunch in a small house. A half dozen Africans and I huddled around a common bowl of rice and some kind of fiery hot meat sauce eating and laughing. At a point, one man spoke in Ibo and several others looked at me and smiled.

"What did he say?" I asked.

"He said," someone explained, "this white man fits in."

I considered it high praise. In a worship service in Benin City they went through an elaborate procedure to choose a Nigerian name for me. Finally they settled on "Osaro." It means "The Lord Is."

In Peru I tried, with humorous results, to translate my name into Spanish. It somehow came out Valle (Valley) so to this day I am called Marcos Valle in Peru. While in Ghana, I found that my name is Kweku, meaning Wednesday Born.

Sometimes it has gotten confusing. Once on my first day home in Georgia from six weeks in Africa, I spoke to a yard full of little black children in Twi. Ah, well, I thought, they think I am a foreigner and they smiled warmly and waved as I walked by.

Over the years I have felt that a sense of humor has proven indispensable. I am persuaded that the Lord has His own.

I boarded a train in Madras, India, late one afternoon and rode all night across the southern quarter of the sub-continent. I watched the sleeping towns slip by as the old narrow-gauge steam locomotive wheezed and snorted its way toward Madura. The caterpillar of passenger cars clattered along in the wake. On the lighted platforms of the depots we passed, I saw people sleeping on benches and on the floor. Here and there a water buffalo in a moonlit rice paddy stood knee-deep in water like an ancient statue slowly sinking out of sight. The palm trees along the rails stood silent honor guard against the full moon.

In my compartment a man complained of being sick. Some fruit was being passed around but he declined rolling his eyes and rubbing his stomach. He was a small, dwarfish man with a slightly hunched back, but he was obviously educated.

"I am a Christian minister," I said. "If I have your permission, I'd like to pray for God to heal you. Is that all right?"

"Yes," he said, "that is fine."

Without thinking I stepped across the aisle way with my hands outstretched to lay them on his head. Perceiving my intention he raised his hands as if to ward off a blow and began to shake his head violently.

One of the other passengers said, "He is a Brahmin. He doesn't want you to touch him."

"I will pray without touching you," I heard myself saying. "Jesus will heal you. In the morning when you awaken you will be well and you will **know** that it was Jesus **only** that healed you and no other God."

I prayed aloud and turned my face to the wall and went to sleep. Before I drifted off I prayed even more. I always feel bolder in such moments than I do afterward in the quiet. In the morning as we began to stir to life, I thought he avoided my eyes.

"How do you feel this morning?" I asked him.

He answered me in Tamil, though he had been speaking English fluently the night before. Again, another in the cabin spoke up.

"He says he is perfectly well," the man said.

"The Lord Jesus has healed you," I told him. "You will **always** remember that."

The Spirit checked me at that point from saying any more, and less than an hour later the little man got off. I have never seen him again and I have no idea what fruit that seed has brought forth. I have chuckled from time to time remembering that high caste Hindu who did not want to be touched by my hands but was quite content to be healed by my God.

Sometimes the travel itself can be both fascinating and extremely wearing. In Peru I traveled from the desert floor to the peaks of the Andes in one grueling day. The coastal desert in Peru is as barren as the Sahara. The desert wind sculpts the dunes daily into modernistic statues and fights the road crews constantly for possession of the coastal highway. Beyond the desert, on one side, the Andes jut dramatically into the sky and on the other side, rugged cliffs plunge down to a rocky Pacific beach. Two Peruvians, one other American and I traveled by bus up that desert highway from Ica to Lima. At Lima we hired a driver and car and began the climb to the mountain city of Huancayo.

At 10,000 feet it began to snow and the drafty, heaterless Ford was an icebox. A sudden attack of altitude sickness was a complete but very real surprise with equally real symptoms. When the car reached 15,000 feet everyone except the driver (thank God) went sound asleep.

High in the Andes we entered the Valle Montaro, an absolutely beautiful river valley at the head of which is the city of Hauncayo. The highway up the valley is beautiful. The little villages that dot the valley floor with red-tiled roofs and Spanish architecture are idyllic reminders of the Mediterranean roots in South America. Small herds of llamas and alpacas and old peasant women in their quaint costumes are in sharp contrast to the unbelievably ugly mines wreathed in abiding clouds of pollution. The rape of the Andes is not in the least clandestine.

In a small Methodist church in Huancayo we found the power of the Holy Spirit was just as real in the snow-capped Andes as it is in lush African forests. How marvelous to see the descendants of the Incas weeping and praising God in joy that the Comforter had come.

One of the most frightening moments in those early miles of ministry came in Bogata, Colombia, when my nine year-old son, Travis, fell desperately ill. An American musical group had gone with me and I had taken Travis for this, his first foreign mission except to Mexico. The Colombians making the arrangements for us had accepted the offer of quarters in several rooms behind a little bar. It seemed an odd choice but their reasoning was that the lady who offered the rooms, not being a believer, might get saved. Furthermore, there was plenty of room and a kitchen. We did not have to enter our rooms through the bar and it was mostly a quiet, sleepy little place where old men sipped cervesa and gossiped.

We had hardly arrived in Colombia, however, when Travis broke out in huge red hives all over his body. His temperature steadily rose through the first day and in the middle of the night he began to vomit. Everyone on the team began to pray immediately and I started dosing him with an anti-vomiting prescription with very little apparent result.

How I struggled at each worship service. A teenaged girl agreed to stay with Travis and he was very brave, but it was tortuous to leave him in such misery. He would try to wave and smile gamely as I left for each service, but the mysterious welts covering his entire body gave him a horrifying appearance. By the third night it was apparent he was getting worse. I had taken him to a Colombia doctor in Bogata but the injection he received there had no results.

"Preach good, Daddy," he said. "I hope a lot of people get saved."

I looked at him there and wanted to weep. Including the soles of his feet, his body was one swollen, painful, stinging hive. His eyes were nearly swollen shut and his hands and feet were easily twice their normal size. I was so confused. What should I do? Should I leave him there — even for the duration of the service? Finally I decided to go but in my mind I was determined that unless he were some better by morning, I would leave the rest of the team with Florencio and take Travis home.

The strange thing was that the ministry times were under a heavy anointing. In midday services at local schools we often saw as many as half the listeners receive Christ. The evening services in local churches were packed and the response was fabulous. In two of the services the buildings were so jammed that people were standing in the aisles and were even seated on the platform! I could not take one step in any direction without treading on someone. People listening at the windows came in off the street to be saved.

I returned, however, to our room to find Travis dangerously worse. I could hardly recognize my own son. His face and body had that red, swollen, raw appearance of having been badly burned. Through the night his vomiting became violent. He could not even hold a teaspoon of Coke for 30 seconds.

He was such a brave little soldier! We made up a game to make light of his appearance in those hours calling him a new super-hero — Tomato Man! By 2 a.m. nothing helped. He worsened rapidly, his fever skyrocketing him into frightening hallucinations.

Hour after hour I knelt by his bed praying, longing for some sign of a break. None came. Suddenly just before dawn the hives turned inward into his throat.

"I'm choking, Daddy!" he gasped. "Please, Daddy, help me. I'm choking."

My God, I thought, my son is dying. He's dying and there is nothing I can do. The thought that missionaries since the days of Pentecost had held fearfully sick children in their arms in lonely outposts was of **no** comfort. I felt very alone and afraid.

I put my face on the boy's chest and screamed out to God in my heart. "Lord," I prayed, "please, heal my son. I cannot believe You have brought us down here to let him die in a dirty little room behind a bar. Lord Jesus, Son of David, have mercy on me."

In a few moments his breathing became more regular and the real crisis passed. I do not know if he really was dying. I know I **thought** he was. I also know he did **not** die. Many "friends" have been happy to tell me that I blew it spiritually by not praying with some particular formula which they have found helpful in such moments. I was frightened and confused and desperate and that was all I seemed to be capable of right then.

As morning traffic began to stir in the street outside I knew that I had to take him home. One of the Colombian brothers told me that if I left, I was just letting Satan have a victory. That was **great!** When folks are already hurting and confused and trying to make the best decision they know how to make, why — oh, why must we shoot the wounded by trying to act "spiritual"?

I do not know if I made the best or most "spiritual" decision possible. I know I felt that, for once I had to decide for fatherhood. I have asked my family to sacrifice so much for the ministry to which God has called me. That once I felt I **had** to show that sick little boy that I was not bound by my work. I **could** leave it. It was an opportunity to show him I could decide for **him,** and I took it.

The trip home was a nightmare. The hives made him miserable and despite as much aspirin as he could keep down, his fever raged almost unchecked. In Miami's airport, Travis finally passed completely out. He did not know who or where he was.

Having no ticket from Miami to Atlanta I laid Travis in the floor and stacked our suitcases around him. Pleading the protection of angels I dashed off to the ticket counter. With a ticket and a wheelchair I raced back, collected Travis and barely made a flight to Atlanta. All the way home he shivered and rambled out of his head.

In a week the boy was fully recovered. The team I left behind with Florencio was blessed with many souls and no irreparable damaged seemed to accrue to the mission in Bogata. The lady who owned the bar did, in fact, accept Christ. I, however, was left with a great deal of ambiguity about the whole trip. Had I missed God? Had I made the right decision? Had I been "defeated"?

I still do not know. I do know this. I came out of it with a greater sense of what the parents in I.C.U. waiting rooms go through. All the pat answers about healing, faith and prayer seem pitifully powerless in the presence of such crunching realities. What is left when all the theories break down? What is left is what I was left with. It is what Paul was left with upon occasion: God's promise has to be **enough.** "My grace is sufficient."

Sometimes in cross-cultural evangelism I have wept. At other times I have laughed until I wept, but I have never found anything else in life quite so fraught with unique learning experiences.

At a huge girl's high school in the state of Tamil Nadu in South India I scandalized the whole school by actually **shaking hands** with the female principal. A man simply does not shake hands with a woman. In Africa I caused untold confusion by waving "good-bye" in the American style which, in that country means "come here." In Amsterdam I attended a Salvation Army service only to find it was "Surinam Night." I sat listening to a colonel preaching in Dutch which was being translated into Surinamese for south American immigrants dressed in costumes exactly like those worn by their West African ancestors. I could not understand a word, of course, and I got the giggles. The Dutch colonel both in appearance and accent bore a striking resemblance to the **chef** on the Muppets! In Italy I watched hundreds in a refugee camp from many countries and faiths sit spell-bound watching a Billy Graham movie and I learned about the hunger for answers in this "refugee world." In villages and towns in West Africa I studied the thousands staring through clouds of insects at a ragged movie screen to watch Bible movies as amateurish as a sophomore play. I saw them weep and howl when Jesus was crucified, and dance in exultation at the resurrection. I saw them hiss at Jezebel and scream in excitement as Elijah prayed down fire. Their touching innocence was such a striking contrast to jaded American congregations that want their gospel packaged with movie stars, athletes and rock groups. I prayed with a Japanese businessman to receive Christ and learned again — Jesus is the Lord over the **whole** earth.

None of this is to say anything except that He has taught me and is teaching me, mile by mile. There are many men more traveled than I. Many have preached to much larger crowds. In my first million miles I have learned two valuable lessons. This shrinking planet is hungry for Jesus — and He will sustain them who go in His Name.

Chapter XIV
Launch Out . . .

IN CANOE FAITH

As he slithered down the mud bank and knifed into the murky river to my left, the alligator looked remarkably prehistoric. He also seemed more than a bit ominous. There are not thousands of alligators visible along the Rio Pichis, but there are enough to make swimming an uninviting prospect. Perched in our canoe like a caged canary I contemplated the journey that had brought me there.

As a missionary-evangelist I have traveled in many countries on most of the continents. I have ridden in enough different kinds of conveyances for a lifetime. I have lumbered across India in an old-time, narrow-gauge steam locomotive. At 125 m.p.h. Japan shot past my eyes in a smear as I rode the famous "bullet train." In rickshaws, taxis, buses, lorries, ox carts, and airplanes of varying sizes I have traveled the mountains, jungles, and cities of the Third World. Each one lingers in memory. Is it, in fact, even possible to forget a harrowing ride in a Nigerian taxi?

Nothing, however, has ever taxed me quite like one mission to Peru in early 1985. Arriving in Lima after midnight my associate and I got a few hours of sleep before leaving early the next morning. The 1958 Ford, which we managed to hire for the journey from Lima to La Merced, looked as if it had weathered Patton's north African campaign. Five Peruvians, two Americans, the driver and our luggage jammed the ancient Ford from boot to bonnet.

The Andes thrust dramatically up from sea level to well over

187

15,000 feet. They are not pretty but they are majestic. These snow-swept mountains are a massive, jagged escarpment separating Peru's lush jungles from its rocky Pacific coastline.

The "highway" from Lima up to the chilly cities like Oroya and Huancayo high in the Andes, is ridiculously dangerous. Often only wide enough for a single vehicle and mostly unpaved, it snakes its way along the cliffs and through snowy passes. It is hardly more than a precipitous rock ledge dynamited out as the Andes' begrudging concession to civilization.

The heaterless car was an icebox and the thin air and hairpin turns held me in a nagging, lethargic nausea. Looking down from the tiny road without a sign of retaining wall I could see literally hundreds of feet to a boiling river in the ravine below. The driver seemed convinced that he was A. J. Foyt.

Twelve hours later we were hungry, half-sick and frozen in La Merced. We slept on our sleeping bags in a small Evangelical Methodist Church and rose at dawn for the trek down to the jungle town of Puerto Bermudez.

Leaving our luggage there and taking only what could be carried in back packs we left before dawn the next morning. Managing to pile into a dug-out canoe powered by a nine-horsepower engine we began to chug up river at a snail's pace. Before Bermudez was out of sight, a driving, penetrating rain had thoroughly soaked us and all the gear.

For the next seventeen hours and many more hours for most of the next two weeks we traveled in one canoe or another. Small planks or bamboo sticks jammed down between the gunnels were the only seats. After the first day I was in touch with certain parts of my anatomy and spirit as never before.

As we fought the determined current I looked at the impenetrable wall of jungle on either side of me. Birds-of-paradise were in riotous bloom with butterflies and birds from a Disney fantasy buzzing the little boat. The jungle has a certain savage grace and I was fascinated by everything around me. Yet the hours — the rain-drenched, then sunbaked, cramped, unchanging hours — seemed to move even more slowly than the canoe.

"O Lord," I prayed in my heart. "Why am I wasting time here? All I have done is travel for days. When will I get **out** of this canoe and **minister?** I know You did not call me down here to squat in this canoe. When will I get to fulfill my ministry?"

188

It seemed that the Lord spoke to me there. As though the others, the jungle, the whole world had fled away, I was instantly alone with God in that little canoe. And He spoke to me.

"No, Mark, you do not understand. This **is** what I have called you to. Today, right now, in this moment, this very canoe is My perfect will for you. The 'ministry' to which I have called you, is to be faithful to Me. Unless you receive this time with joy and faith I will not be able to use you later in what **you** call ministry. Do you only love Me on the platform or do you love Me now —right **here** in this canoe?"

In Paul's last letter, 2 Timothy, he wrote, "I have fought a good fight, I have finished my course, I have kept the faith."

It is important that at the end of his life and ministry, having won thousands to Christ, planted churches and written most of the New Testament, Paul said only, "I finished."

Such exquisite simplicity flies in the face of much that is happening in contemporary American religion. Glamorized, glitterized Christianity is threatened by the humble believer who simply serves God daily. In such an atmosphere the door is wide open to a spiritual elitism that is utterly repugnant to the gospel. The result may well be an entire generation of spiritual wimps who lack the plain old Christian grit to hold on in the canoe of daily life.

Much of the modern philosophy of ministry is intoxicated with "success" more than it is informed by the Pauline admonition to "endure afflictions." Hence the Biblical virtues of obedience, faithfulness, and perseverance in Lordship are often lightly regarded as quaint relics, or worse, held up to naked scorn.

The great test of the mission field is not usually in dying bravely before a firing squad. There is that, to be sure, but perhaps the greater part is the call to deny the lust for the sensual stimulation of great fame, great success or even great challenge. On an Amazonian tributary or in the teeming jungles of America's suburbs, real ministry, and real Christianity, is less to be found on the platform than in the canoe.

This is not an attempt to rationalize that contemptible complacency that accepts stagnation and calls it endurance. And none of this is to say that the pastor of a successful American church in the suburbs is missing God. Not in the least! I often wonder, however, if we are not creating an ambiance so saturated in the success syndrome that many pastors could not even hear a call to the mission field if it came.

In the face of the deep hurts and hungers of a world lost in darkness, blithe platitudes are a pathetic insult. Those ministers who, in the crucible of their own lives, have laid hold on canoe faith will offer enduring light while neon cowboys mouth syllogistic formulas for prosperity.

Canoe Christianity is not just for missionaries. It is for the housewife, businessman and pastor. Canoe Christianity means having and keeping faith which is **real** and enduring in the face of a bathtub full of dirty diapers and a broken washing machine. It is a sustaining grace in the rainy season. Canoe Christianity gets up and goes to work week after week because that is the mature, responsible thing to do. Platform religion quits summarily because "I just didn't feel led to work there anymore." Canoe Christianity is simply that quiet, disciplined, orderly, frugal, holy living that finishes the course.

None of this is to deny miracles or blessings in ministry. God forbid! Yet, true missionary faith clings to a God of miracles —not the miracles of God. There is a time for blessings and, thank God, a time for preaching to thousands. There is also a time to catch hold of His nail-scarred hand and keep on chugging up river because that is His will for today.

Paul spoke of "finishing the course." It is impossible to finish a race without running all the intermediate steps between the starting line and the victor's crown. Every marathon runner knows the excitement of beginning a race. The starting gun sounds and boosters shout encouragement. Even more wonderful is that time of arriving at the finish line to cheers and backslaps. But those sublime moments are impossible without running out the long, weary miles in the woods when no one is watching or cheering and your track shoes are full of water and your legs and lungs are screaming with pain. Just to keep on —that's real victory.

In 1986 Alison and our three children accompanied me on a truly grueling missionary journey. For nearly two months we traveled and preached across Africa and South India. In a little less than eight weeks we were in more than one hundred worship services, traveled thousands of miles, ate local food, often even drank water from open wells, and lived with more difficulty than we ever had before, as a family.

We knew the possibilities were endless for Satan to attack in such a trek. Some of "Job's friends" discouraged us, of course.

"How can you put your children through such an experience?" they demanded. "What if one of them gets real sick or even dies?"

How can such questions be answered? God is calling. That is all the answer there is. We had not plunged off half-cocked. We had prayed for two years before undertaking such a strenuous family task. We knew it would be hard, and we were not hiding our eyes from the possibilities. I had watched Travis almost die in Colombia two years earlier. Yet we kept coming back to that one truth. Trust and obey!

This trip was, of course, even harder than we had contemplated. Through the hardship and difficulty, however, several wonderful things happened; things which had not happened for us as a family on any of our sweetest family holidays.

First of all, my personal admiration for my wife and children grew daily as I watched them handle the stress of heat, fatigue, culture-shock, and homesickness like true soldiers of the King. It was a new and unique experience for me to watch, with profound respect, as my own family matured right before my eyes.

The children had learned choruses in several languages through my previous journeys. We were amazed at the absolutely stunning effect it had on the crowds when three little blond haired, blue-eyed foreigners stood ram-rod straight and boldly sang out in Twi or Tamil before congregations that often numbered into the thousands. The Africans, especially, were absolutely thrilled.

In India one old man told me, "I cannot even explain the emotions I feel when these little children sing in my language."

Yet it put the children under the constant stress of being **surrounded** by large and sometimes quite unruly crowds who were somehow overstimulated by their presence. The African and Indian children just literally went wild to touch our children's skin and hair. Sometimes they became a seething swarm of bees tugging and jerking the children first one way and then another.

One night someone in the crowd pinched Emily quite painfully causing some real fear in all three. We had totally underestimated the effect of the children, especially in the villages, and were therefore more than a little unprepared to deal with it. Looking back on it now I see that I handled it poorly but I was frankly astonished by it all.

It is a stressful thing for three children, 11, 8, and 6 to be at the center of a maelstrom every time they take a step. A stroll down an African street became a scene like the Pied Piper in a matter of minutes, and an Indian fishing village threatened to erupt into near riot as a knot of dancing, leaping, shouting over-excited youngsters almost lost all control at the sight of the three diminutive whites.

The constant physical drain of the ministry's work schedule which necessarily included them, combined with strange surroundings and strange food to add to the strain. At night we often slept in hot rooms under serious mosquito attack. In India we spent almost every night sleeping with the five of us in three single beds shoved together.

From Tirunelveli to Madras we traveled by train. The jolting, lurching, journey for seventeen hours was an unforgettable experience. We found ourselves in Madras, totally exhausted and facing five worship services in less than thirty hours.

Two nights later we rode in an ancient van from Madras to Salem. It was probably the ten most miserable hours of our family's life so far. The road was a nightmare. We bounced, crashing from pothole to pothole for ten hours until I was sure the van would disintegrate.

I looked at my beautiful wife, fatigue like a heavy mask on her face, sitting erect with our luggage piled around her, a sleeping child on her lap. She would have looked more at home at a debutante's ball yet she never complained and she met my every solicitous remark with a reassuring smile and a game comment.

That is canoe faith. What victory did she have on that hot, rattling tin-can journey into misery? Why — she finished!

"Launching out" can mean leaving the snug security of the beach to ply deeper and unknown waters. I have heard God call like that. The only appropriate response in the face of such a command is to catch a deep breath and make the necessary leap in faith.

I have also heard God tell me to dig in and hold the fort when, for all appearances, the situation was hopeless. Only in the exercises of such tough-minded canoe faith can we overcome the fleshy, pseudo-spiritual nonsense that aborts relationships, babies, and divine commissions in the name of the "leading of the Spirit." We must be willing to hold on when holding on is the only victory possible. We must learn to endure when enduring gains us nothing but public derision and scorn from the spiritual butterflies flitting from blossom to blossom in search of the blessings of Abraham.

Missions and ministry are not all miracles and dramatic breakthroughs. I love to read stories of some church that grew from 12 to 5000 members in five years. How exciting! God give us more. Yet my real spiritual juices start to flow in response to some pastor who lovingly declares the whole council of God to a congregation who rejects his message and drives him out. The contemporary spiritual sissies just cannot relate to that. Paul did. He constantly admonished Timothy to just such prosaic virtues as endurance, contentment and courage.

We live in an age of quick fixes and bail outs. Plea bargaining has replaced justice and expediency has conquered excellence. Without a careful cultivation of the deepest respect for canoe faith Christianity we will raise up churchmen who are spiritual quitters.

The modern mentality demands divorce at the first squabble and justifies infanticide on the unborn whose only sin is that they dared to be inconvenient. We end marriages and pregnancies willy-nilly rather than face the moral test they imply. Certainly this might even be expected of the world. Yet when this kind of thinking invades the church, it erodes the stern Apostolic faith that in blood-soaked arenas joyfully endured. Sometimes launching means venturing into the unknown. Sometimes it means knuckling-down to persevere when persevering seems illogical, if not impossible.

It is better to grow spiritually in a doomed struggle than to succeed easily and grow morally soft in victory. It is a desperate mistake to contrive to shield our families from the very hardships that may shape them in maturity.

I looked at my son's exhausted form sound asleep on the bench seat next to me in the Bombay airport. A tiny frown played across his features and he groaned in his sleep. He was completely fatigued. We all were. Yet I knew we would recover. So would Travis!

Meanwhile I cherished the memory of Travis, a mere eleven-year-old boy, preaching spontaneously on an African street corner. I relished the mental picture of the little fellow standing on a stool shouting the gospel, through a shocked interpreter, to a swarm of children. How surprised I had been to hear the boy give an altar call! I was even more surprised when seventeen children and one grown man came forward at his invitation and accepted Christ.

I suppose the Bombay airport is not ideal for a nap. And no one enjoys seeing his children so utterly exhausted that they can hardly sleep. Yet my family came out of that taxing two month journey with a unity, a faith, a love and a confidence in God that was worth every bone-bruising mile and every sleepless night.

Only a few verses after Paul writes his own epitaph he dismally signals the sad end of a backslider. "Demas hath forsaken me, having loved this present world."

I am confident that at some point Demas was a bright-eyed, eager young evangelist ready for great ministry **or** great suffering. Perhaps he watched Paul cast out demons or heal the sick or preach in a packed gymnasium and he said, "Count me in!" Perhaps Demas even saw Paul endure a great hour of brutal persecution and nobly set himself to face that test. I believe that Demas most probably failed because he simply loved the world and lost his soul in spineless, disdain for the long, dusty roads and lonely nights by mountain trails.

This is not a call to some kind of drab, joyless, grindstone Christianity that cannot dance when the horse and rider are indeed thrown into the sea. It is simply to say that we must add to all that, the tested mettle of a scarred warrior who can write from a prison cell, "Rejoice, and again I say rejoice!" To the discouraged pastor, to the downcast missionary, to the believer whose colorless suburban life lacks utterly the spectacular — begin now to praise Him for the tedious lackluster hours in the canoe. There is your crucible. There is your cross. And there your victory. Keep the bow upstream and believe Him for faith to finish.

Chapter XV
Launch Out . . .

FORSAKING ALL ELSE

In the little Nigerian town of Owoyibo we had a grand crusade. We saw marvelous miracles and hundreds of salvations. As a result, however, we got away on the final night much later than we intended.

Armed violence is an outright commonality on Nigerian highways. Since the Biafran civil war, bands of heavily armed men terrorize lonely roads, isolated houses, even whole factories. Four Nigerians and I rode in a dilapidated Peugeot on a deeply eroded, one-lane dirt road that stretched interminably in the darkness. A high bank on either side sprouted lush foliage that brushed the sides of the cars. The deep ruts filled with mud made sudden acceleration impossible. It was a scene from everyone's worst nightmare.

I realized that a single man with a gun would hold us completely at his mercy. My pulse was pounding in my throat. The car was silent except for the heaving breathing of the five of us. A slight sprinkle began to dot the windshield when one of the pastors spoke in a soft whisper.

"If we can just reach the main road," he said. "I'll feel so much better when we're on the main road." I realized they were as afraid as I.

I began to claim every promise of protection I ever read in Psalms. "God," I prayed, "I **know** You are not going to let me be killed out here on this road. I claim Your protection. I **know** You will not let me be killed."

Then it seemed as if the Holy Spirit spoke to me.

"How do you know?" I thought He said. "How do you know I won't? Peter was crucified upside down and Paul was beheaded. I loved them. They were My servants. Are you better than they?"

These thoughts brought sheer terror upon me. What could it mean? I had a fleeting vision of myself face down in the mud. I could almost **hear** the crack of a carbine. My wife did not even know what country I was in. I could be murdered and my body hidden forever in some muddy jungle. My babies might never know what had become of me.

"Lord," I prayed, "what are You saying? Are You telling me I am going to be killed out here?"

"I am telling you," I thought He said, "that I do not have to tell you. I am the Lord thy God. Are you willing to quit claiming promises long enough to put your life, without any reservations, in My hands?"

I was as shaken as I have ever been in my life. I remembered Paul's testimony that he was "persuaded that (God) is able to keep that which I have committed unto him."

"I am Yours, Lord," I prayed silently. "I am uncertain and confused, but I belong to You. Where I do not, I long to belong to You."

In that moment it seemed that God's power filled that little car like the Shekinah Glory. Such peace — such radiant, thrilling peace came over me that I was almost overcome.

God's protection was with me that night, yet something inside me did die just a little. I know it must go on dying regularly, daily. I pray that it will. It must.

I am beginning to believe that time after time in one way after another the Lord issues the same call. Launch out into the deep! Whether for salvation, baptism in the Spirit, a new challenge in Spiritual formation or a call to service — the command remains the same. The Lord calls on one to leave business and enter the pastoral ministry. He leads another out of the pastorate and into foreign missions. The deep place for one may be to stay — for another, it may be to go. As the Spirit of Jesus speaks into any heart only that man can know. The Lord's word for one may be to crucify pride and trust Him by standing fast in a situation that seems to offer no hope of success. By the same token, God may tell another to leave obvious success and launch into a new and uncertain future.

It is utterly impossible, and probably counter-productive, to try to list all the possibilities. That is hardly the point. The Holy Spirit is not trying to distribute comprehensive manuals for handling every conceivable crisis. He is rather brooding restlessly over our lives, longing to take us into the deepest waters of faith. From salvation, to sanctification, to soul winning, to fasting and prayer, the leadership of the Holy Spirit will often be counter to reason and will always lead toward new levels of dependence on God. Launch out! If Jesus is in the boat there is naught to fear. "Whether the wrath of the storm-tossed sea or demons or men or whatever it be, no danger can swallow the ship where lies the Master of ocean and earth and skies."

The fields are white unto harvest. The power of God is ours! Shall we, like craven children, hug the beaches? God forbid! We are soldiers of the mighty King.

Catch hold of the hem of His garment and launch out into the deep!

To Barbara & [illegible]
With appreciation for a lot of years of fun & friendship — and sincere wishes for your health & happiness. Also, if you've had it in the kitchen, try it somewhere else.
Love
Teddi

Have You Had It In The Kitchen?

Have You Had It In The Kitchen?

by Teddi Levison
and Mickie Silverstein

GROSSET & DUNLAP, INC.
A NATIONAL GENERAL COMPANY
Publishers   *New York*

To our husbands ——
who have not yet asked for
equal time for rebuttal

Contents

Introduction

If anyone had told us eight years ago on that dreary afternoon while we were teaching each other the bossa nova and drinking spiked iced tea that we would one day be interviewing the greats of the world, writing a monthly column for a sleek, sophisticated award-winning local magazine, seen by millions on television, heard by multitudes on radio, in demand for everything from judging beauty contests to speaking before civic groups to appearing on national television for guest appearances, asked for advice on everything from fashion predictions to our solution on ending the United States' involvement in Vietnam, and most unbelievable of all, winning for our station the coveted George Foster Peabody Award for distinguished news reporting, the highest honor given in broadcasting (never before received by a woman in the news category), we would have suspected that his tea had been over-spiked.

However, although we never became proficient at the bossa nova, the rest of that seemingly improbable success story did happen to us, and perhaps this book will give you the incentive to make it happen to you. That's right — *make it happen!* No gin-induced hallucination or fistful of four leaf clovers ever landed a successful career. It is a long, hard and sometimes painful crawl up that ladder, and a slippery one, too.

Taking on the business world with a brand-new career or picking up the threads of one you left behind is doubly difficult when you are also committed to a husband and children and the reigns of domesticity. It is to you women, who want to trade in your dust mop for a briefcase, and still play the traditional roles of wife, confidante, mother, nurse, housekeeper, cook, keeper of the exchequer, chauffeur, and general handyman, that this book is directed. Through a lot of floundering around, and a little luck, we have learned many shortcuts in traveling the path between our two worlds and we hope this book will save you part of the struggle.

One word of caution, however. We can take you by the hand, lead you up the ladder of success rung by rung, tell you what to do when you get there, and how to keep from falling off, but if your family isn't behind you, forget it! The most important prerequisite to tackling the business world is the understanding, or at least the acceptance, even grudgingly, of your husband and children. So, for their patience and endurance, we affectionately dedicate this book to our families.

PART I

So You Want To Have a Career . . . .

Cutting the Cord

So the day of reckoning has finally come. After the third load of laundry, the fourth cup of coffee and fifteen minutes on the phone with your old college roommate who is just passing through town — on her way to a Women's Chamber of Commerce convention at which she is to receive an award for Business Woman of the Year—you've decided you've had it. No more suburbia, no more neglected, overworked, under-appreciated, unpaid slavey. Housework isn't what you want to spend the rest of your life doing, redoing and undoing. It's time to untie the apron strings, slip into a gray flannel business suit and offer your talents to the outside world.

Although the situation above is somewhat apocryphal, it is a fact that more and more women are entering the business world, not because of economic necessity alone, but simply out of personal desire. According to recent U.S. Department of Labor statistics, women make up 38 per cent of the total labor force; 43 per cent of all women over age sixteen work; and of the twenty-nine million working women, eighteen million four-hundred thousand are married. More than ten

million of these women have children under eighteen
years of age, a jump of 460,000 over last year's figures.
One fourth of all wives with children under three years
old are in the labor force. The Labor Department notes
that more and more women have been entering the
ranks of the employed for years steadily, regardless of
the level of joblessness in the country or prevailing
economic conditions. And yet in spite of these impressive statistics, for too many years American women
have been made to feel guilty if they wanted a career
outside the home. Most of the experts (usually men)
were busy telling us that we were being "fulfilled" by
bearing and rearing children, tending the home fires
and using our creative energies for "womanly" pursuits
like gardening, candle-making or gourmet cooking.

But what about those of us who hate grubbing in the
dirt, can't stand the smell of herbs and flunked
creative arts in school? What about the thousands of
women who are fascinated by finance, who were professionals in some field before marriage and who feel
that the limited horizons of home and hearth are just
that—too limiting? Increasingly they have been heed-
ing the sometimes strident, but nevertheless persuasive
siren call of the women's liberation forces to get out of
the kitchen and into the labor force.

Going back to work can be an exhilarating, enriching, rewarding experience. It should be. It can also
be exhausting, nerve-racking and emotionally draining, and it probably will be at times. There's no point
in kidding yourself. It will take every ounce of imagination, discipline, self-sacrifice, organization and intelligence you can muster to juggle all the parts of your
life without neglecting anyone while doing full justice
to all. (The mere logistics of managing children and
home are mind-boggling, and succeeding chapters will

attempt to help you sort out the usually imperfect solutions.)

Now at this point you may ask, "Then why should I bother?" Well, if you have to ask, then you probably shouldn't bother—you're not ready. You're only ready IF: You honestly feel that you're not a complete human being unless you're pursuing an interest outside your home and family; you're trained for a profession that needs you, or are willing to work toward one; you feel that your family will be better off if you're more than "just a mommy," or "just Dan's wife"; you realize that what your family sacrifices of your time can be made up three-fold by your becoming a more interesting, vital, aware, self-sufficient woman; you can get over, or live with, any guilt feeling about "abandoning" your family in favor of your own selfish pursuits. (We all go through that stage, although a University of Michigan study showed that full-time housewives spend only two hours a day directly communicating with their children, whereas working mothers spend one hour and eighteen minutes, *only forty-two minutes less time*).

And the most important IF of all—if your husband supports you in your endeavors, if not actively, at least passively. We think that most husbands deep down still harbor the desire for the sweet little housewife of yesteryear whose day revolved around the house and neighborhood and whose excursions were limited to the grocery store and shopping center with an occasional daring foray onto the neighborhood tennis court or golf course. However, more and more educated men, particularly those under thirty-five, are beginning to realize that we women are indeed capable of almost anything we put our minds to. After all, we sit side by side with men in college; we read the same books; we make the same (often better) grades; we read the same magazines and newspapers, see the same movies and plays, vote for the same politicians. How in the world can we be expected to stop our minds, turn off our spirit and retreat into the house, never to be heard from publicly again just because we change our name? We urge more husbands to realize that their lives can be enriched by a partner who really understands what he means when he says he's had a hard day at the office because she might have had one, too!

Once that premise is accepted, the rest is easy. Sit down with your husband, preferably over a relaxing drink, after the kids are in bed, and tell him exactly how you feel and what you want to do. Thrash out the pros and cons. Explain your needs and enlist his support and help. His life is going to change too when you go to work, so he might as well know it in advance. He might not like it; he might argue; he might rave. But calmly and firmly stick to your guns and don't be dissuaded by his objections. Remember, you're not a little girl any more. Your husband is not your father, and you do not owe blind obedience to him at the expense of your own needs. (The word "obey" is no longer in the marriage ceremony.) You are a grown woman and you and you alone must determine how you are going to spend the rest of your life. (Of course, this presupposes that you have in mind adequate arrangements for handling your family life while you are away. Your husband does have a right to expect the house and children to be reasonably well cared for in your absence.)

One word of caution, though, before you take the plunge. Be sure that what you want to do is worth the effort. If you're professionally trained and have only to pick up the threads of a previous career, you have lesser problems. But those of you without any training who want to do something exciting and personally fulfilling, will have to sit down and assess your talents, as we did. What are you interested in? Do you have any talents that can be put to use? Any particular skills that can be marketed? If you married before you completed your education, perhaps you should consider going back to school to get a degree. But get the degree in a specific field. We know an awful lot of liberal arts graduates who've never advanced past glorified file clerks. The point is, know who you are and where you want to go. You might have to try several fields before you hit on the right one, but always keep in mind that it's a vocation you want, not just a job. There is nothing glamorous about pounding a typewriter all day in the secretarial pool, or clerking at the suburban 5¢ and 10¢ store, or cashiering in the supermarket. Most of these women are working because they have to and might gladly trade places with you stay-at-homes.

Now of course a great many women work because they *do* have to. These women have many other problems, the most immediate one being their low economic status. Although we are writing primarily for the woman who does not have to work for purely economic reasons, many of the suggestions and advice we give here applies to them, too. After all, working wives and mothers all face pretty much the same problems, it's just the degrees that differ. It's just much easier for the woman who can depend on her husband for full economic sustenance to hold back and give herself all sorts of excuses why she shouldn't go to work. On the other hand, a woman who does not *have* to work can take the time to prepare herself for a really meaningful career. If you don't have to work to put food on the table, it's a lot easier to find work to feed your soul.

This book is directed toward the serious, intelligent, aware woman who realizes that motherhood and a rewarding career are not mutually exclusive but can be complementary, each bringing new dimension to the other. It's not a question of having to work or not. For many women it's not even a choice anymore — it's just a fact of life. They want to be part of that great big, fascinating, troubled world out there. They want to use every ounce of talent, energy and brainpower they possess. It's no longer enough for many of us to be on the outside looking in. There is nothing ennobling about cleaning house or washing dishes. They're just necessary but boring jobs to be gotten over with as quickly and effortlessly as possible.

Betty Friedan in *The Feminine Mystique* put it very succinctly: "The more a woman is deprived of functioning in society at the level of her own ability, the more her housework, mother-work, wife-work will expand.... The time required to do the housework for any given woman varies inversely with the challenge of the other work to which she is committed. Without any outside interests, a woman is virtually forced to devote her every moment to the trivia of keeping house." She bases this on the simple principle of Parkinson's Law (by C. Northcote Parkinson) : "Work expands to fill the time available for its completion." Mrs. Friedan reformulates this law for the American housewife: "Housewifery expands to fill the time available, or motherhood expands to fill the time available, or even sex expands to fill the time available." This, she feels, is the reason why in spite of all kinds of labor saving equipment, the modern housewife probably spends more time on household tasks than her grandmother. Much of it is just busy work and most of it can be done in a fraction of the time you now probably spend. We often ask ourselves in puzzlement, what do some of our friends *do* all day? How can they always profess to be so busy when we do the same things they do, plus hold down a full-time job, write a book, make speeches, read prodigiously, work on various civic committees, and still find time to polish our nails, set our hair and shop for the latest fashions? We're no paragons of virtue either. In fact, we're rather models of disorganization, always seemingly one step ahead of disaster, but somehow it all gets done. When you have something more important and personally rewarding to look forward to, namely your career, it's amazing how fast you can zip through necessary chores.

So make that decision to get up and get out right now! The children won't suffer; your husband won't leave you; your mother-in-law will eventually accept it; and the new sense of self-worth you attain will be inestimable. Some people call us selfish. We prefer to think that a woman who willingly splinters her life between her husband, home, children, and job, leaving precious little time for herself, is one of the most unselfish, self-sacrificing creatures on earth and should be applauded and encouraged instead of patronized and reviled.

And we hope that one of these days, after your career is successfully launched and you've found that your children didn't become delinquents and your husband has finally admitted his pride in your accomplishments, and your envious friends are all marveling at your fascinating job, you'll be able to ask yourself. "Was it worth it?"—and the answer will be a resounding YES!

Assess Your Abilities

Now comes the moment of truth—exactly what can you do? If you have your teaching certificate or your medical degree or your master's in sociology, and you've just been waiting to take the giant step back into the mainstream of activity, then you have jobs awaiting you. But if you've only had a couple of years of college or, like too many women, you unthinkingly took a degree in liberal arts or American history, you'll find your background isn't worth 50¢ on the job market. We know—it happened to us. Our parents were very anxious for us to graduate from college—in *what* didn't seem to matter. Nobody ever really asked us, "What do you want to *do*?" Consequently, we had no idea of our abilities and real interests until we started, years later, the slow, painful process of "learn as you go." You can bet we'll direct our daughters toward different goals.

In this frantic world, talent, brains and training are prerequisites for almost any exciting career. If a woman knows who she is, where she is going, and how she's going to get there while she is still in college, then it's only natural for her to continue those goals after marriage. As the Dean of Women at one large city

10

university put it, "I'm afraid that the days of the general liberal arts degree are over for any woman who wants more out of her university training than just four years of marking time." And a placement counselor at the same school noted, "It's heartbreaking to tell a girl who has a straight A average and a degree in English literature that she'd better take a secretarial course if she wants any kind of job. These days you have to have a degree in a specific field of interest to even begin the climb up the ladder in a profession."

Many young women are beginning to recognize this. For instance, recent statistics from the American Bar Association show that, although only 2.8 per cent of the nation's lawyers are women, 7 per cent of the total enrollment in law school today is female, and the number of women in first-year law has doubled in the past few years. Other professions reflect equally impressive gains. Although only 6.7 per cent of today's physicians are women, some authorities estimate that by the end of the decade 15 per cent of medical students will be female.

So O.K., that's great advice for your daughter's future, but it's your present we're talking about now, and where are you going?

First of all, assess your personality. Are you a leader, an innovator, assertive, poised? Perhaps public relations is for you. Are you precise, interested in detail work or statistics, do you like figures? Maybe market research or stock brokerage will be your field. Do you like working with children? There is a tremendous need for day-care centers and nursery schools all over the country. Most states do not require a teaching certificate for licensing day-care centers. Innovative ideas in early learning techniques are making older methods obsolete anyway. Visit some of the better centers in your city; send for as much literature as you can find; talk to mothers and experts in the field.

Real estate is a marvelous field for an enterprising woman who likes people and doesn't mind working odd hours. In our city a majority of the residential real-estate sales people are women. You can make a lot of money in a growing city, but it's a pressure cooker kind of job. Some women thrive on it and become extremely successful—others can't take it. To be really successful, you must work some nights and every Sunday. Your phone at home will ring constantly, and you are always at the beck and call of your clients.

According to one of our friends, who was making $15,000 to $20,000 a year working full time, "I wouldn't recommend it unless your children are grown and independent. It'll drive you insane unless you've got nerves of steel. If you can take all the abuse on the outside and come home, cook meals and care for your children, you're a miracle woman." And yet this same friend also admits, "I would recommend real estate highly to the woman who can handle it, because I don't know another business where you can have the freedom of movement. It's exciting, you're constantly meeting all kinds of people, and every day is different."

Generally speaking, real estate is great for divorcees or widows or women whose husbands travel frequently. It might be too disrupting for the average household. But again, it's up to you.

Another practically limitless field is interior decorating. There are several good home-study courses available which award a certificate at the conclusion of the course. Or you can take a course locally if one is offered. This is a good field because you can do as little or as much as you want. You can work out of your home on your own, or work for a department store or interior design firm. The large office supply firms also employ decorators to work with business clients, but it is unlikely you would be hired without some prior experience in the field. Again, get all the information you can, ask anyone who knows anything about the field, and read everything you can find.

There are also public service and civic jobs, although they are usually hard to land—working with Community Chest, an art museum, Welcome Wagon, Newcomers Club, chamber of commerce, various community services (but watch out here—most of the above will be delighted to have your services on a volunteer basis, for free). Each large service organization, however, usually has a paid executive director or a small full-time paid staff, and that's what you aim for. In fact, if you've had an impressive background in volunteer work all these years, this is a perfect place to put your talents to use. The feeling of self-worth you get when you find someone will actually pay for the same abilities you've been giving away free all these years is really amazing. As our friend Grace, who is now executive director of a community mental health organization, put it: "I'm not making much at this job because the city can't afford it, but the fact that I'm paid at all and am considered a professional with all the responsibility and respect that go with it is wonderful. I'm not working any harder now than when I was organizing for mental health on a volunteer basis for the Women's Club. In fact, it's easier because before I had to do it all from home with little or no help, and now I have an office, a secretary and a professional staff to call on. Although I know we accomplished a lot through the Women's Club, somehow I always felt unappreciated—as though I was just spinning my wheels. Now I feel a sense of great accomplishment."

Although we are in no way putting down volunteer work, much of it is make-work. Unless women are really dedicated to a particular cause, most will find organization work unfulfilling and boring after a few years.

If you're not sure what you want to do or can do, we suggest that you sit down and realistically write down your assets, your liabilities, your talents, your training, your personality traits, your interests. How old are you? Did you work before marriage? How do you look—vibrant and trim or overweight and drab? What do you want out of life? What is important to you? And most important of all, how hard are you willing to work to reach your goal? You might have to start on a lower rung of the ladder in order to gain experience and ease yourself back into the business world. You will occasionally be frustrated and disappointed. Are you willing to chance it? You will also have, in many instances, to compete on the job not only with men but with young, unmarried women who are willing to work with boundless enthusiasm for longer hours than you.

Many women want to go into the so-called glamour fields—advertising, public relations, broadcasting, publishing, television, movie production, fashion. Naturally, these fields are also the toughest to crack, and if you live outside the main centers of New York, Chicago and Los Angeles, positions are very limited. However, we are the living proof of the exception to the rule, so if you're determined to conquer one of these fields, gather up your ammunition, storm the barriers and plunge in. Determination is an asset almost as valuable as talent, and the woman who refuses to take no for an answer can often talk her way into a dream job.

Most other really meaningful jobs require some sort of training. Don't be afraid to take the step of going back to school for special training, or college for a degree or graduate work. Probably the field most open to women in today's complex urban society is work in social service, in government programs, economic planning, city and state government. There's a number of programs funded by various government agencies, private foundations, or churches, such as Model Cities, OEO, Head Start, Urban Coalition, consumer groups, VISTA. A degree or background in social work, economics, urbanology, journalism or education is usually required. Jobs in these fields, although not usually well paying, can be extremely rewarding and meaningful. Working with all strata of society and being a part of the great social and cultural changes erupting throughout our country is very challenging and gives most women a sense of really being where the action is.

One of our acquaintances is a perfect example of volunteer work leading to full-time employment. She majored in philosophy in college, didn't graduate, married young and never worked. She was always actively involved in community work and, as her children grew up, she found herself more and more involved in city programs for the disadvantaged. She entered a program sponsored by Economic Opportunity Atlanta (a local branch of the government-funded Office of Economic Opportunity) and trained along with other volunteers for six weeks. She then spent six months as an unpaid worker at an E.O.A. center. Her diligence, understanding and plain hard work landed her an offer as paid coordinator at $8,000 a year. The money isn't important to her, but the fact that she is paid at all is. "Several times I was offered a salary," she told us, "but each time I said, 'I can't, I'm not qualified.' It never occurred to me that someone would think my work important enough to pay for it." She also pointed out, accurately, that women usually think so little of their talents they need the reinforcement of a salary.

Often, you will find you have more talent than you think. Some women are already practically running a business at home by helping their husbands and they never realize how easy it would be to transfer their talents to their own pursuits. A perfect example of this is a neighbor of ours who for years kept the books, sent out the orders and filed the receipts for her husband, a manufacturer's agent. Like many salesmen, he had an office at home and travelled a great deal, showing several lines. At first he couldn't afford a secretary, so his wife, who formerly was a bookkeeper, filled in. She did such a good job and was so efficient that he made no effort to replace her with a paid employee. In the meantime, she took on more and more responsibility until she was really running the entire business end of the operation. All this time if anyone asked her what she did, she replied, "I'm just a housewife," because that's really how she thought of herself. It never occured to her that she was really an unpaid bookkeeper, file clerk and secretary and that if her husband lost her services he would have to pay dearly to replace her. She found it out finally when she went into analysis. As part of her therapy, she quit working for her husband and started her own business running a secretarial service for *other* manufacturers' representatives. The story has a happy ending. Through mutual therapy, the husband realized his wife's frustrations and willingly accepted her new role. In fact, now he is one of her clients, paying a very good price for what he had been getting free all those years. (She *does* give him a discount for her services.)

Another woman had a consuming interest in the occult. She is a very high-powered and charming person with great magnetism. At a party she got into a deep discussion with the vice-president of a new shopping center. Her knowledge of and interest in astrology, witchcraft and the metaphysical fascinated him. A few days later he offered her the managership of a new store in the center devoted to the occult arts. Although she had never worked before she plunged into this new challenge with her usual enthusiasm and is now ecstatically happy presiding over her metaphysical marvels. Her husband was so happy that she found an outlet for her energies that he bought the business for her and now they are making plans to franchise other stores. Although he couldn't care less about astrology, he is mighty impressed by his wife's business acumen.

Sometimes it's easy to turn a craft hobby into a paying business. We know women who run knitting shops, needlepoint boutiques and weaving emporiums. In fact, one acquaintance makes such magnificent rugs and wall hangings on her loom that she has won several awards. Her work is in great demand and it commands a high price.

Another business that started as a hobby is furniture antiqueing. One shop in town is run by two women who will "antique" anything you bring them. They will also copy a design off wallpaper or material and hand-paint it on furniture, lamps, and such to match the decor of your room. Often their children help out and the whole family can be found happily painting, sanding, and shellacking away. All of these women and many more like them took a skill or hobby that they were enjoying anyway and turned it into a paying enterprise.

If you plan to go back to school, realize it is going to

be tough. One of our friends, a doctor's wife, went through four years of college with three children who were in grade school at the time. (Now she's teaching disadvantaged children.) She likes to joke about how the four of them did their homework together at night. In a more serious tone, she'll admit, if pressed, that it was rough at times. It's not easy for a woman of thirty or forty to study at the college level with the same ease as an unencumbered kid of twenty. It's even more difficult to embark on serious study if you've let your mind drift in a state of limbo for the past ten or fifteen years.

Another acquaintance, also with three young children, took her master's and later, doctorate, in economics and is now an economic consultant and planner with her own firm. One of our close relatives went back to school to take a degree in psychiatric social work while her four children were still quite young. Another finished her nurse's training. One glamorous acquaintance of ours who looks as if she never did anything more exerting than to go to the beauty parlor is now in her second year of law school (it's taken her three) and is determined to stick it out to her degree.

We could go on and on, but by now you get the point. If you really want to do something badly enough, somehow, someway, you'll do it. The difficulties of a woman attending school full-time are quite similar to those of the working wife and mother. You still run into all the problems of the absentee *hausfrau* plus the hours you will need for studying at home (if you can concentrate with two or three screaming kiddies playing hide-and-seek under the table), or at the library if you can escape.

The extra years you spend preparing yourself for a profession will be well worth it the rest of your life. Skills, talent, experience and thorough preparation are always marketable at any age in any field.

We hope the foregoing advice has set you in the right direction for your new dimension in life. However, if you're only discouraged by now because none of your talents or training fit any of the suggested fields, and you just can't get up the enthusiasm to go back to school, and besides, you're just bursting to plunge into that exciting, rewarding, paying business world *right now*, don't panic—just read on.

If You Can't Find a Job That Suits You, Invent One

This is a critical point in your development of the new you. At the first realization that a fascinating, exciting and rewarding job is not magically waiting on their back porch when they open the door to bring in the milk, many women sigh, slump back into their housecoats, turn on the daily soap opera, and tearfully contemplate the inequality of women and the discrimination the fairer sex is subject to in the job market. To this we say, "Baloney!" When we began our careers, no one could have been less aware of the unlimited possibilities for women if they will only leave the bridge tables and search them out.

We were young wives with three children between us, immersed in gourmet cooking, decorating, bridge lessons and club work. In fact, only the slightest stirrings of dissatisfaction with suburban tranquility were beginning to make themselves felt. Neither of us is a college graduate, nor had we had any special training in any particular area. One of us had never worked before, the other for just a few years in public relations before marriage. We were both fairly disorganized, useless before 9:30 A.M. and not well inclined toward taking directions from anyone other than our husbands, maybe. What we did possess were inquiring minds, a delight in the unusual or offbeat, an awareness of the world around us, a latent writing ability which had shown flashes in our variety of organization work, a flair for publicity, and an ability to relate to people.

One afternoon, after attempting to teach each other the bossa nova while waiting for a rum souffle to finish baking, we looked at each other—both in Bermuda shorts, tennis shoes and with that natural drabness that only no makeup can provide—and simultaneously said, "What'll it be? There has to be more to life than two shots of rum and a bossa nova at three in the afternoon."

It was about that same time that we were in the process of reading Betty Friedan's *Feminine Mystique*, and the more we read, the more we realized that she was writing about us. After realistically evaluating our talents, training, interests, the devastating realization hit us: There was really nothing available in the job market that we wanted to do or were qualified to do. That left only one avenue—what did our city and the people in it need that it didn't have or needed more of?

We searched the yellow pages, the want ads, our brains—with no success. During conversation one of us mentioned having to attend a convention the following week with her husband—wishing something would save her from going because there would be nothing to do. Well, thunder and lightning didn't crash down from the heavens to give us the signal, but we both got the message. What the city needed was a convention service that would plan conventions—from agenda to activities for wives.

We won't bore you with the details of the many hours spent telephoning, making appointments, writing out ideas, and finding someone to foot the bill. But we will tell you that, within thirty days, we were in business. We worked hard, badgered businessmen, sweet-talked hotel keepers and banquet managers, and never saw a profit. That enterprise bombed. (It would probably succeed today, but we were a little premature.) It took one year, and in that year we learned one thing: Life was too short and could be too exciting to while it away taking dancing lessons.

The next step up the ladder came in the form of a political fund-raising party. Our convention business was taking its last gasps, and we were feeling that tinge of depression and disappointment that sets in when things don't go in the direction you have pushed and shoved them. We knew that we would have to find the right thing—it wouldn't find us.

We got to the party, which was held at the estate of some very wealthy patrons of the art of politics, and after paying our dollar for admission commented that, for only a dollar, you could actually feel you were invited and wanted—not just there to get perhaps a glance at those at the top and hope that some of their glamour would rub off on you. It was sad and funny to see the hundreds of bejewelled and tightly collared couples straining to see and be seen.

One of the guests was the articles editor of award-winning *Atlanta* magazine. In conversation with him, we told him that the whole thing should be written up. He said, "Write it. If I like it, I'll print it." We did, and he did. It was this and a few more ideas written and accepted that landed us the job of "Town Talk" editors, a regular feature in *Atlanta*.

"Town Talk" was an around-town potpourri of news, human interest features, personality sketches, business articles and unusual items. It was a dream job while we were galavanting all over town, interviewing celebrities, tracking down little-known oddities, covering political events and the like. Sitting down and pounding out twenty to twenty-five typewritten pages of copy for the column every month was a little less glamorous, but the feeling of creativity attained from looking at your words in print is akin to giving birth to a baby.

We had been pounding happily away at our typewriters for almost a year when we were invited to be guests on a local television talk show to discuss our column. It was after that appearance that the ambition bug took a big chomp. We liked being in front of a mike, and we were going to be there again as soon as possible. One week later, we were interviewing the host of a new local TV show. A few days after that we received a call from the station with an offer to book the show (that's setting up guest appearances). We agreed—with one condition: that we get our faces in front of that camera at least once in a while. It wasn't long before "once in a while" wasn't enough, and through hard work (booking 15 guests per week), with perseverance and some nagging, we convinced the management that what that show needed more than anything was two hostesses—a job which, in addition to booking the show, included doing cooking demonstrations, serious interviews, and an occasional song-

and-dance routine, not to mention coddling a temperamental host.

We were still doing the "Town Talk" column—and, with that load, there were days when the thought of a leisurely bossa nova lesson seemed almost appealing—but not quite. (Incidentally, one of us had already had a third child by then, and many of the shortcuts for those either too busy or too lazy to be a full-time housekeeper were already being tested.) We loved the job, even though it meant being made-up and on camera at 9:00 A.M.—something we would previously have thought an impossibility. (If nothing else, we've learned that *nothing* is an impossibility if you want it enough.)

Well, as they say, the best laid plans—and as you know, a show biz career can be short-lived. Our sudden exit from television is described in other chapters.

Our entrance into our present job came after pounding the pavements, with sheer determination and the conviction that we were capable of doing just about anything we set our minds to. By this time we were pretty well known in town, due to our column and the television exposure. Still, openings in our fields were scarce.

Eventually we made contact with the manager of a new all-talk radio station that was soon to go on the air in Atlanta. He was anxious to hire us, but had all the slots filled with the exception of a Saturday morning show. We took it and, within a few months, had talked our way into a daily two-hour show, plus doing part-time news coverage of press conferences and other feature reporting.

At present, after almost four years on WRNG Radio we have built our show into a top spot on the station (which is now pushing No. 1 in the market) and have worked into fulltime news coverage, doing mostly features and documentaries (for which we won the 1970 George F. Peabody Award for news). We are also regularly invited to speak before various civic groups, make personal appearances locally, and have appeared on several local and national TV shows. We have also been featured in *Time* magazine, and our latest effort is this book. As for the future, we feel that our careers are only in midstream—more books (we have already started on our second), maybe a syndicated show. If the opportunity is available, we'll be there to take advantage of it.

We're by no means the only women who have been determined to succeed in a career and have made it. And many others have ingeniously devised their own jobs through their own imagination and determination. One young mother of two that we know personally and professionally started out by having exercise classes for her friends (she had studied physical education and nutrition), went on to a weekly spot on our TV show, and now has her own TV exercise show every week in addition to professional classes for which she is nicely remunerated.

Another friend—and this is a real success story— enjoyed dabbling in découpage. She dabbled her way into a new, simplified process for découpage which is now patented and bringing her and her husband a healthy income. The side benefits of her dabbling took her around the country for TV appearances, promotional tours, write-ups in national magazines, and all the accoutrements of success. Again, it was determination, drive and hard work that she thanks.

Two other women right in our town opened a custom dressmaking shop without any experience with a needle and thread. What they did have was a flair for design, a good fashion sense and a desire to enlarge their previous sphere of bridge games and carpools. They borrowed money to rent an old vacant house, coaxed their friends into giving a hand with cleaning, painting and decorating, and hired a woman to do the sewing, then advertised their skills by wearing their own creations.

Antique shops are also a good business possibility for women, especially if you have an interest in art and history. A friend of ours developed a casual interest in antiques, acquired through decorating her house, into a thriving, successful business. She and her partner (who also has a family) share the responsibilities of purchasing, bookkeeping, joys and aggravations of their work. Incidentally, their extensive research into the history of antiques has stimulated numerous interesting conversations on the social level—not to mention the free advice they provide for their friends in establishing the quality of their antique pieces.

Another friend on the West Coast, an avid tennis player, could never find tennis clothes to suit her taste, so she began to design her own. Soon her friends were coaxing her to make their tennis clothes. Before long she had rented a small building, hired two seamstresses, enlarged her stock to include matching sweaters and racket covers, and did quite nicely while at the same time running an equally well-organized household.

There is no end to businesses that start small and wind up making a real impact. As a matter of fact, 4,000 new businesses open each week in this country.

If the own-your-own-business route isn't for you, there are plenty of other avenues open with the only prerequisites being ingenuity, stamina, drive, initiative

and plain hard work. Two young mothers we interviewed could never think of interesting ways to spend
time with their children. They decided that many
other young mothers had the same problem, so they
got together, did some extensive research into all the
nooks and crannies in their city, and wrote a *Guide to
Entertaining Children*, complete with illustrations. Another mother of two came up with the idea of an
offbeat guide to the city she lives in—everything from
restaurants to knitting shops—done in a unique pam-
phlet. It is so successful that she has updated it each
year.

One of the most successful women we know is a
wedding and party consultant. She is the mother of
four young children and got started in her profession
because of her knack for unusual parties which she
gave regularly in her home. She now earns over
$25,000 a year. (P.S. She was a college dropout after
one year.)

A great career for women who enjoy teaching, but
don't have the credentials for academia is operating a
charm school. This is an area where personal charm,
poise and grace steal the stage from book learning. It is
particularly interesting to direct these charm classes to
young people in their teens, and very rewarding to see
them make the transition from bumbling tomboys to
something that resembles a girl. Advertising in suburban papers brought an attractive mother of two teenagers whom we talked to enough business to require
her to find a partner (also the mother of two, one only
three months old) and expand her charm school into
larger quarters.

One of the best examples of inventiveness happened
right on our own show. We were discussing the need
for a press representative in the mayor's office, and one

woman called in claiming she would like the job. She hung up the phone, went to city hall and talked her way into one of the most interesting careers we know of.

Another unique job is that of private detective. There are only about six women who are licensed in the United States. Most private detectives don't handle cases that involve violence. One of the six licensed ladies quips, "All that hardboiled stuff in books and movies is nonsense. I have never had a gun pointed at me in anger. Most of my work is insurance investigation, missing persons, domestic situations, and such." This type of career can be based at home and leaves time for domesticity when you're not sitting all night at a stake-out.

And why not try a traditionally male job? What's wrong with a lady car salesman? Women are a natural for this one—especially if you're articulate and like people—and the only training necessary is the gift of gab. Another traditionally (but why?) man's field is the home building contractor. This requires some specialized training, but who knows the needs of a home better than a woman? We know a gal who hired herself out as an interior consultant to builders—a job she invented—and now has more requests for her services than she can handle. Another mother of five teen-agers and wife of an architect buys old houses, remodels them (with some occasional help from her teenage sons) and sells them at comfortable profits — again, no training needed, only good taste and imagination.

Another pretty blonde friend of ours, the mother of two, landed herself the job of press secretary to the governor's wife. After that governor had served his four-year term of office, she had sufficient contacts to land an equally stimulating job. Another acquaintance had a similar position, but with even more responsibility as press secretary to the lieutenant governor. When her boss was voted out of office, this attractive grandmother redirected her talents into public relations.

A number of women we know have discovered their business talents after the death of their husbands. They were reluctant to get their feet wet in the outside world as long as they had a man to take care of them. What a shame that their husbands couldn't share in the joy of their accomplishments. One mother of four took over a thriving veterinarian business after her husband's death. She is not a pet M.D., but runs the business end of things very successfully. Another late blooming female entrepreneur took over the management of her husband's variety store business and has doubled the volume in three years.

There are also several women who have assumed their late husband's insurance clients and continued to serve as their agents. This is an excellent field for women, and one that you are nicely remunerated for.

It would have been so much more fulfilling for these women to have shared these accomplishments with their husbands instead of waiting until it was too late and they had no one to share their success with.

What it all boils down to is your ingenuity. Look around your city and assess its needs. You may be surprised to find that one of them is you.

Selling Yourself
*(Or How To Make Little or
No Credentials Look Impressive)*

Once you decide what you want to do, you face the problem of actually going out and doing it. This is no time to be shy and self-effacing. There's an old adage that if you don't blow your own horn, no one else will, and like most well-worn sayings, it's true.

Summon up all your self-possession, look proudly in the mirror and chant ten times, "I'm terrific, I'm talented, I'm going out and take the world by storm, and I'm not going to take no for an answer or settle for second best." Then do it! Sure, you'll be nervous calling on strange people and trying to sell yourself, but you'll find that each time you do it, you develop new confidence for the next time.

Use every means possible to find out about job possibilities in your particular field. Remember that nice young man you met at a cocktail party last month whose firm has just landed a big research contract in your particular field? Call him up, remind him of the meeting, and ask for an appointment. Even if he can't use you, very often you'll find that one prospect will lead you to another. Follow the want ads, the trade publications, look in the yellow pages. Use every personal contact and friends of friends that you can find. Write letters of inquiry or send résumés to companies you're interested in. Call the placement bureau of your university if you're a local graduate.

Use employment agencies only as a last resort, as very often they charge you instead of the company.

Besides, they serve as a buffer, and we much prefer to get our own foot in the right door.

Try to see prospective employers in person. It's too easy for them to say no over a telephone or to file your letter in the wastebasket. Once you're sitting face to face with the prospect, pull out all the stops. Use your wiles; drown him (or her) in charm, act sure but not superior; enumerate your accomplishments, back- ground and training in a matter-of-fact but confident way. Remember: You *know* you're good and would be an asset to this particular organization. Always be prepared with a complete typewritten résumé of your background, including letters of reference, press clip- pings, technical material you've written, or whatever. In other words, it's time to lose your amateur stand- ing — if you're entering business, be businesslike!

Another important point. They would never teach it to you in business school, and maybe it's not exactly ethical, but it doesn't hurt to stretch the truth a bit. Suppose you're after a copywriter's job in Cleveland, and where the application asks for previous experi- ence, you put "Copywriter—Andersons Department Store, Des Moines, Iowa, 1962-'63." If no one asks, it's not necessary to mention that Mr. Anderson is your uncle and you only helped out with copy and layout every so often when they needed extra help.

If you want to be really blatant about it, you can make up all kinds of previous jobs in other cities. Your record will rarely be checked unless, of course, it's a sensitive position you're applying for.

But a word of warning here. You can lie, finagle, or talk your way into a job, but nothing less than talent, skill, hard work and production will keep you there. Getting the job is one thing—keeping it is quite an- other.

Your Appearance—Get With It

If you have ever stood in front of a full-length mirror and not quite recognized yourself, then this chapter is especially important for you.

For some reason, getting married and having children does something to your appearance. Besides the stretch marks, sagging bosoms, lumpy hips and flabby arms, a lot of housewives look like a slightly out-of-focus TV image.

There have been innumerable articles written on how to transform your college wardrobe into a suburban matron's dream, or how to be a well-dressed working girl on $12.50 a week. Also, quite a few on what's right for the career woman—usually from Cardin or Channel with a price tag somewhere around one month's salary.

We think a woman should look as glamorous and young as possible, whether she has a career or not. Any woman who believes her husband when he tells her that he likes her looking plain, with no makeup and in a cotton housedress, is crazy — and often lonely — waiting for her husband to come home to her homemade chicken soup from a office full of well-groomed, "with-it" women.

Those of you who are already in the mainstream of

the business world know what an important part
your appearance plays in making the right impression
at the right time. A friend of ours who runs a successful modeling school told a group of students she was
working with on self-improvement that only God and
your mother tells you to come as you are. The rest of
the world judges you on the way you look, first—and
then on your accomplishments. This is true for men as
well as women—just look at the increase in men's cosmetics in the last few years.

Some jobs require more attention to appearance than
others. Naturally, if you are closeted in a room for a
year writing a novel, you don't need your false eyelashes. But when you take that book to the publisher,
put them on, along with the rest of your makeup
(don't say you don't need any; everyone over twenty-
five does!), and something on your back that doesn't
look like your daughter made it in sewing class.

We are not saying that you have to religiously follow
every fashion whim of the moment. On the contrary, if
you have confidence in yourself, you will develop your
own ideas of what looks right on you—not "a look," but
a lot of looks that are all you. In other words, if you go
to work in an old tweed skirt and an angora sweater,
accessorized with one strand of pearls and black suede
pumps, your brain will have to work three times as
hard to make up for the rest of you. *We* don't believe
in the classic look for anyone under 60 with a nice
shape. If you are moving in an ever-changing, mobile
world, move with it—and that includes the way you
look. If you are determined to be the classic type, do it
with flair, perfect fit, and a whiff of your best perfume.
When you are in a field that deals with people, this is
especially important.

This doesn't mean you have to throw your old

clothes away—they can make the transition with your help. A few nice accessories can update almost anything. A beautiful silk scarf, an embroidered vest that goes over everything basic, a pair of sleek boots, a bright-colored raincoat with matching hat—items like these can perk up a closet full of mistakes. Incidentally, don't forget banlons — we swear by them — especially if you travel a lot. We have both been known to take two-day business trips with one Banlon on our back and one in our briefcase.

For those of you who are fortunate enough to have a Prince Charming (or husband) who will treat you to a new wardrobe with which to kick off your new-found glory, here is a basic list of essentials that we have found work for us and a lot of other working wife-mother combos:

Two go-to-work outfits — preferably two-piece separates;
Two well-tailored pants suits;
One fun "with-it" outfit (gauchos, etc.) ;
Four skirts;
Four tops that interchange;
One vest or weskit;
Several Banlon or jersey dresses;
Two around-the-house pants outfits;
Three after-five dresses (or dressy pants outfits) ;
One hostess gown;
As many unusual scarves, belts, jewelry, and such, as you can collect;
One pair of boots;
Three pairs of day shoes;
One pair of silk pumps for evening;
One pair of sandals for evening;
Sneakers for weekends and loafing;
One raincoat;

One evening coat;
One daytime coat.

It goes without saying that soiled clothes with missing buttons or dandruff-flecked collars are not chic.

Once you have the problem of what to wear off your mind, consider the other time-saving ideas you can employ while careening between conference room and the kitchen. We feel that hairpieces are a necessity for any woman who leaves her house at least once every day (what we ever did before that invention is a mystery to both of us). A wig and a fall (both of inexpensive synthetics that look more like hair than hair) should keep you from looking like the right end of a mop during your waking hours.

Fortunately, while you are sleeping the problem is your husband's. (Nothing short of being presented to the Queen in the morning would cause either of us to go to bed with a head full of curlers.) If your hair rebels at sleeping uncurled and uncovered, electric rollers will revive it — but you will have to sacrifice about thirty minutes of sleep in the morning to do the job. Another worthwhile investment is a professional hairdryer. It's far more relaxing to wash and set your hair at home at your own convenience than to try squeezing two precious hours at the beauty parlor into an already tight schedule, and also cheaper. If you are all thumbs when it comes to your hair, ignore the previous advice and find the two hours, even if it's at a salon that stays open once a week at night for working women.

Don't forget to manicure your nails, personally or professionally, once a week. We recommend light polish—it doesn't show chips.

In regard to makeup, this is generally a matter of

individual taste. We go the whole route when we have time—false lashes, liner, the works. If you are not in one of the so-called glamour fields or are allergic to eyelash glue, soft makeup, using a little eyeshadow, liner and mascara, along with rouge (again, if you're over twenty-five, you need it) is fine. As for certain Women's Lib groups' declaration of no makeup, any woman who has ever been caught answering the door bare-faced and stringy-haired to find that it's her boss calling, or worse yet his wife, knows the importance of those paints and powders.

Incidentally, don't turn into an old bag the minute you walk through your front door at night. Your husband and kids have as much right as your boss to see you looking human. We make it a practice to slip on a pretty hostess robe when we get home—they're comfortable and attractive, and a lot sexier than Bermuda shorts or blue jeans.

The rest of your grooming is so basic that if you don't know it, you're not ready for the outside world. B.O. and halitosis do not inspire love and affection from your co-workers or your boss, and you'd be surprised how many well-groomed women offend their co-workers in this way. Most people need to bathe every day—some don't. But everyone's teeth need the brush twice a day, at least. If that stale-breath and wet-dog aroma waffs up to the top, your best friends won't tell you, but your boss might—and not what you want to hear.

Getting your appearance together will be one of your easiest hurdles. Once more you will be enhancing not only your image in the business world but also the image of you in your husband's eyes—not to mention in your own mirror.

PART II

Once You Have
Your Foot
In The Door . . . .

How To Make Your Boss
Think You're Indispensable

One thing you will consistently find in the business world is that your co-workers, and especially your boss, will always be expecting you to "act like a woman." They don't mean this as a compliment. What they do mean is that they expect you to complain more, chatter or bicker with the other women in the office, take longer lunch hours, find innumerable excuses to show up late or not at all for work and, in general, cop out. If you have even the brains you were born with, you will see to it that they are disappointed on every one of those expectations. It is a fact women do have to work harder, be more competent, and "prove themselves" far more than their male counterpart. The old saying that in order to succeed in business a woman must "work like a dog, think like a man, and act like a lady" isn't far from the truth.

Don't overlook the possibility that you may have a woman employer. In this case, you can either be very fortunate, or up the creek without a paddle. The right female boss will be more willing to accept you as a competent equal, more respectful of your abilities, and more likely to promote you, even over a male co-worker

38

if you deserve it. The wrong female boss will be suspicious, jealous, overly critical, and a bitch to work under. This one is up to chance and luck.

Many employers complain, and with some justification, that women are not as reliable as men. You should immediately set out to show your boss that you are the shining exception to all the problems he's had with women he's dealt with in business. In other words, don't come in late, take long lunch hours, or constantly request time off to attend to family business, such as dental appointments and the like, until you have proven your reliability beyond a doubt. For example, last year a severe ice storm hit Atlanta, closing down schools, offices and stores. The broadcasting business, however, never closes, even in the wake of natural disaster. We are responsible for two hours of air time that takes no recognition of ice and snow. We could have easily pleaded impossibility and hoped that one of the men at the station had snow chains or skis—but we didn't. We managed, with the aid of a fire poker to inch down long, steep driveways (the car would never have made it), and hitchhiked to work.

We have also dumped runny-nosed kids at each other's houses, met our husbands a day late for vacations, and even dragged our kids to work with us if necessary, in order to fulfill our responsibilities to our job. In return for this, we are allowed a flexible schedule (except for our two hours daily on the air) which allows us all the freedom we need. Once you prove yourself to your employer by doing a better job than he expected, then you can begin to make a few demands yourself. He will be far more likely to accept your taking the afternoon off if you have worked through lunch for a few days or volunteered to go over those extra briefs at home in the evening. You might also point out to him that the Department of Labor statistics show that women take less sick leave, have less absenteeism and more loyalty to the job than men. However, in spite of your best laid plans, emergencies will arise.

The main argument we have heard from businessmen against giving younger women responsible positions is, "What if the kids get sick, or Johnnie needs an operation, or Susie has an accident at school? We can't have those kinds of disruptions in our office." This is difficult to answer unless you think of it this way. Would that same executive say to a male applicant, "What if you have a hangover and show up late some morning?" "What if you have a flat tire and have to be towed into a garage, forcing you to cancel an important business meeting?" "What if your wife gets ill and you have to leave the office to rush her to a hospital?" Of course he wouldn't! Life is full of the unexpected, and every one of the above examples are common enough to have happened at least once to every businessman. These emergencies are part of everyday living, and every office makes exceptions for them. Why single out women? So, don't let any prospective employer cow you with that "What if" business. Just ask him what arrangements the office makes for male emergencies and how many days sick leave you're entitled to, and sweetly tell him you're sure you'll be able to function within those limits.

Now, back to those emergencies. There will be times (hopefully very few) when getting to the office will be impossible. If Johnnie falls down and breaks a leg on the way to school and your husband can't help out, then, of course, Johnnie comes first. You will have to make a decision here and we dislike even having to suggest it, but if the attitude at your office is negative, then we feel it is best to lie. It's a shame that this is sometimes necessary, but until attitudes change you might as well face it. If you call and say, "Johnnie broke his leg and I'm rushing to the hospital emergency room and probably won't get in the office today," your boss might think, "There, I knew I shouldn't have hired a woman with kids for this job; they're too unreliable" (completely overlooking the fact that for the last six months you were the only person in the office who never missed a day). But if you call and in a choking voice gasp out, "I woke up with a 104° fever, a terrible pain in my chest and a sore throat," you'll get lots of sympathy and a stern admonition to stay home for a few days until you get over it. After all, the boss remembers how miserable he was last month when he was laid up with the flu! We know it's unfair, and we know it's hypocritical, but we also know that prejudice dies hard, and in the meantime you don't want to jeopardize that exciting job. Of course, the foregoing is a last resort tactic. Hopefully, you will become so important in your chosen profession that you can honestly say, "I'm taking the afternoon off to attend Susie's ballet recital," and all you'll get is a pleasant nod.

The above is only to be invoked when it is really impossible to do otherwise. We assume that you will manage to get to the office under all but the most severe circumstances. Real emergencies don't come along too often. We've been working nearly eight years and only once or twice have we been unable to cope. We do not consider pains, headaches, nerves, cramps, hangovers, minor colds or visiting relatives grounds for copping out of a day's work. But for those unavoidable times when the emergency is one of your kids, whether to lie or not to lie is up to you, your business relationship and your conscience.

How To Be One Of the Boys
While Wearing
Your False Eyelashes

In this chapter you will probably find the strongest opposition to the anti-man jargon of many radical feminists. We firmly believe that women should employ every trick and technique inherited through the ages, from Cleopatra on, to get where they're going. This doesn't mean we advocate hopping into bed with your boss—which is usually bad strategy. What we are saying is that, like it or not, you will be working in a male-oriented business world, where the female image is still not the equal force that we would like to see it.

Many men still regard women as charming little creatures who should gaze adoringly and marvel at the wisdom of men. Even when a woman has moved into the executive arena, most men of the generation you will be working for appreciate femininity in a woman. Women have been getting the best of men through charm and feminine wiles for centuries—so who are we to knock it?

In case you haven't noticed, the male executive today spends almost as much time preening and primping as his female cohort — and at this writing, more grooming products are purchased by men than by women, not to mention the great influx of men's hair styling shops, men's hairpieces, and men's haberdashery, which today's woman is hard put to keep up with. The man of today makes no bones about his desire to make an attractive appearance, and you're kidding yourself if you don't realize that men use their sex appeal in business whenever it's deemed advantageous. So why shouldn't we?

An architectural engineer whom we talked to—the mother of a small baby—wears her false eyelashes to work every day, and her co-workers have never seen her bare-faced. And she has indicated that a little extra charm and a flutter of those lashes were instrumental in assignments from two important clients.

As for our own business, we could devote an entire book to the many times that feminine charm has got us a scoop that our male cohorts would have given their double-breasted blazers for.

For example, in covering the state legislature, which we generally do as part of our reporting duties, we find it heartwarming to watch representatives and senators trip over each other to be first at the microphones of mini-skirted reporters while time-seasoned male capitol correspondents shrug their shoulders in resignation.

Then there was the time when we managed an exclusive interview with Governor Nelson Rockefeller, then a Presidential candidate in town for the day, several hours before his general press conference (during which he called a halt to all questions while one of us replaced a broken tape on our recorder). And if we had a dollar for every important guest we cajoled into an appearance on our show, even though his schedule "wouldn't allow it," we could buy our own radio station.

We have found that, as much as Women's Lib is

trying to overcome it, most men think of women first as sex objects, and then, maybe after a few rejections, as people. You could be talking about a million-dollar real estate merger with your boss, and while you are thinking interest rates, don't be surprised if he is wondering how you would be in the sack.

Don't get the idea that you can bat your eyes and sweet-talk your way up the ladder if you don't have a firm foundation to balance on. Nothing can replace competence—not even the assistance of a 38-24-36 figure. You may be able to charm your employer into giving you that big chance you've been working toward — but if you flub it, all the Chanel No. 5 in Paris won't do you any good.

Too many women in the Lib movement forget that men are not our enemies, they are merely a product of generations of role playing, and that they need our help to realize that we are ready and willing to share the burdens of our own destiny with them. But let's tell them in a soft voice, echoing from a Mona Lisa smile. And perhaps, eventually, they'll realize that there is no combination quite like a woman with both beauty and brains.

Is Sex In the Office a No-No?

We're not going to tell you naively that women don't sometimes use sex to get ahead professionally. They've done it from time immemorial. We are going to tell you, however, that it's not necessary, it's self-degrading and often backfires. If a woman has to sleep with her boss to get ahead, she'll never know whether she could have made it on her own.

Offices are like small towns—rumors spread like fungus, and everyone knows the business (true or false) of everyone else. If you're having an affair with a member of the staff, you'll be the last to find out that everyone in the office has known about it all along.

Subtle suggestions will sometimes be made that sex could boost your career. Sometimes it works out and you might get to the top of the ladder, but then everyone knows how. That reminds us of the story we were told about the former fashion director of a major department store. She started as an assistant buyer and soon after began her other career as mistress to the president of the store (they were both married). She proceeded smoothly, and just as she was reaching for the top rung (a vice-presidency), her lover died of a sudden heart attack. The new president wasn't interested in her sexual charms, and her job performance had never been worthy of her title, so she was demoted and subsequently fired.

Another acquaintance of ours had a dream job in public relations for an international firm. It called for several brief trips to Europe a year, plus entertaining fascinating people from all over the globe. The only trouble was, her boss, a Frenchman, was the most interesting man of all, and an affair soon ensued. He, although very married, was used to such liaisons and could handle them. She wasn't and became emotionally involved. Her job suffered. Her marriage almost broke up, and finally the strain of it all caused her to have a nervous breakdown. Of course, she could never come back to that company. She was a very talented woman, with a marvelous opportunity, a terrific job and a great salary, and she threw it all away because she didn't keep her cool. Eventually she'll get another job, but it's unlikely it will be as good.

Because we pride ourselves on being good reporters, it wouldn't be fair to tell only one side of the story. Although it is true that ninety-nine out of one hundred extramarital office remances end unhappily, every so often one does work out into something permanent, like marriage.

We know of several such instances. A dental technician we know fell in love with her employer and although they were both married an affair ensued. One day his wife caught them after hours making love in the contour dental chair. A scene followed and eventually the dentist made his choice. He divorced his wife and married his technician. They now work side by side among the drills and couldn't be happier. Another close friend of ours (male) in public relations had a wife and four kids and a charming executive secretary. After years of loyal service, our friend found she was not only important to the company, but had become increasingly important to him. After the last child went to college, he divorced his wife and married his secretary. She doesn't work for him anymore, but she freelances in public relations just to keep her hand in.

The top executive of the leading television station in a large midwestern city fell in love with the station's weather girl, and both their temperatures zoomed. Although they were married to others, it was very convenient to be together because of her irregular hours. (After all, she didn't *have* to come straight home after the 11 o'clock news!) Eventually that liaison, too, led to marriage.

A brilliant woman psychologist we know found herself falling in love with one of her patients, an equally brilliant but troubled writer. Eventually, because of professional ethics, she had to tell him the truth about her feelings and terminate the professional relationship. They were then free, however, to pursue a personal one and although she lost a patient, she gained a new husband, and he wrote a story about the whole experience.

One well-known married politician and his assistant campaign manager had the ideal set-up. She had a dream job, travelling all over the state and country on speaking and campaign tours, setting up press conferences, scheduling his appointments and writing speeches. The nature of her job took her away from home quite often, so while her husband and his wife were waiting patiently in their respective suburbs, the politician and his aide were traipsing around the country together. It does get lonely in a strange hotel in a distant city after the thunder and glory of the speech-making has subsided. What could be more natural than for them to turn to each other, first for a late dinner, then a few drinks, then inevitably, more. They haven't married each other yet, but they're constant companions and it's known and accepted among their friends and followers. There is nothing clandestine about their relationship. He's only staying married because it looks better for the voters and his wife would rather be Mrs. Somebody, than Mrs. Divorced Nobody. Our friend likes it this way because she frankly admits she loves her job, and if she married her lover, she couldn't continue to be his press aide and manager! But it's real love between them and if he ever loses an election or decides to retire from the political arena, we have no doubt they'll marry.

So although it can happen to you, it probably won't.

What is more likely to happen if you get involved in an office romance is told in the sad saga of a very good friend of ours. She was talent coordinator of a top syndicated television show. The show's star is a charming rogue, twenty years her senior, who is known to occasionally down one too many. Every time he got inebriated he would call on our friend to come nurse him back to reality, which she willingly did. Eventually she divorced her husband and she and the star consumated their rather sick relationship in marriage. Neither her job, nor the marriage lasted. They began to argue and a couple of times he beat her up. Management was afraid of scandal, so she got booted out and while he's still smiling out from the TV screen, making scores of feminine hearts flutter, she's looking for a new job and a new husband.

You can bet that if management finds out about your office love affair and decides it looks bad for business, he won't be the one to go — you will.

Sex is as available to the working woman as paper clips, but if you're going to indulge, at least don't be incestuous — keep it out of *your* office. (More on that in a later chapter.)

If you're offended by every pass, however, you're in the wrong ball game. In the business world you are thrown into close daily contact with men. Some are going to flirt; they are going to notice you. Depending on how informal your office is, they are going to make good-natured suggestive comments. If you are in one of the so-called glamour fields, as we are, you are usually very conscious of your looks, and the men will comment and admire. We say, let them! Their appreciation is good for our ego, and our appreciation of their admiration is good for theirs, so everyone is happy.

Once in a while a man you work with might make a

comment or suggestion which you consider offensive. This is no time for you to put on your virginal, school-girl airs—you might make a permanent enemy of him. Instead, handle it tactfully. Let him know firmly, but pleasantly, that he's out of line. Make a joke out of it, if possible. Give him a chance to retreat gracefully. If he wasn't insecure in the first place, he never would have come on so strong.

You will find that many men in business feel they must constantly prove their manhood by either putting women down or treating them as sex objects. They are feeling more and more threatened as increasing numbers of women assert themselves professionally and socially, so to prove their "superiority," they make a pass. We feel sorry for these men—as much victims of society's role casting as women—and once you understand, it's easy to be forgiving instead of furious. Besides, we still like men. Most of them are pretty nice and noncompetitive, and we've never found a replacement for the sparks generated between a man and a woman.

We enjoy kidding around with the men in the office, and if the kidding is often about sex, why not join in? In a way, it's a compliment that they feel so free to talk about anything with us. It means we're accepted as equals, as human beings, not put in a separate category of "women." We personally don't talk like longshoremen; it just isn't our style. But we have no objection to the men around us using colorful language if that happens to be *their* style.

The whole secret of male-female relationships is to be comfortable around each other. In other words, let them flirt, admire, lust, suggest, swear, or leer. We don't mind, as long as they also let us do our job, recognize our abilities, promote us on the basis of performance, not sex, and pay us accordingly. If they occasionally feel the urge to pat our fanny or comment on the size of our bust, or the shortness of our skirt, we pass it off good-naturedly. After all, it's their problem—not ours!

Keeping Friendly With the Office Staff —At a Distance

One rule that we have steadfastly maintained throughout our career is keeping our business lives and personal lives separate. Getting chummy with your co-workers can result in far more aggravation than it's worth, and very often a confidence shared with a fellow employee can come back to haunt you when you least expect it. Your office is not the place to confide domestic shortcomings and quarrels with your husband, nor to gossip about anything or anybody. After all, you're not at a cocktail party, and you're supposed to be working, not partaking in an all-day coffee klatch.

We also try to stay away from informal, chatty lunches with our co-workers. If the occasion does arise, keep the conversation business-oriented. This applies to socializing in the evenings, too.

It's a good idea to keep your business relationships and the social relationships you share with your husband separate. Inviting the office staff to a yearly Christmas party, or something of that nature, is within acceptable limits — but if you go beyond that, you're asking for trouble.

It's also a good idea to keep your mouth shut about the plans for advancement you have and all the devious means you're going to use to get that promotion, raise, or whatever you're after. You will have enough on your hands trying to get to the top in this competitive world without giving your competition the master plan for your success.

There is one exception to the "keep your distance" rule—and that is your boss. We don't advocate a romantic liaison with the top brass (the "why nots" are covered in another chapter), *but* lunch with your boss is a great opportunity for him to receive the full impact of your charm, wit, intelligence and any other qualities you can present over the consommé. As for social evenings with your boss, his wife and your husband—the fewer, the better; it can cause an uncomfortable atmosphere at the office for both of you.

We know of several instances when social relationships with the boss have led to semi-disaster. One copywriter for a successful ad agency felt compelled to keep up with her boss socially. She cajoled her husband into joining her employer's country club, she nagged him into moving to the other side of town where the boss resided in suburban splendor, and even insisted that they use the same expensive caterer to help with the constant entertaining that she felt she must do because the boss's wife was a popular hostess. All of this led to the draining of her husband's income not to mention her own and eventually to the realization that keeping up with the head of the firm was not as important as keeping yourself and your family happy. She didn't stop working, she just stopped social climbing. Another example of too much chumminess at the office can be found in an unfortunate incident involving an attractive young magazine editor. She was having some rather bizarre marital difficulties which she divulged to one of the secretaries in her office one morning over coffee and danish. The secretary expressed the expected sympathies and after the coffee break promptly went to the boss with the tale—slightly embellished, of course. The boss was a conservative and straight-laced type who wanted his publication to have the same image that he did—so, exit Miss Editor with the big mouth.

It goes without saying that the worst faux pas you can make is to let slip to your co-workers that you're looking for another job, or that you're dissatisfied with your current position. If you are loose-tongued and dull-witted enough to let this slip you may very well find yourself with an unemployed period in the interim.

To sum it up, while you're on the job keep a smiling face, an alert mind, a good sense of humor and a buttoned lip. Keep your problems to yourself and you will have a lot less of them.

How and When To Ask For a Raise

We could write a complete book on the financial inequities women have been subjected to merely because of their physiological makeup. We do devote a teeth-gnashing chapter to that subject later in the book. There is one financial area we would like to

mention while on the subject of your relationship with
your boss—and that is how, when and why to ask for a
raise.

A lot of working women we've talked to have actually admitted that they're afraid to ask for a raise.
Several have even said they not only were refused the
raise they asked for, but also were given their walking
papers. One young woman even had a male co-worker
suggest to the boss that she was worth more money,
only to be told that "women will work for less than
men, so we pay them less."

Unfortunately, this tight-fisted employer was right.
Women, because of years of conditioning to their sec-
ond-class citizen role, have always dutifully accepted
whatever meager pittance they were accorded by
chauvinistic employers who think a pinch on the rear
and a wink will compensate for sickly pay envelopes.
Thanks to Women's Lib and a few liberated men, this
medieval practice is beginning to change—but you
must spur it along. In other words, even if you have to
take a lower-salaried job to get your foot in the door,
keep both eyes on your goal and push for it. Ask for
more money the moment you feel that your performance deserves it. State your request firmly, with
confidence, and list the reasons for it.

Incidentally, don't be cajoled into accepting a
higher title or boosted status in the firm in lieu of more
pay. In nine cases out of ten, a person's monetary
compensation measures his success, not the title on his
business card.

Also, don't be silly enough to think that you will be
offered a raise just because of excellence, almost always, you have to ask. Most employers have a way of
overlooking little details like how good you are until it

is brought loudly to their attention. We have received various salary increases in our career, and never at the insistence of the boss.

If you demand a raise and can prove you deserve it, but your boss gives you that flack about the men needing more money, or you have a husband to support you, you can do what a friend of ours in the publishing business did when she found she was making considerably less than the men beneath her in experience and performance. She and a few other female co-workers went on strike. And when that didn't work, they brought a federal suit against the company for job discrimination. This is a pretty extreme measure and one that does not endear you to present or future employers, so use it with caution and only after everything else has backfired.

Before asking for a hike in pay, it's a good idea to find out what other employees are making; you can do this by straight-forward questions or by bribing the accountant. If one doesn't work, try the other. And if you find no one else in the office is getting rich either, don't get cold feet; they probably haven't had the nerve to ask for a raise either.

Want an Affair—Get a Job

Although this book is intended for the serious, married career aspirant, it's a fact that if you're looking for a little fling on the side or if you'd like to trade in your old, used husband for a shiny, new one, the business world is a good hunting ground. Depending on the kind of job you have, we guarantee you'll meet men— fascinating men, interesting men, dynamic men, rich men. You'll also meet plenty of plain, dull, ordinary ones. But at least you won't be sitting in suburbia lacing your coffee with bourbon, dreaming erotic fantasies and casting hopeful eyes at the milkman.

Through our job we have met and observed men from all walks of life—politicians, actors, writers, artists, business and professional men, athletes, social workers, civil rights activists—you name it, and one thing is for sure: Although married, plenty of them are available. In our early innocence we admit we were mildly shocked when we witnessed some well-known married politicians and other pillars of the community openly cavorting and not seeming to care who knew. We soon learned that far from hurting their careers, it seemed to enhance it in the eyes of their peers, as long as there was no scandal. We're hardened to it now; in fact, we've been the objects of quite a few advances from men in high places ourselves, men whose names and faces you would recognize.

Don't get the idea that having an affair with a prominent man can further your career. It's more likely to backfire. While society smiles indulgently at male indiscretions, it frowns disapprovingly at female hanky-panky. There's another, more important deterrent: your career. Remember it? With all this talk of forbidden love, we forgot about it for a moment, didn't we? That's the trouble with extra-curricular romance. It's hard enough to juggle a husband, children, home and job, but throw in a lover too and life will become as complicated as a three-hundred-piece jigsaw puzzle. So our advice to you based strictly on pragmatism is, don't. It's simply too much trouble and the emotional strain is liable to be reflected in your work. However, we don't feel we're our sisters' keepers, so if you still insist on tasting of life's forbidden fruits, it's easy. Here's how.

The best way, of course, is to get a job with lots of public contact. There are attractive men everywhere out there. You might meet him at a client's office, over a business lunch, at the ticket counter or in the elevator. In our field the ubiquitous press party is a fertile meeting ground. We admit most of them are pretty dull, but there's always that special one . . . .

If your job entails traveling, fine. Maybe your future lover will be occupying the next seat on the plane. We've met several charming men that way. And, of course, even if an affair isn't your goal, it's always nice to have an escort to dinner when you're in a strange city on business. (It's up to you how far it will go. A smile and a thank you are really all that's necessary; after all, you've shared your scintillating company with him, haven't you?)

The closer you are to the top and the more respected you are in your field, the more desirable the men will be and the more desirable they will find you. Most successful men are impressed by a woman's equal success, especially if she has managed to retain her femininity.

So if you're still determined to live dangerously—stay attractive, concentrate on getting ahead, take advantage of every opportunity to meet men, and keep your antennae out sending subtle vibrations. We guarantee you that within six months the right man will pick up those vibrations and send some of his own back to you, and you're on your way. He'll be married, of course, but then, so are you, and remember—we warned you!

Two For the Price Of One—
Our Job Solution

Let's not kid ourselves. Despite your new-found importance and independence, despite your glamorous new image, despite the exhilaration of being where the action is, leading three lives is often hectic and frustrating. In fact, in our high-pressure type of job, we would find ourselves pushed close to the limits of our endurance if we had to do it alone. We invented our own solution, which we feel could be applicable to many other nontechnical jobs. We share one job, one salary, one office, two bylines and double glory. In fact, when we were written up in *Time* magazine, after winning the Peabody Award, our boss at the time, Ray Stanfield, was quoted as saying, "We never know which one will show up, but one of them always does."

We started our career sharing the same billing, and no one has ever questioned the unique arrangement. Our daily routine is such that we can easily split our duties as long as we keep each other and the office informed as to who's doing what when. Sometimes it's a little disconcerting to those we work with, and sometimes our business associates aren't sure which one of us they're talking to, but mostly it works out very well. We realize (and we know our bosses are quite aware of it) that each one of us puts more than half of her time and energy into the job, so they are really getting one and a half times the amount of work for a single salary. However, the freedom our unique arrangement provides us makes up for the inequity.

As long as we happen to work this way, we have turned our broadcasting duo into a valuable public relations asset. As the first female broadcasting team in the country, we do make all public appearances together. We also write and produce documentaries as a team, attend interesting press conferences (and parties) dually, and usually do our show together at least once a week so we don't lose our double image. The rest of the time we split it up so that one day one works, and the next day the other does. Or maybe one of us will do the show and then the other will cover the news and the office in the afternoon. We also split up the chapters of this book, writing separately but conferring constantly and then going over each other's work to tighten, correct or suggest deletions or additions.

For us this arrangement works perfectly, and we think it's the ideal solution for other career-minded women as well. There is no reason, for instance, why two women couldn't share a copywriter's job, or an administrative position, or a social worker's case load. Just because it hasn't been done before doesn't mean it isn't a good, workable idea. All it takes is two women who have similar training, temperament, creativity, approach to the job and a responsible attitude. It's really just like any other business partnership.

Look at it from another angle. If two persons form a partnership and open up a retail store, no one thinks a thing of it. They run the business together, taking alternate days off, if they have other obligations elsewhere. Maybe one works in the store in the morning, the other in the afternoon. On Saturday, because it's a busier day, they both work together. One partner handles the bookkeeping, the other the buying. They share the profits equally.

Or take doctors. Our gynecologists have several partners. If one is busy, the other sees the patient. If it's time to deliver a baby and one doctor is unavailable, one of the others officiates at the birth. In other words, they work interchangeably, and they inform new patients of the arrangement on the first visit.

Now, if doctors can work out that type of an arrangement with the most intimate kind of relationship, why can't the same technique be applied to almost any job in almost any company? It's just not done, they say? Phooey, we say. It's time it *is* done, and if you can talk yourself into a "sharing" career, by all means do it.

Evidently some of the experts (women, naturally) agree with our concept. Dr. Estelle Ramey, Professor of Endocrinology at Georgetown Medical School, Washington, D. C., is quoted as saying, "We need a whole new kind of social engineering. . . . We need to work out ways women can work while their children are in school—perhaps two women sharing the same job at different hours." Three cheers for Dr. Ramey!

This brings us to another one of our pet peeves. We can't count the number of men who've patronizingly marveled, "I can't understand how two women can work so closely together and get along so well. Don't you two ever fight?" Of course we do! Don't two men who are close business associates have disagreements and personality conflicts? You bet! In fact, we get along better and work together more harmoniously than most of the men we know. You have to be attuned to each other, share similar goals and carry your part of the responsibility. You also must be considerate, have mutual respect for each other's intelligence, trust one another and be willing to compromise on disputed points. In short, you have to be mature adults—gender has nothing to do with it.

We get so tired of hearing the refrain, "But women don't really like each other." It's been drummed into our heads since we were little girls that women have no loyalty, that they will cut each other's throats for a man, that they are constantly in competition with each other. Sadly, all too often it's been true, because we were never allowed to trust each other. Happily, in the business world, you'll meet a different kind of women. A busy, productive career women wants to get the job done as professionally as possible. She doesn't have time for grudges or gossip. She's intelligent, organized, articulate and usually commands respect and admiration from both men and women. In fact, you'll often find she's by far the most interesting person in the office.

We have been fortunate to meet many women like this, and find their company stimulating and delightful. A many-faceted women usually has a great variety of interests. She can talk with equal enthusiasm about fashion, art, politics, economics, her home, marriage, the stock market, her profession, her husband's job, her children's school, urban problems, the high cost of living, foreign affairs, and a myriad of other subjects. In fact, at a party, after five minutes of conversation, you can usually tell which woman is the careerist (even if she doesn't mention it) and which is the stay-at-home. The career woman is usually most interesting and very likable. We think it's because she likes herself and is vital, involved and never bored. How many men can say that?

Business, unfortunately, hasn't yet come around to realizing the fantastic wealth of wasted talent locked up in the American woman. Whenever a woman has a talent or special training that's at a premium, she finds her employer is usually more than willing to make concessions to land her. But you've got to be pretty special to command that kind of treatment. In the main, companies are just too rigid to change outmoded regulations and are thus dooming thousands of potentially productive women to frustration and bitterness. What's even worse from industry's point of view, they are depriving business of the brains, enthusiasm and fresh approach women could bring, if only the way to the labor force were made a little easier.

Why do office hours have to be nine to five? Maybe you'd be just as productive from ten to four or eight to three. Or maybe you could accomplish your office work from nine to twelve and take the rest of it home to finish at your convenience. When we think of the time wasted by so many male business executives with their two-hour, three-martini lunches, their endless and usually fruitless staff meetings, and the general shuffling of papers in so much busy work, we honestly think that most eight-hour days really produce about three hours of actual work.

One friend of ours, a successful attorney in a large firm, schedules all her appointments in the morning. At 2:00 she goes home with a briefcase full of work and continues with her paperwork and dictation at home. She may work far into the night at times, and she always puts in eight or ten hours a day, but after 2:00 she does it on her own time, at her own pace, and she's home when the kids come in from school. The dictation is ready for her secretary first thing in the morning, and the office can always reach her at home if any questions arise.

Many women (and men) prefer to work at night. One x-ray technician we know loves her late hours at a suburban hospital. She works from 11:00 P.M. to 7:00 A.M. Her husband travels and is usually home only on weekends. She sleeps after the kids go to school and is awake and unhurried when they return after 3:00.

Most jobs really require little actual time at the office, and the higher up you go in the executive suite, the more flexible your hours will be. We didn't say you'll be working *less* hours, just that they'll be easier to juggle. Reports can be written at home; manuscripts can be read at home; copy and layout can be written and designed at home; phone calls can be made at home; designing can be done at home, and so on. Outside of working with highly technical equipment, there is no job that can't be done partly at home. Try to talk your boss into letting you try it. When he finds out that you're producing far more than the office-bound men, he'll probably tell them to go home too!

We are night owls. Most of this book was written after 10:00 P.M. and far into the night. We do most of our research and reading for our show at home. There have been a few mumbles at the office, but our ratings are high, our show is respected, and we're always available when needed. We're also willing to work odd hours when a big story is breaking. So management realizes that it all evens out. We honestly feel that most people are much more productive when allowed to work at their own particular pace. This is as true for men as for women, and modern business would be wise to recognize it. This is particularly true for the so-called "creative" professions.

So, work it out any way you can—full-time, part-time, sharing, splitting hours between home and the office. You'll find out what works best for you. Now all you have to do is talk management into it!

You Can Turn Being Fired Into an Advantage

Yes, it can happen. You've done all the right things and made all the right contacts, and finally landed the job. Even your horoscope promises success (which it will occasionally no matter which sign you're born under). But one horrible morning, mixed among your fan letters and invitations, is the pink slip—you've been canned. It's happened to us—more than once—and each time we wadded up our astrological charts in complete despair, positive beyond a doubt that we had hit the bottom before we reached the top.

The most mind-blowing ax fell after we had just begun to enjoy the egotistical bliss of being minor celebrities through co-hosting a daily T.V. show (along with the tall, dark and handsome host). One day, after an unfortunate choice of words uttered on the air by one of our guests, followed by an explosion of calls to the manager from little old ladies in tennis shoes, there was a soft knock on our office door by the program director, followed by an even softer, almost apologetic statement: "Today's your last day, baby."

Believe it or not, and we didn't at the time, this can be the proverbial blessing in disguise. It can be a period of reevaluation, reassessment, and sometimes redirection. It was for us. It led us into an area of more serious programming, to our own daily two-hour interview show, to investigative news reporting, and to the coveted George Foster Peabody Award for news reporting (the highest honor given in radio and T.V.).

Your unexpectedly jobless state is not something you look forward to when you wake up in the morning, but, the sooner the better, puff up your deflated ego and go out and find yourself another job. And be sure that it's one step higher on the ladder than the one you were removed from by that shortsighted clod who didn't know genius when he saw it.

Unless you are a model of versatility, you had better stick to the same field, or something related. The more credits you line up in a specific area, the closer you come to the peak of your particular profession. Incidentally, don't be embarrassed or ashamed if you are fired from a job. Many of the top names in every field of endeavor have been given the boot at one time or another. In fact, a successful author we know never got around to writing his first book until he lost the job he had worked at for over twenty years. Another acquaintance, after being fired from what she thought was her dream job, entered law school and is now a successful attorney, making more than her former boss.

Several women we know have been fired from top jobs in advertising agencies because of all the layoffs during the recent recession. One of the women started her own agency on a much smaller and more personal scale, with far fewer employees, and is doing very well. Another used her creative abilities to establish a consultant firm for art galleries (a job she invented). Both women, now self-employed, no longer have to worry about finding that little pink slip in their pay check envelope. Our own field, broadcasting, is known for its tenuous nature and sudden dismissals. There are countless examples in both radio and television of broadcasting personalities who have been given their walking papers by one station only to go on to an even more successful career at another. One friend of a friend of ours on the West Coast was dismissed as a television weather girl because the station decided to become more scientific in their weather reporting and hire a professional meteorologist. She was beside herself at the thought of no longer being in front of the cameras. (That sounded familiar to us!) She was offered an off-camera job at the same station, but she decided to try her luck at doing commercials. She is now the successful voice and face selling countless products, many of which appear on the station that fired her.

Another good example of turning adversity into good fortune is seen in the case of an attractive mother of two teenagers who was one of the buyers for a large department store. Her avocation was politics. Her political views were quite liberal and she was quite vocal in espousing them—too liberal and too vocal for her conservative, establishment-oriented boss and the image that he had set for his store. She was politely informed of her dismissal, due to what was termed as "personal conflicts which interfered with her job." She then decided to make politics her *vocation*, instead of her *avocation*, and is now a well paid, respected and highly sought after campaign manager and speech writer for politicians. Eventually, she intends to seek elective office herself—and she'll probably make it.

Whatever you do, no matter how hot your temper, or

how big your mouth, never, never speak ill of your former employers, or for that matter, anyone else in the business world who may some day be able to give you a boost up that shaky ladder. This is not easy to do! Shove your fist in your mouth if you must, but don't bite any hand that may possibly turn up later with something in it you want.

This works both ways. We have a soft spot for a former television news director whom we had spoken to concerning a television news job. He had no openings, but he was so encouraging and just plain nice that it spurred us on. The following year when *he* received the pink slip, we returned the favor by putting in a good word for him at our station.

By the way, don't hesitate in using any and all your contacts in getting the new job. Most business and professional people know that a favor given is often returned when most needed, and those dimly remembered rules of etiquette grandma tried to teach you are not to be laughed at either. A note of appreciation for a favor is remembered by even the most hardened tycoon.

So, heed these words, and before you know it, you may be sending that thank you note to the guy who fired you!

PART III

The Gray Flannel Apron

If You're Planning
To Lead Three Lives—
Get Organized

The woman who wears two hats is often quite likely to find herself in need of two heads, four hands, and six pairs of legs. If your mind's eye portrays the career woman of your dreams—the new you—as impeccably groomed, perfectly coiffed, impressively chic, and calm, cool, and confident from sunup to sundown, blink once and conjure up the view many career women face when the front door closes behind them at the end of the day. They are home, and it's time to change hats.

Rather than peep through the keyhole of some fictional lady executive, let us apprise you of the 5:00 P.M. scene that confronts two real life careerists, with a combined entourage of five children, assorted pets, malfunctioning appliances, visiting relatives, and the whole bit commonly known as domesticity. Our particular business usually gets us home by around 5:00 P.M.— just in time for Mary Poppins to plop on her hat and fly away on her umbrella. Also, just in time for the combined vocalization of anxious children who have been waiting eagerly to tell Mommy what they have done all day, and what they want to do for the next six months.

This is where our first rule of "Six Rules to Avoid Insanity" comes in. Tell those adorable dimpled faces to button their lips until Mommy has fifteen minutes alone in her room to make the transition, pull herself together, change clothes, and maybe have a quick martini. Lock the door if you must, because, as far as we're concerned, this is a very important part of any working mother's schedule. However, don't think that because the troops have temporarily retreated that you've won the war. When you emerge from your fifteen-minute sanctuary, be prepared to listen and pay attention to your children for at least fifteen minutes before getting them bathed, straightening up the mess they made while you were unwinding, and preparing dinner for them, your husband, and possibly the six guests he called you about at the office that afternoon.

There are a few tricks you can use to give the impression that you've spent all day preparing for your husband's nightly arrival. Naturally the ideal situation would be to arrive home about two hours before he does, take your unwinding period, slip into an elegant hostess gown, spend an hour chatting with the children, and greet your husband at the door with a pitcher of perfectly chilled martinis. Unfortunately, that scene is usually only in the movies. But you *can* do it with mirrors. After your fifteen minutes with the kids, start getting dinner under way while one of them sets the table. Clean up as you go. Nothing is more depressing than getting up from a fairly relaxing dinner and facing something that resembles an army mess hall before the K.P. show up. Also, before you leave the kitchen throw together tomorrow night's salad, slice the fruit for breakfast, and reset the table. It will be a lot easier then than at 7:00 A.M. (Several career wives we know spend a couple of Sundays a month cooking for the freezer. It's a grind at the time, but you sure will appreciate it later.)

After dinner give yourself fifteen minutes to relax and talk to the children while you have your coffee. Check homework, etc. Then at the appointed time, banish all children to their rooms, or somewhere you're not, and spend the rest of the evening with your husband. We strongly recommend that you not overlook this advice, or you may find it necessary to dispense with this book and find one advising "How to Continue Your Career After Your Husband Walks Out."

Incidentally, there are two schools of thought concerning whether or not to dine with your children. Some career mothers feel this is a good time for family togetherness and worth whatever indigestion it may bring. Others prefer togetherness before and after dinner, but reserve the dinner hour for conversation with their husbands, so it's up to you.

There does come a time somewhere between 10:00 P.M. and 2:00 A.M. that the day is finally over and it's time to go to sleep. One working friend of ours gets into bed exactly one hour before she plans to turn out the lights and uses this time to do her nails, pluck eyebrows, and make lists of everything she has to do the following day—all of this to the soothing strains of stereo music.

Lists are great for busy people. Everyone in your household should make them and tack them up on a central bulletin board. If each family member makes a weekly list of needs for the week, it will save your nerves and your time, both of which will become more precious to you than food and water.

Scheduling doctor and dentist appointments all at

once for several children may provide one miserable afternoon—but only *one*. If everyone in the family, including your husband, goes through his own closets and drawers once a week to check for cleaning and repairs, you won't have to do it. In other words, don't do anything around the house that you can get some-one else to do. Don't leave all this to chance either. Put a list inside everyone's closet door stating what is ex-pected of him each day and week. Discipline works in the army and in jail, and it can work for you too!

Everyone has one particular time of day that is es-pecially gruesome. For some it's that period of pre-dinner confusion. For us it's that mind-shattering alarm that tells us in no uncertain terms that it's time to get up. Morning can be the hardest time to accom-plish any type of organization. But with a little scream-ing and a couple of Bufferin, it can be done. First of all, have your clothes and the children's laid out the night before—from underwear to accessories. If you can, try to drag out of bed a few minutes before every-one else and have a cup of coffee alone, and, if pos-sible, get the kids off to school before you start getting dressed. Trying to put on false eyelashes while tying little shoes and buttoning dresses can cause loss of sanity and eyes.

Incidentally, any child past five years of age is old enough to put together his own breakfast, and the older ones can serve the little ones and Dad. (Remem-ber, most of it was put out by you the night before.) As far as we're concerned, the Europeans have the right idea, with just juice, rolls, coffee, and maybe cold cereal in the morning. If your family insists on a farm-er's breakfast, let them make it.

We say that togetherness at the breakfast table is for the birds and those with the disposition of a saint.

Most mornings we would be good company for a gorilla. If you fall into the same category, don't inflict yourself on the family and vice versa. We believe in everyone doing his own thing in the morning and everyone meeting again at a more civilized hour. But again, this one's up to you—your tranquilizer bills will tell you if you've made the right decision.

On the subject of shopping—for groceries, clothes and the like—you can cut the time and aggravation in half with a little ingenuity. First of all, do all the shopping you can by telephone. Your fingers walking through the yellow pages will let your legs off the hook. We find grocery shopping on Sunday or one night a week more relaxing, less crowded and a nice time to take the little ones "out with Mommy." As for clothes, twice a year junkets with the children, with occasional fill-ins, should be sufficient. Again, do it all at once—condense the agony. If it costs more for pick up and delivery on cleaning and laundry, it's worth it. You can make up the difference by cutting back on nerve pills.

Now for the most important point of all. It's too late for us in this area, because we were married before the onslaught of the Women's Liberation movement. But for those of you who have recently married or who have husbands who are willing to make the new scene, the picture today is sharing of household chores between working husbands and wives. A law student we know with a doctor husband and two children says that she and her spouse alternate days of cooking, cleaning, ironing, the works—and it's working out fine. We won't stress the feminist movement too heavily here, but if you can get your husband to share the household duties with you, do it—we can't.

There are some areas in which even the most chauvinistic male will usually pitch in and help. Changing an occasional diaper, clearing the dishes off the dining table, and taking over marketing responsibilities once in a while shouldn't set your husband to screaming for the return of his masculinity. Also, quite a few men have working schedules that bring them home before their wives. If this is the case in your household, there is no reason why your husband shouldn't put up the roast and even load up the washing machine without feeling demasculinized.

One designer we know has convinced her husband that no one can iron his shirts as well as he can himself. Another high-powered lady executive has cajoled her husband into thinking that his culinary ability far surpasses hers; therefore, the important dishes in their meals deserve his touch. Maybe you're not as persuasive as these wily females, but nevertheless, don't let your spouse completely off the hook without a struggle.

We don't guarantee that reading this chapter will transform you into an organizational wonder and magically solve all the problems of handling a career and running a home, but we hope it will set your own gears in motion. We suggest you start with these "Six Rules to Avoid Insanity":

1. Don't let anything short of disaster interfere with your fifteen minute unwinding period.

2. Don't do anything around the house that you can get someone else to do — and do anything short of taking food out of the kids' mouths to get regular help.

3. Spend at least a couple of hours a night alone with your husband.

4. Make lists for everything and have the rest of the family do likewise.

5. Lump no-fun chores, such as trips to the dentist barber, etc., together. Take all the children at one time and get it over with.

6. Do your household chores, cleaning, laundry, marketing, etc. when it's convenient for you (Sundays, evenings, 3:00 A.M. or whenever), not necessarily when your friends and neighbors are doing them.

POSTSCRIPT: Allow yourself one day a month to completely fall apart — if necessary.

Don't Feel Guilty— You Have Nothing To Apologize For

Every woman who has ever strayed from the confines of her vine-covered split-level in suburbia to the exhilarating and downright hectic world of business has occasionally experienced that gnawing question, "Should I really be doing this? Is it fair to my family?" A majority of the women we surveyed with our informal questionnaire (which you'll hear more about in a later chapter) at some time experienced some guilt about their career. Rather than go into a dissertation on the psychological and sociological reasons for a woman feeling guilty just because she is living up to her capacities, let's just accept the fact that she does and then examine the reasons why she shouldn't.

First of all, you have nothing to apologize for—you are merely doing what the male species has been enjoying from the beginning of time—using your mind and your talents to develop your potential to its fullest. It would be a criminal waste of human potential if you did not become what your capabilities allow, even though society may frown on you. And many times society, with its traditional values, does make it pretty rough for women who choose to stray from the established ideals. As Dr. Estelle Ramey, Professor of Endocrinology at the Georgetown Medical School put it, "They're treating our middle-class women as though they had a disease. A master's degree is a symptom. Intelligence is the virus. It's absurd to put a healthy woman on chronic medication to dull her brain until her children are in school or she gives up herself." What a waste.

And why is it that the very people who fight the hardest against women expanding their lives are other women? Is it that many career homemakers are so unsure of their own status and insecure about their own contributions that they feel threatened if they see other women breaking through to wider horizons? We think so. If a woman is truly fulfilled and happy in her role, she won't feel the need to put down those who dance to a different drummer.

We have found that some of our severest critics are women. In the many speeches we give to civic groups on the subject of a woman fulfilling her potential, the hostility expressed during the question and answer session by many of the women can be cut with a knife. The questions they ask (which are discussed in a later chapter) are almost always negative. They look for

every angle imaginable to find flaws in combining a
career with housewifery. Strangely enough this phenomenon is not true with groups of professional women
that we have spoken to.

Mothers, fathers, mothers-in-law, fathers-in-law,
aunts, uncles, sisters-in-law, and other assorted members of your family may also cause you a few
headaches concerning your double life. One woman we
know, a psychiatric social worker, was besieged by
phone calls at her office from her mother. Every call
was a well-meaning dissertation on why the woman
should be home attending to "woman's work" instead of
out in the world worrying about other people's problems. She's still getting the phone calls, which she politely acknowledges, while continuing to do a good job
at her own thing—at home and at the office. Another
career-homemaker combo is forever receiving invitations from her sister-in-law to "bring the kids over for a
good home-cooked meal." The invitation is usually accompanied by sympathetic clucking about the impossibility of handling a career and a home simultaneously,
and how tired she must be all the time. It's true she is
tired occasionally but she is also completely happy in
her role, competent at both jobs—and a good cook.
Another working mother was harangued by, of all people, her housekeeper. That lady dropped insinuating
remarks about her absence from home and the
amount of time spent with the children at every opportunity. She now has the same job, but a different
housekeeper.

What really matters, in the long run, is *your* coming
to terms with your own doubts and misgivings and
then providing an atmosphere of communication with
your husband and children where each of you has the

opportunity to develop and expand individually and together.

Actually, most of the working wives and mothers that we know say that their families take tremendous pride in their accomplishments. Children adapt far more easily than their parents to almost any conditions, and the conditions of children with working mothers are not so different from those of the tots of stay-at-homes as you may think. We can't think of anyone of our acquaintance who stays home all day and indulges in constant creative interaction with her children. Most nonworking mothers spend nearly as much time shopping, at the beauty parlor, doing charity work, talking on the phone, carpooling, playing bridge and just doing busy work around their homes as working mothers spend in the office. And never have we heard one full-time homemaker express one moment's guilt about the time she expends in these areas.

You might also be interested in the fact that the majority of juvenile delinquents in this country are from homes where the mother in *not* a career woman. This disproves the claim of the foes of Women's Lib who say that much juvenile delinquency can be blamed on the working mother who should be home with her children.

A technical director of a local radio station, the mother of two youngsters under four, put it bluntly. "Don't kid yourselves, ladies. Your company is not always as desirable for your children as you may think it is. I think basically children of working mothers are more self-reliant and in a positive way. Because, if you are doing a good job at mothering, you let them know how important they are to you, how much you love them, and at the same time teach them they are capable of performing many tasks by themselves. Teaching self-reliance does not mean neglect, and my children are happier when I'm working because I'm happier."

"But everyone else's mother is bringing homemade brownies to the PTA meeting." Just about every working mother with kids old enough to talk haŝ heard some form of those conscience-pricking words. Our advice to you is to smile lovingly at your little gourmet, pat him on the head and proceed to the bakery where 89¢ will buy you about a dozen brownies that are good enough for any kid who would probably choose a hot dog over Chateaubriand. It is amazing how many women spend precious hours of the day preparing fresh from scratch vegetables, cakes, pies, and such, that are gulped down unappreciated by hungry children without so much as an exclamation over the hollandaise sauce, or else rejected completely in favor of a hamburger.

Children and husbands have been trained by society to expect our culinary abilities, skill at bathing a dog, dexterity at zipping jackets in a hurry, ability to charm the boss when he comes to dinner, talent with knitting needles, warmth in the boudoir, adroitness in diapering a squirming baby, and sometimes even our ability to discuss the events in the morning paper. We were not expected to cope with the world outside our back fence—and when we do, the initial shock may resemble an earthquake, but once accepted, the family's former appreciation broadens to make room for *all* of you, not just "Mommy" and "*Mrs.* John Doe." For example, one woman who has a demanding career in the art field quotes her seven-year-old as saying, "You're not just a mommy. You paint pretty pictures for people to look at and be happy."

One of our own children, a rangy twelve-year-old

(then younger) became very teary when it was announced that our TV career had been terminated. "What will you be if you're not a TV star?" he blurted out.

By and large, children adjust very well to the working mother and very often look at their mothers with the same acceptance as given to their fathers. A busy doctor we know says her four children accept her career as part of her personality and would think it strange if she were any other way.

Another purveyor of guilt for working wives and mothers is the traditional ladies' magazines. They have portrayed today's woman just as they portrayed yesterday's woman—as fluffy, simpering, passive, able to almost achieve orgasm over a new household detergent, and completely contented in a world of babies, lemon-waxed furniture and double ovens. In fact, as Betty Freidan was reported as saying, "The only passion, pursuit or goal a woman is permitted is pursuit of a man." She went on to say that women are portrayed as living in a world crammed full of food, clothes, cosmetics and furniture, "But where is the thought and ideas, the life of the mind and the spirit?"

The man of the house is very often the purveyor of guilt for many women. In our questionnaire we asked, "What advice would you give to other women contemplating combining a career and marriage?" And incorporated in over 75 per cent of the answers was, "Make sure your husband knows what he is getting into—that he is sure of his masculinity and won't resent your success."

One highly successful career woman told us this story. "My husband never said he objected to my working. He doesn't even now, after fifteen years. But he is constantly throwing little digs at me about the hole in his sock, dust under the bed, my missing a PTA meeting, or a dozen other insignificant items that normally wouldn't bother him. I don't make as much money as he does, but he has been in several different jobs without really finding his niche—and I feel very guilty that I am so content in my work."

The problem that this woman faces is not uncommon. A lot of husbands who profess delight at their wives' accomplishments publicly show quite a different face in the privacy of the domain. Snide comments about the feminine appeal of a pretty stay-at-home neighbor, flip remarks about unimaginative dinners, and, most painful of all, "You should be around in case the children need you." Be prepared for some antagonism from your husband and don't let it set your guilt pangs in motion.

Your former bridge-table friends are likely to be cat-eyed with envy at your exciting new life. However, it is doubtful that they will shower you with praise. Instead, they will probably make snide remarks about your kids walking home in the rain, or the fact that you missed that fabulous sale at the department store. Let them sniff at the table you didn't have time to dust; let them belittle your job; let them cluck over your poor, neglected husband—because you know you wouldn't trade places with them for all the split-level dream houses in suburbia.

Remind yourself that you are a living, breathing human being, with a mind and the ability to use it, and while your husband and children are an important part of your life, they are not, and shouldn't be, the only part, any more than you are the only part of theirs. What we're really saying is, Why should a woman be the only member of society expected to live her life solely through another person?

We can't think of many children who would stay home from an activity that they wanted to attend because their mother was lonely and wanted company, nor can we conceive of many fathers feeling guilty about being in their office working instead of watching the kiddies in that afternoon baseball game. Yet we women are flooded with remorse when our children complain that they missed going skating because we weren't there to drive them. It's pure insanity, and it's a custom perpetuated by almost every woman who sits at home at the beck and call of her children—who, in turn, may someday return the favor in the way that the 15-year-old daughter of a stay-at-home mother did. The youngster was having a telephone conversation with a friend and the mother, in the next room, could hear only her daughter's comments. The topic of the discussion was unimportant, and that's just how the mother felt when she heard her offspring say, "I'll ask my dad. Mom doesn't know anything. She just stays home all day." In relating this story, far from showing any anger at her daughter's words, the woman asked, "What did I do wrong?"

If that little incident doesn't hit home with you, try this one. Another friend of ours was also the perfect stay-at-home wife. She made her own curtains and slipcovers, her kitchen always smelled like a bakery, and she probably never missed a PTA. One thing she is missing now is her husband who divorced her and is now married to a career girl who worked side by side with him and still does.

Another friend, an executive in a major city, said that guilt actually forced her to divorce her husband even though she still loved him. He was struggling in his field and too unsure of his masculinity to accept her success. She is now married again, has a child and has moved even higher up the ladder with her new husband's approval.

Naturally, these are extreme cases chosen to illustrate the point. The real answer can only come from within you when you realize that feeling guilty about dividing your life so that part of it belongs to you is a natural feeling—and if you accept it without letting it overwhelm you, it will fade, just like a toothache or a cold. It will probably return, but so will the cold.

Whose Career Comes First—

(Or Don't Overwhelm Your Husband With Your New-Found Importance)

Almost every single respondent to our questionnaire clearly stated that her husband's career was dominant and that when there was a conflict between the two careers, his usually won out. One conflict that kept popping up in the survey was what to do about vacations when his was convenient at one time and hers another. Some of the couples solved this by taking mini vacations—one weekend every couple of months instead of the traditional one or two weeks. A few preferred vacationing alone or with a friend occasionally, letting their husbands use their vacation time for fishing, hunting or other so-called male endeavors.

The basic problem of which career comes first is much more complex than vacation schedules. It is psychologically rooted. In every partnership there is a dominant partner, even if it is evident only in very subtle ways. Up to now in the male-female relationship society has granted the upper hand to the male. There's no doubt in our minds that this is changing— but we don't think it has yet made the transition in the age group that this book is directed toward. The men of our generation, even the seemingly liberated ones, secretly resent their role of breadwinner and supreme ruler gradually slipping away. Therefore, we feel that if you are planning to retain your status as a happily married career woman, you will probably find yourself making concessions when it comes to decisions about his job versus yours. You will more than likely be the one that has to give up an interesting job because he must transfer to another location. Usually job transfers mean promotions and salary increase, on the plus side, but they may also mean the temporary loss of your income, uprooting children, moving problems and the like, which you might point out to your dominant partner.

Just keep in mind that life is a series of compromises in every area. Unfortunately, it's usually women on the giving end. *But* men have to make them too, and if giving in on traditionally male decisions will make for more harmony at home without doing much damage to your own status, it's probably worth it.

Several young couples we spoke to who are contemplating combining a career with marriage have found the way to combat these difficulties that crop up after the honeymoon is over. They look at marriage as a contract between two people, each stating before the union what they both expect from the partnership and where the basic responsibilities shall be divided. Every year the contract is reappraised and changed if necessary. We think this is a great idea—unfortunately, they came up with it a few years too late for us.

You will probably find your own self-esteem a few

notches higher when you are really out there making it on your own, but don't overwhelm your husband with your new-found importance. Quite a few of the women we surveyed said this was one mistake they made at the onset of their return to the business world. Remember, even though you may be a high-powered, decision-making executive eight hours a day at the office, you are still Mrs. John Doe and Jimmy's mother when you cross back into your other world. Whether you feel it's unfair or not, you will have to retain your role as wife and mother at home if you want to remain both. As far as we're concerned, this means underplaying your career role in the presence of your family—at least part of the time.

The traditional role of a woman has always been to be at home waiting eagerly for her husband's arrival at night, with a chilled martini and his slippers ready to hand him as he walks in the door and a cool hand to soothe his tired brow. When a man has been raised for generations with this image in mind, it's hard to break him of it. We aren't saying that you have to be an Americanized version of the geisha girl, but, if you're smart, you won't greet your husband at the door (or arrive there simultaneously) still in your business suit and immediately bombard him with the fascinating day you had at the office. You will listen to his triumphs and tragedies first—boring as they may be. You will then serve him his dinner. Then, after you or, as we recommend, the kids wash the dishes, you will sit down and tell him what your day was like.

Some women are even lucky enough to have a husband who will listen. One of the women we surveyed wasn't. She wrote, "When I start to tell my husband about my day at the office, he gets a glazed look in his eyes and focuses on something above my head. So I gave up, and we talk about politics, world events, or his job."

Most husbands aren't this narrow-minded and will, generally, at least pretend to be fascinated by your office tales. Naturally it's terrific when you and your husband are in related, not competitive fields. Another of our questionees works as a designer in her husband's business and she marvels at the fact that "There isn't enough time in the day or evening to discuss everything we want to share with each other."

Another area where a man's ego can be bruised by his executive dynamo partner is in the social arena. When you are out with other couples, they will invariably talk about your job, especially if it's more interesting or unusual than your husband's. This can be a real thorn to a man, particularly if he has any doubts about his own status. In our field, this happens all the time because of the public nature of our job. People are constantly running up to us at parties, on the street and in restaurants to ask about a particular show or to fawn over us with false or sincere praise. It's probably a pain in the neck to our husbands, but, fortunately, they are successful enough in their own fields to accept it.

Very often the husband of a newly born career woman will encounter a reversal of a very old theme. Remember the stereotype of the little woman fearfully wondering if her husband is being ogled and seduced by glamorous secretaries? Now the man of the house is apt to have a few misgivings about his suddenly sophisticated wife being wined and dined at three-hour, four-martini business lunches by handsome and lecherous junior executives. Jealousy is a very human emotion—don't laugh at your spouse if he shows tinges of green. Just cross your fingers and point out that you always have a sandwich at your desk and that all your co-workers are over sixty and bald. If he won't buy that, you may have to gently explain to him why you must do some of the same things he's been doing for years—and that at your office, you're just one of the boys.

Many of the working wives we talked to said they understood their husbands better since they began working themselves. They became more aware of the problems that crop up in business and more sympathetic toward the minor irritations that their husbands put up with during the business day because they had them, too.

Career women are often more understanding about money and how hard it is to earn it. You will probably find yourself far less willing to part with the greenbacks you sweated for than you ever were with your husband's hard-earned cash. Incidentally, one of the worst mistakes you can make is to refer to your earnings as "my money"; even if you feel it is, keep your mouth shut. Several of the women we interviewed said they had considered their paycheck to be *theirs* for *their* extravagances and luxuries. This caused a few husbands to comment that maybe their salary should belong solely to them. This can get to be a bit sticky, considering that most women are still paid considerably less than men.

Most of the women we questioned shared a bank account with their husbands and everything went into one pot. If you make more money than your husband, as a few of the wives we talked to do, you will most likely have an ego problem on your hands. But as one woman said, "I have consistently made more money than my husband. I think he resents it, but when the bills are paid every month and the checkbook balances, he manages to endure the pain in his ego."

To sum it up, all we are trying to say is, just remember you have a husband. He's the guy you chose for better or worse—and, assuming you want to keep him, don't make his life miserable in the process of making yours more enjoyable. Your job and your children make demands that must be met. Your husband usually gets what's left over, which too often isn't much.

How To Keep Your Friends Without Ever Seeing Them

You will find it necessary to develop a split personality in order to be a successful career woman and a successful member of the suburban social arena. You will not be able to see your friends as much as you did when you were lady of the manor. Gone will be the narcissism of sleeping until 10:00 or 11:00, the morning coffee klatches, the luncheons, the bridge games, and the leisurely afternoons of shopping. There will also be less time and energy for extensive entertaining, which may eventually eliminate you from the scene when your neglected friends plan their parties.

To this myriad of losses we say, "Good riddance!" Most of us waste our time playing bridge with, talking to and entertaining hordes of people that we couldn't care less about, and the feeling is probably mutual. As a working woman, you will find that you are much more discriminating in your extracurricular activities. You will find yourself entertaining people whose company you actually enjoy, and you will also find your

desire to be entertained, or even to go out just for the
sake of going out, considerably lessened. We have
found that we are no longer compulsive about going
out on the town every Saturday night, or telephoning
friends so the gang can all go out together. In fact, we
often welcome a quiet Saturday night at home, with a
good steak, a bottle of wine and our husbands.

We aren't suggesting that you become a weekend
recluse or a hermit. Of course, there are some friends
that you would like to hang on to—and when you do
throw a party, it's nice to have someone to invite. It's
not easy for your friends to remember who you are
when they only catch a glimpse of you rushing to and
from work, and even your staunchest admirers may
take offense when you just don't have the time to
spend hours on those long phone conversations you
used to enjoy.

There are a few tricks that will help you keep a foot
in the social scene and pacify your friends until you
can get around to your social amenities. For one thing,
try to telephone your close friends at least once a
week, even if it's on your lunch hour or after dinner at
night. You will remind them you're alive, and you can
avoid lengthy discussions by just being honest. Tell
them you are in the middle of sewing Jane's Girl Scout
uniform, or whatever, but you were thinking about
them and wanted to say hello and how are you. You
may be surprised how much your friends appreciate not
having to gab for an hour, especially if it's about *your*
fascinating experiences.

A friend of ours, a busy social worker, spends an
hour a month going through a list of her friends' birth-
days, anniversaries, etc., and sends them a card with a
little personal note on it. "My friends marvel over the
fact that, despite my busy routine, I take the time to

remember them," she says. It's a nice gesture—for relatives, too—and takes less time than you think. You can even do it under the hairdryer.

Another idea is to have a friend meet you in town for lunch occasionally if your schedule allows. You can always cut the time to reasonable proportions by saying you have to get back for an appointment. This allows your friends to see you in your other role, which may seem strange and foreign to them, yet under the familiar circumstances of a chatty lunch.

Of course, there are weekends when you can join the girls for bridge, or the like, but we generally find ourselves too busy with errands and family that have been neglected all week.

Entertaining can be a real thorn in the side. Somehow spending hours perfecting a gourmet dinner loses its appeal after a hectic week in the business world. There are plenty of ways to get around that. The answers to this problem were quite varied in our questionnaire. Several women said they entertain frequently but have the dinner catered so they don't have to lift a finger. This is great, though expensive. We feel it's worth the money to enjoy your own party. And don't be embarrassed because you haven't cooked the meal with your own hands—your guests are there mainly to be with you. If they are interested only in the food, they can go to a restaurant.

As one teacher we questioned admitted, "I used to lie and say I had concocted the casserole or souffle that had really just been delivered by the caterer. But I was stuck so many times when asked for the recipe that I gave up and admitted I wasn't super-chef, and no one seemed to mind."

Your method of entertaining is a personal decision, depending on your help situation, your fondness for the kitchen, and the setup of your home. One of us finds small dinners for eight to twelve every few months, plus a once-a-year cocktail buffet for about fifty, usually work out well. The other prefers informal buffet dinners for twenty or thirty.

Most of the women we talked to agreed that the large cocktail party was impersonal and a waste of time and that a small group of carefully selected people conversing around a table was far more enjoyable and much more of a compliment to your guests.

A few of our questionees said they had no time to entertain since they began working. We can't buy that. Everyone has to eat dinner, and a few more around the table, even if the meal is spaghetti, isn't that much trouble. Entertaining is one of the gracious areas of life, few of which are left, so unless you hold down three jobs, or hate people, don't eliminate it.

Incidentally, several of the wives who answered our survey mentioned that they often took couples *out* to dinner, or to a play or sporting event. This is fine once in a while, especially if it's a business-social occasion, but we still maintain that it's a much nicer compliment to someone if you invite them to your own home.

Another idea that popped up in the questionnaire a number of times was Sunday afternoon parties where parents and children were invited. This gives your kids something to do besides bug you during the party and also solves babysitting problems for your friends. If you're a real togetherness type, this sort of thing can be very enjoyable; neither of us is. We prefer good adult conversation, good wine, minus the hoopla that seems to surround kids.

Needless to say, entertaining during the week is sadistic when working. If you must entertain someone on a week night, this is the time to take them out to dinner, and even that can be an effort after a long, harrowing day.

One thing we can't stress strongly enough, is, don't brag to your friends about how simply marvelous it is to be working and how dull your old life was in retrospect, especially if they're still living it. If you bend their ear long enough with your new-found experiences, you will soon find yourself being avoided even when you don't want to be. Other women who lead less interesting and rewarding lives are going to be jealous of your abilities and success. Some of them will completely ignore your job in conversation; others who are curious as to what's out there in the big world will ply you with questions and hang on your every word. Don't be surprised, though, if, when you walk out the door, they have a field day dissecting you. Of course, not all your friends are going to turn on you just because you are now working. The worthwhile, genuine ones will accept your new life style as a new part of your personality and admire you for it, even if the admiration is tinged with a grain of envy.

Many of the women who responded to our questionnaire found their social lives more and more involved with women who also had careers. This eliminates a lot of the jealousies and antagonisms. However, if you are like we are, plenty of your friends are still homebodies, and the less you emphasize the differences in your life and theirs, the longer they'll remain your friends. After all, you should be able to converse about something besides your job. We know a woman in the fashion field who finds it impossible to relate to anyone or anything not concerned with fashion—that's all she talks about, and as a steady diet that can be every bit as boring as discussing the merits of a laundry detergent.

So try to be as conversationally versatile as you hope others will be. Most women who work have very little trouble in this area. Being exposed to the business world and all its nuances is a very broadening experience. In fact, we have received more of an education through our show and interviewing various experts in almost every field than we did in our school years. We find that we read even more than we have to (if that's possible!) because our curiosity about everything has been expanded. You will more than likely do the same. Regardless of your field, working at a career you like stretches your mind, and it becomes like a sponge, eager to soak up everything you put into it. You will become a far more interesting human being.

Getting Out Of All Those Volunteer Jobs You Never Wanted In the First Place

There's an old proverb: "The busiest man has the time to spare." True, like most old proverbs.

The working wife and mother seems to find the extra time and strength to take on any volunteer jobs that are important to her. The woman who has been active in her church will somehow find the energy to continue, even though on a more limited basis. Those women interested in health or service organizations will invariably continue as active participants, despite a full-time job and all the myriad other demands on her time. One friend of ours, a busy administrative assistant in a large firm, agreed to call a list of twenty-five women for charitable contributions. Not only did she have difficulty finding any of her nonworking friends willing to share the calling job with her, but it took her several calls a day over a two-week period to even find the women at home to answer the phone call.

In spite of our hectic schedule, we make time to speak to various civic and youth groups as often as possible. We are particularly interested in working with the young and the disadvantaged, so that's where we place our extracurricular emphasis. The point is, we haven't given up our community responsibilities to lead a completely hedonistic and selfish life "doing our own thing," and most of the other working wives we know haven't either.

But, oh, the joy of being able to say no when asked to do something you're not the least interested in. You can say completely without guilt, "I'm awfully sorry, but I'm working full-time now and I just don't have a minute to spare." Of course, the asker can't cajole or convince such a busy woman—all she can do is cluck sympathetically and ask someone else. You can smugly sit back and breathe a sigh of relief.

It isn't the same if you're not working. Then you're a sitting duck for every boring volunteer job your friends can dream up, whether it's collecting money door-to-door or running the local paper sale. If you beg off, your friends call you selfish behind your back or shame you into accepting the job. After all, you're not doing anything special with all your free time. We know from experience. Before we started working, we went the whole route—program chairman, bulletin editor, projects director, chief cook and bottlewasher—you name it. All in the name of charity. We tried to convince ourselves that it was important, and some of it was, but most of it was a waste of time and an utter bore.

And the funny thing is, we hated working with women. They were often undependable, selfish, petty and gossipy. You meet an entirely different kind of woman in business. In organization work you have to take what you get. In business a woman doesn't last long who displays the above traits, so you frequently meet a superior person. We didn't fully realize how many terrifically talented women there were all around us until we got into this field. Of course, there are bitchy women in business just as there are nasty men, but compared to the service organizations we've been involved with, they're in the minority.

This is not to knock volunteer work. Many jobs would not get done if housewives didn't do them. Certainly the hospitals, churches, schools, welfare organizations and community projects of all kinds would suffer immeasurably without the volunteer support of thousands of women. Yet, it's so nice to know that you have a built-in excuse for not getting involved in any of it.

As for who will do the work if women like you don't, a very wise older friend of ours puts it this way: "I never feel guilty about turning down a volunteer job. I know that for every one I refuse, some other woman is always waiting in the wings to fill it."

Coping With Car Pools

How did we women ever get trapped into the suburban syndrome? We think we must have been brainwashed to have allowed ourselves to live stranded in the wilderness on an acre or two of land, with no public transporatation and no way for our children to get around without our acting as a one-woman taxi service. We, for instance, live in typical houses in a typical American suburban area—which, translated, means too much property to keep up, no sidewalks, kids have to ride a school bus to school, no public transportation, and no way to get them anywhere without driving them. They can't even ride their bikes any distance because of hilly terrain and lack of sidewalks for safety.

Many of our friends with several children put 100 miles on their cars daily while driving to ballet, piano, scouts, Little League, the library, et al. Well, if they want to spend their lives being unpaid chauffeurs, let them. We decided we had more to do with our lives.

On the other hand, we realize that it's really not fair to your children to deprive them of everything. It's not their fault we foolishly choose to live this way. So we compromise. Music lessons are taken on Saturdays. Car pools take care of Scouts and Little League, and that's it. Our kids understand that we work and know that they have to decide which activities are really important to them and which they are willing to forego. It's amazing how resourceful children can be if they really want to be. One of our boys worked it out so his coach takes him home from football practice, and one of the girls who wanted to stay late to be in a school play cajoled her teacher into bringing her home after each rehearsal.

If you work fairly near home and have a flexible schedule (which we strongly advise), then you can run home occasionally to fetch and carry to lessons. We're extremely fortunate that our office is five minutes away from home, but the nature of our job is such that we never know where we'll be at any given time. You can try to arrange car pools with other mothers, but that doesn't always work out. One of our friends, a busy heart specialist, hires a driver who comes every afternoon at 3:00 and drives her three grade-school girls all over town to their various lessons and activities. Another acquaintance sends her older child by taxi to and from his lessons. Another busy executive employs a housekeeper who can drive, which is an ideal solution. You might also consider hiring a responsible teenager to drive the children on their appointed rounds.

Here again the unfairness of the typical marital role of woman versus man comes in. Why should the mother be the one solely responsible for seeing that the kids get taken care of? Many fathers work odd hours, conduct their business from home, or have their offices in the neighborhood. Try to get your husband to help out with the driving, if possible. One teacher friend of ours has that kind of husband. A physician, he drives the children to school on his way to the office, and, on his afternoon off, he takes them to their music lessons. He says he enjoys it because it gives him some extra time alone with his girls. He's the same man who encouraged his wife through four years of college, and on our questionnaire she gives him plenty of credit.

One of the women we work with also has an ideal

husband. His shop is close to their home and school. The children walk there after school and he brings them home in the evening. As she puts it on our questionnaire: "They have shop facilities; they have a lake, a creek, woods and my mother-in-law close by (in case of illness). I feel my boys are benefiting from this. What better care can little boys get than from their own devoted father?" She's the same woman who answered the question, "What does your family think of your working?" with, "They think I am prettier, smarter, younger than ever!" She also confided, "My marriage has improved 100%. I am a person—not a utility now!!!"

These men are a rarity, unfortunately, and for most of you, like us, the burden of chauffeuring the kids is going to fall squarely on your already over-burdened shoulders. The solution you come up with might not be perfect—but if you really want to, you *can* find one that will work.

All the foregoing presupposes that you are already firmly established in your split-level suburban trap and have no intention of moving. Personally, if we had it to do again and knew we were going to turn out to be career women, we would never choose this kind of velvet prison. We would live, instead, in a large apartment, town house, or older home in a convenient, close-in location. We would have very little property to worry about; we would locate within walking distance of school, busline and stores. Our children would have much more freedom of movement and would not have to rely on us every time they wanted so much as a candy bar. They would be happier because they could exercise self-reliance, and we would feel less guilty about depriving them of needed activities.

We think this is a very important consideration for

any woman who is planning a full-time career. If at all possible, move to the most convenient location you can find, even if it's less fashionable.

If you have small children and haven't yet thought about the magnitude of the problem, then we hope this chapter has convinced you to stay in town. When we think of the wasted hours that our friends spend driving all over the city for the benefit of their children, we're amazed. Don't they ever stop to wonder, "Is this what life is really all about?" We think they do and that they very much resent the role they're forced to play.

So, if you're embarking on a career and haven't yet settled down in a permanent home, give very careful thought to where you're going to live. If you're already inconveniently located, then work things out the best you can. Explain the problem to the children; enlist their understanding; but don't apologize and don't feel guilty!

Where Is Mary Poppins?

If you have children, this is the most important chapter in this book. Unfortunately, it's also the most difficult chapter to write, because none of the many options open to you as working mothers is perfect. No matter how well you have organized your career and the rest of your life, in the child-care department you have to rely on someone else, and that's the one flaw in the fabric.

The number one choice for mother substitute would be just that—a motherly woman who was kind to your kids, loved them as you would, listened to their problems, dispensed wholesome wisdom, who also cleaned house with a vengeance, cooked up epicurean delights, neither drank nor smoked, and never missed a day of work. Wake up from that dream, lady—no one like that exists any more, and if she did, *we'd* hire her. So let's be practical and list the options open to you by starting at the top and working down.

Most working women with homes to run need some kind of household help. Except for one paragon who does all her own work, all our respondents had help at least twice a week and about half employed full-time help. We ourselves have full-time household help and find it a tremendous benefit not only in keeping house, but in knowing that someone responsible is there with our children each day. Even if your children are in school, it's a tremendous feeling of relief to know that someone is home waiting for them. As one woman economist was quoted recently in *The New York Times*, "I'm paying so that somebody's there when they get home from school, or if one of the children gets sick, as well as to take care of them during school vacations. For me it's an insurance policy." It's also darn nice to come home to a table already set, a clean house and dinner in the oven.

In line with our policy of never doing anything around the house we can get someone else to do, we heartily recommend full-time help, even if it takes most of your salary. And it probably will. The average rate for a full-time housekeeper is around $75. per week and social security (call your local office about this), although it varies as much as $20. more or less in different sections of the country. (But then the salaries paid to you for the same job will also vary with where you live, so it evens out.)

We think full-time help is particularly important when your children are small. And right here we want to impress upon you one very important rule. The working mother has to be very careful of the emotional stability and the personality makeup of the woman who will spend so much time with her child. The woman's cooking and cleaning ability is strictly secondary. Time and time again our working friends will comment, "Agnes' cooking is lousy and she can't iron but she's terrific with the kids, and I'm lucky to have her." Or, "I don't know what Gertrude does all day— the dust on the table tops is so thick you could write your name—but I don't care. Just as long as she stays happy." You will find that working women will put up with almost anything in order to keep reliable help. And does it really matter if the linen closet is straightened or the floor mopped that day? What really matters is little Johnnie or Susie being cared for and loved.

To find good help, contact several agencies, put your own ad in the paper, and read the "Situations Wanted" section. There are several nationwide agencies that import domestics from Europe and the West Indies. It's a rather complicated process and you're sometimes stuck with an unhappy, homesick and completely untrained girl, but it's certainly worth a try if no help is available locally.

If your children are older and you can't afford a full-time housekeeper but still want some help through the dinner hour, you may be able to find a student who will live with you for room and board and a nominal salary of $10. a week. She won't do any heavy housework, but will help you straighten up, make beds, cook and do the dishes. She will also babysit at night. In our city, several medical, dental and technical schools place their students this way. Many of our friends use these girls and are quite happy with the arrangement. She is more like a member of the family than a servant. There are drawbacks here, too, of course. You may get a "lemon," and each time the girl completes her course (usually six months), she leaves and is replaced by another, which makes for a lack of continuity.

The arrangements ingenious women make are really remarkable. One of our friends in a large midwest city gives free room and board and a token salary to an older career woman who has no family. This woman gets home around 3:30 and stays with the children, starts dinner and helps out generally. There is a maid three times a week, so no heavy cleaning is involved. Our friend is delighted with the arrangement and the children look on the boarder as another grandmother. The woman, on the other hand, is no longer lonely after work and is saving what would be her rent money for her retirement.

Another acquaintance hires a babysitter to come in at 3:00, when the kids come home, and stay until she arrives. When we were on television, our show went on at 9:00 A.M. We had to be at the studio in full makeup and hairpiece at 8:30, which meant leaving our houses at 8:00. Our children were quite small then, so we each hired a regular babysitter to come in at 7:30 and stay until our maids arrived at 10:00.

Right here we must interject another very important rule: Keep a list of good babysitters whom you can call in a pinch. When Gertrude calls up at 7:00 A.M. and says she has to rush her sick mother to the hospital, on the very day when you have the most important appointment of your career at 9:00, and two kids at home with the flu, the feeling of panic that comes over you is akin to being left adrift on a raft in the middle of the ocean without a paddle. If you have fifteen or twenty names in your little black book, one of them is likely to be available. If you have a mother or in-law you can call on in an emergency, of course, you're lucky, but the way things are going, she'll probably be out working, too!

We have left day-care centers for the last because they are a whole subject in themselves. The United States is woefully behind other technological countries in providing good, reliable day care coupled with innovative schooling. The standards vary widely from state to state and there are no real guidelines. Many so-called day-care centers are merely old-fashioned nurseries run by women with no training and no background in child psychology or education. Those centers are little more than custodial and too often are over-crowded and under-staffed. The horror stories we have heard on our program about some of the practices in these places would curdle your blood. However, the picture is changing as the pressure from emancipated women becomes greater. More and more modern centers are springing up all over the country. Many of them are franchised, with rigid controls and innovative facilities.

A center, of course, is only as good as the people who run it, and that is why it is imperative for you to look beyond a fancy façade and find out just whom you are leaving your child with all day. We cannot stress this strongly enough. If your child is under three, the important thing to you, if you choose day care over private arrangements, is the type of care provided. Do they change the babies often enough? Are they taken outside in good weather? Are there sheets on the cribs? Are the children picked up and allowed to crawl around, or are they left in their cribs all day? Is the staff adequate? Does the director have a real love of children and a sense of commitment? Are the facilities reasonably clean? These might seem like elementary questions, but don't take anything for granted. Check and double-check! Be very suspicious of any center that does not allow you to look around at any time. Before you choose one, or soon after you have enrolled your child, pay a surprise visit. A good center will welcome your inspection, a marginal one won't.

After age three, more attention should be paid to the kind of schooling your child will get. There are many excellent centers employing one of several Montessori methods. Some centers use the British Infant School or "Free School" method. Some use a combination. Many exciting things are happening in early education circles today, and if your child is fortunate enough to be enrolled in one of these schools, it will be a very enriching experience.

The nursery-kindergarten that our two youngest go to has school until 2:00, and the rest of the day is devoted to free play until time to go home. Mothers come in at various times to pick the children up and the center is open to 6:00 P.M. Some centers pick up and deliver the children at their homes. Costs for day care range from $14. to $35. per week, with the good ones ranging toward the upper end of the scale.

There is one big lack in child care in this country that badly needs rectifying and that is after-school care when the child enters public school. Suppose you found a wonderful day-care center and sent your child there through kindergarten. Now he's six and entering first grade. What happens when he comes home at 2:00? Unless there is a good after-school program, you're back to the question of hiring full-time help or a babysitter. Some very large cities have programs of this type, where the child is picked up at his school and taken to a play ground, but most cities, ours included, don't have any, though some of the day-care centers do take children up to twelve. Most of the places that take older children after school are in the lower-income areas of town where women traditionally have had to work to supplement the family income. Good centers have been a lot slower coming out to the suburbs.

Since the job that we are directing you toward in this book will be a meaningful, fairly high-paying one, a combination of day care and regular help or a full-time housekeeper while the children are small will probably be well worth the money spent. If the children are older, then part-time help will suffice. It all depends on what you want to do with your time and your money. We would go without lunch and new dresses for a year in order to hire someone to do our housework, but again, it's your choice.

You might notice that we have neglected to mention the husband's role in child care. Again, as usual, the burden seems to fall unfairly on the woman. Statistics show that men contribute all of 1.6 hours a day in helping around the house, whether or not the wife works. Men who are willing to share the responsibility with their wives are rare, although we know several who do. One university professor we know sets his hours from 7:00 to 3:00, while his wife works the traditional 9:00 to 5:00. He's home with the kids in the afternoon, and if one of them is sick, he and his wife decide who can best take off that day. As often as not, he does. If you've got a liberated husband, nurture him carefully. If you're not yet married, check out your future husband's philosophy before, not after, marriage.

In the meantime, if you know where Mary Poppins is hiding, send a note up the fireplace: "Beautiful room, bath, telephone, TV, radio, two delightful children, undemanding husband, and practically invisible housewife need you. Our home is your home. High salary, small demands. Your every wish is our command. We only ask that you show up regularly."

Oh, The Inequity Of It All!

We won't exasperate you with a lot of statistics about the unfair treatment of women in the business world. We'll throw a few at you here to make our point, but for the rest, there are many in-depth studies available which you can easily obtain. They all come up with one basic fact: Women *are* discriminated against. They get the worst jobs, the lowest pay, and the least promotions. They are the last hired, the first fired, and they are constantly having to prove their worth. There is mass resistance to giving women equal pay for equal work and even more resistance to awarding jobs that really *are* equal to begin with. Men are not about to let women invade territory that has long been exclusively theirs without putting up a fierce battle.

Here are some of those statistics we promised: The median earnings of women employed full-time is 42 per cent below that of men. In some jobs, such as sales, it drops as low as 60 per cent. While women make up 38 per cent of the labor force they account for only 1 per cent of the engineers, 2 per cent of executives, 7 per cent physicians, 13 per cent of proprietors outside of retail trade, 15 per cent managers, and 21 per cent of professionals outside of health and educational services. The biggest discrepancy is in clerical and service jobs — 63 per cent of all working women are engaged in these lower paying occupations.° The wage gap between male and female workers is widening, not narrowing. More women proportionately than men are entering the labor force, but the opportunities have not increased proportionately, thus forcing more competition, which in turn keeps salaries down.

The above is meant as a warning to you to be on the lookout every time you talk money with your employers. At first you may be so happy to get an exciting job after years of nonproductiveness in the career world that you'll take anything, and we wouldn't blame you a bit! But after a while the glamour wears off and no matter how terrific your position is, it's still galling to realize that you're working your heart out and the guy in the next office, who hasn't had a new idea in ten years, is making 40 per cent more than you do.

If things get really bad, you can always file a suit with the Federal Equal Employment Opportunity Commission (several thousand women have since it was created in 1964 as part of the Civil Rights Act). Most of us are practical enough to put up with it, while letting management know our feelings and quietly working in every way we can to equalize things. Each step up the ladder brings you closer to your goal of full equality. If you get proficient enough in your profes-

°Survey by the Chase Manhattan Bank, New York

sion and develop self-confidence and *demand* fair treatment, you may eventually get it.

Now that's just one area working against us women. Another more immediate one is child-care expenses and unfair income tax laws. This is where it really hurts. Although it is imperative to hire household help or to place preschool children in a day nursery, or both, none of that is deductible (unless you and your husband make the combined grand total of $6,000 a year, in which case you might be better off on welfare). We strongly feel this rule must be changed. It is simply not fair or practical to expect a woman to turn over most of her salary for the privilege of exercising her right to participate fully in society. Instead of encouraging her, our tax laws actually dissuade her, because it is true that you can find yourself working just to pay the housekeeper.

Here's an example: An advertising director of a large lingerie firm and mother of a nineteen-month-old son makes a salary of $20,000 a year. She pays a full-time nursemaid $5,500, a cleaning woman $1,105, $3,000 for her working wardrobe, $1,000 for taxis, $400 for nondeductible lunches and about $7,000 for taxes (in her husband's higher bracket). That leaves her just $2,000 a year profit from her salary. Seems ridiculous, doesn't it? Certainly part of the nursemaid and cleaning woman's salary should be tax deductible, as well as part of the clothing expenditure — none of those expenses would be necessary if she didn't work. We want to warn you here that husbands sometimes use the above as leverage in citing why you shouldn't work. "It will cost you money in the long run," they'll say, or, "Isn't it silly to put in all those hours knocking yourself out and then have nothing to show for it?" Yes, it is too bad, but you didn't make the tax laws, and they are no excuse for not getting out into the world and doing what you want to do to make it better. Maybe if enough women go back to work, their husbands will realize it's really costing *them* money, and then we'll get the tax laws changed.

A Little Dust Under The Carpet Never Hurt Anyone

We have never yet met a busy career woman with a husband and family whose housecleaning habits would qualify her for the Good Housekeeping seal of approval. This is not to say that all lady executives leave their glamourous, plushly carpeted offices and return home to a suburban version of Tobacco Road. What is meant is that unless you are a compulsive house cleaner, neither you, your family or your friends will suffer if your linen closet isn't neat and color-coordinated and your coffee table doesn't glow with fresh lemon wax. It is virtually impossible to have a spotless, orderly house at all times if you work, unless you really have recruited Mary Poppins — and even then Miss Poppins isn't likely to do the job the way you would like it done.

All but one of the women we polled had some household help — but most of them admitted that things were usually a little dusty, and underwear and handkerchiefs weren't ironed. One mother of two young children related, "My husband used to complain if I didn't iron his handkerchiefs; now he's glad if I take them out of the dryer and put them in his drawer." One best-selling author we know removes her towels from the dryer and literally flings them into the linen closet, letting them fall where they may. Another respondent echoed, "The last time I ironed was to bring on labor with my second child." A third said, "My daughter thinks everyone lives in a constant state of disarray and I'm not going to tell her differently." One woman we spoke to said she brought in half the income and her husband halved the housework with her. We have found that this type of sharing is rather unlikely in the past-thirty-five generation. We do suggest, however, that if your husband expects your house to be in a constant state of readiness to be photographed for *House Beautiful*, that you present him with a broom and a mop along with that cold martini he probably expects to have waiting when he gets home.

As for your children living in a less than sterile atmosphere, we guarantee they will never know the difference. Kids like dirt anyhow — it's good for their psyche — and if they don't, and they're over two years of age, they can use a dust cloth as well as you can.

There are plenty of ways to give the impression of order in your house, which are discussed in an earlier chapter on how to get organized.

A few basic hints that are helpful are:

1. It's easier and not much more expensive to have walls and woodwork repainted every year or so rather than having them scrubbed down.

2. Throw away things you don't need. Don't be a saver.

3. Don't look in the children's room unless it's an emergency.

4. Use lots of artificial plants. They give a nice effect and cover up spots on the rug.

5. Carpeting is easier to keep clean than wood or vinyl floors.

6. Keep a lot of decorative hampers around to stuff things in.

You will probably find that you get a compulsive urge every year or two to clean out all the drawers and cabinets, wash the walls, the whole works. We usually resist it, but it does ease the conscience of those whose mothers taught them that cleanliness is next to godliness.

Incidentally, the next time anyone tells you that a woman isn't physically capable of doing a man's job, tell him to try pushing a vacuum cleaner over yards of two-inch thick carpeting, cleaning twenty-eight picture windows inside and out, moving a room full of furniture to clean behind it, and changing the linens on six beds — all after coming home from work.

How To Turn Mother Hubbard's Cupboard Into a Five-Minute Gourmet Dinner

You have just come home after eight hours crammed full of all the pressures and problems that are routine

in the business world. Food is the last thing on your
mind, but you have a husband and a few hungry
children who do have it on their minds, and they want
their dinner—and not the TV variety either. Just about
then the awful realization hits you—that stop you knew
you had to make on the way home, but couldn't
remember for the life of you, was the grocery store.

This chaotic scene has happened to us more times
than we care to remember (despite our once-a-week
shopping intentions), but, to the amazement of our
husbands, we have never yet resorted to peanut butter
sandwiches or TV dinners—and you don't have to either. Once you discover the shortcuts, making an acceptable dinner out of next to nothing comes easy.
There are two staples that are essential. Rice and
noodles. With these two basics, you can create as many
magic tricks as Houdini. The second requirement is a
good supply of packaged sauce mixes—spaghetti, stroganoff, mushroom, onion—there are dozens of them.
And the third is a good-size freezer which you have
stocked with meatballs, various packs of seafood and
chicken chunks, hot dogs, individually wrapped steaks,
hamburgers, chops, chicken parts, a variety of frozen
potatoes, vegetables, fruits, extra bread, grated cheese,
packaged bread crumbs, and anything else that will
defrost in an hour, or that you can cook while still
frozen.

One clever instant cook we talked to serves a casserole three times a week. On those days, she partially
cooks the rice or noodles while she's drinking her
morning coffee, and refreshes the pasta with a dollup
of wine when she gets home, tosses in some frozen
shrimp or meatballs, mixes up an instant sauce, tosses
the whole concoction into a casserole and into the

oven—presto! Five minutes and she has meatballs stroganoff.

If you are too conscious of your waistline to dine on casseroles very often, we find that small steaks, chops and chicken parts all cook very nicely when still frozen—but give them an extra 30 minutes or so. You can also create a very elegant-looking dinner with a couple of cans of tuna tossed with a few canned white grapes and some toasted almonds and a touch of canned white sauce. Run it under the broiler, give it a fancy name, and accompany it with a nice white wine.

Some of the women we surveyed said that breakfast presented more of a problem than dinner. French toast, waffles, pancakes and popups—all are waiting for you ready-made in the frozen foods section. Instant cereals, both hot and cold, pre-packaged cocoa mix, and instant breakfast concoctions can all be handled quite nicely by the kiddies without your supervision.

If you're the type that likes to do her own cooking when you entertain, keep in mind that some of the most famous hostesses serve their famous friends spaghetti and French bread, or a big pot of beef stew, or even hot dogs with all the trimmings. In fact, we received a beautifully engraved formal invitation to a frankfurter roast—and that's what we got, along with baked beans and champagne. It was great!

Here are a few recipes that have held up under being thrown together at 5:45 P.M. to the background music of screaming kids, TVs, ringing doorbells and telephones—and have yet to let us down.

Veal Rosireta

6 veal chops	Garlic salt
1 can stewed tomatoes	Parsley flakes
1 can mushrooms	Pepper
Dried onion flakes	Marjoram

Brown veal chops in pan. Add the rest and simmer one hour. Splash some white wine in, if desired.

Coq au Vin (*Also a great party dish to make a lot of on the weekend and freeze.*)

Cut-up fryers	1 cup white wine
Garlic	2 or 3 tomatoes
Butter or margarine	(canned are O.K.)
Salt, pepper,	Mushrooms
marjoram and thyme	1 finely chopped onion

Saute crushed garlic in butter. Add chicken and brown. Add salt, pepper and marjoram, wine, chopped tomatoes and simmer one hour. Remove chicken. Add chopped onion and mushroom. Cook ten minutes. Pour over chicken. Serve with rice or noodles.

Five-Minute Sukiyaki

1 flank steak	Frozen pea pods or
Soy sauce	frozen Japanese vegetables
	Mushrooms

Slice raw flank steak on angle into strips. Sprinkle with soy sauce. Put in a big frying pan with a little oil and other ingredients. Cook quickly to sear meat and cook vegetables crisply. Serve with Chinese noodles, rice, and more soy sauce.

If you really want to give your husband the illusion that he's dining at La Pavillon, you can use a little culinary trickery. To name a few:

1. A few toasted almonds sprinkled on fish or vegetables.

2. A handful of croutons (from a box) tossed on the salad or plopped in the soup.

3. A snippet of dried or frozen chives on anything they'll show up on.

4. Globs of parsley decorating everything.

5. A glass of wine with everything.

6. Instant pudding served in a champagne glass.

7. Use herbs on everything.

8. Cook everything with wine, pour some in your casseroles.

9. Eat by candlelight (especially if you would rather not have him see the food). Seriously, this does wonders for an ordinary meal.

10. Have some flowers on the table, even if they're fake.

11. Garnish with mushrooms—they look impressive.

12. Don't ever serve frozen souffles, etc., in the container they came in—put them in your own and smile mysteriously when asked if you made it.

As a postscript, it's not a sin to pile your kids in the car occasionally and take them to the neighborhood hamburger stand—children usually prefer a hamburger to a gourmet concoction that takes hours to prepare. Our children consider it a special treat to be served a burger special and french fries, and would prefer it to home cooking any night of the week. In fact, a friend of ours has the kids believing that Chinese TV dinners are party treats and they can be bribed into perfect behavior by the promise of one of those twelve-minute specials. We haven't been able to bamboozle our brood into begging for TV dinners, but we have convinced them that food they can cook themselves tastes even better than anything we serve.

Needless to say, husbands have more sophisticated palates and convincing them that frozen pot pies are comparable to Chateaubriand isn't as easy. We don't think a man should balk at being served scrambled eggs and bacon in an emergency, but, in general, you had better have the semblance of a decent meal on the table. Follow our twelve shortcuts and you should be able to satisfy even the fussiest culinary experts, at least part of the time.

What About the Kids?

Probably the most frequently asked question of the working wife and mother is "What about the children?" This is a sore subject for many working women because of the underlying guilt feelings that society and our parents have ingrained into our subconscious.

We say "What *about* the kids?" There has never been a conclusive study made indicating that the children of working mothers don't fare just as well as those of women who are waiting at home with milk and

cookies when the kiddies get home from school. Did it
ever occur to these women that maybe Johnny doesn't
really care whether he is greeted at the door every
day, because he would just as soon go back outside
and play with his friends, do his homework or listen to
his records? Oh, sure it's nice to have Mom there to
pour a glass of milk, hang up jackets and put away
school books — but would it really stunt Johnny's development if he had to do these things for himself, plus
take on the responsibility of maybe setting the table or
watering the plants.? By the time he got finished with
these little items Mom would probably be home. "But
you should be available in case your child needs you,"
insist many indignant mothers. Well, in the thirteen
years that we have been mothers with a combined
brood of five children, we cannot think of one single
incident when the children had anything arise that
could not wait a couple of hours. Naturally your child
can break a leg, but this can happen while you're at
the grocery store.

Children are like sponges; they will soak up every
moment of attention you give them and then ask for
more. You are not doing them a favor by constantly
giving into their demands for your time. The American
child is probably the most over-indulged, over-
protected and under-estimated child in the world. He
expects to receive more than he gives, and he usually
does. Very little is expected of him except maybe a few
A's on his report card and clean hands at the dinner
table. Could it be that the low expectations we have of
our children and their ability to stand on their own
two feet is one of the reasons for our present generation
of troubled youth? A child coddled, spoiled and smoth-
ered with attention at home is often dismayed to find
that that big world out there is not waiting to receive

him with outstretched arms and milk and cookies the way Momma always has.

There comes a time in every person's life when it suddenly dawns on him that he is not the center of the universe, that other people are entitled to a share of pie also. The sooner this is made clear to a child the better off he will be and the happier you will be. The sooner you demand from your child that he respect the desires and wishes of other people, yourself included, the better equipped he will be to function in society. Who said that a child must participate in five different extracurricular activities to which he must be driven and picked up, or that he must be entertained at a movie or skating or bowling every weekend, with you as the chauffeur? Plenty of children expect this, and more. They express dismay if their parents don't fit *their* schedule around Junior. How many homes do you know of where everything in the family revolves around the kids? Why? When this is true, when do the grown-ups get their chance at bat? After the game is over, or they're too old to play?

Studies conducted by child expert Benjamin Spock have shown that Russian children whose mothers usually combine motherhood with a job outside the home (in areas such as medicine, science, education, industry, government, art, etc. — not typing pools) seemed more stable, better adjusted, and more mature than American children whose full-time mothers spent their time lavishing attention on them and worrying about them. Dr. Spock said that Russian women are more sure of themselves as mothers than their American counterparts and less dependent on the advice from child care experts in raising their offspring.

The damage a mother can do her children by overprotection has been well documented. A detailed study was made by Dr. David Levy of twenty mothers who had done emotional damage to their children by over-indulgence. In many cases the mothers used the child to satisfy her own need for love and affection. She even dressed up and freshened her hair and lipstick as she would for her husband. Dr. Levy attributed these characteristics to the fact that the mother had no other life outside of her child — her ambitions for herself had been thwarted by motherhood.

A number of studies have been done indicating that the role of the middle class American housewife has had a smothering effect on the American child, and yet so many women use the excuse of their children's needs rather than taking a chance on themselves. They find it easier to live through their children's achievements, forever pushing them to achieve more, do better, accomplish all the things they would like to have done. How many children do you know who are dragged to a myriad of lessons, forced to practice and continually nagged by insistent mothers who have grandiose dreams of Johnny or Susie doing all the great things she didn't do and probably never will?

What we are saying is that when that guilt provoking question is tossed at you, "What about the kids?" you should be able to honestly answer "What *about* them?" — knowing that your becoming a totally complete and fulfilled person is setting an example for your children that is more important than all the home-made cookies in the world.

Kids Can Be Self-Sufficient— If You'll Just Let Them

It's remarkable how self-sufficient children can be if only adults expected it of them and trusted them more. All the children of working mothers we know seem extremely poised and self-reliant—often more so than their more pampered peers. If children are given responsibility, they will usually accept it, especially if started young. The self-reliance of career women's off-spring is no accident. More *is* expected of them. Because time is so limited, everyone must use the little available more efficiently.

The kids can clean their own rooms, straighten the bathroom, put away their clothes, fold the laundry, set the table, clear the dishes, and generally help out. The older ones can look after the smaller ones and everyone can be taught to respect Mommy's privacy when she's working at home. Because you're not around all the time, your children will be much less dependent and will learn to develop their own inner resources. You will have more dimension, and it will be reflected in them. Dinner table conversation will probably be more stimulating and the people you entertain at home through your career will probably expose your children

119

to a much wider variety of experience than they would have otherwise.

If you teach them and trust them, your children will be able to cope with many situations that arise while you're working. If Susie gets a headache at school, she's going to think twice before calling you home from the office. Chances are she'll decide the headache's not really so bad after all, and she can hold out until 3:00. She has just experienced a lesson in self-control. If Johnnie just *has* to get to a ball game two miles away, he'll figure out some way to get there, even if he has to walk. He has just used his ingenuity. And so it goes.

The more you expect of your children and the more you respect them, the more self-reliant they will be. The day before we wrote this chapter, a severe ice storm hit Atlanta. We were due at a television taping at 7:00 that evening, and just as we were leaving our respective houses all the electricity went off. Already late for the taping, we had no choice but to grab some candles, hand them to our twelve-year-olds and leave them to cope with dinner, Daddy, and their younger brothers and sisters. They handled things calmly and efficiently, as we knew they would. Thank God for self-sufficient children!

Make the Most of the Weekends

When you boil all the guilt-making rhetoric down, you'll be surprised to find that, once the kids are in school, nonworking women don't see much more of them than you do. The only real difference is the two-and-one-half hours in the afternoon when you're not there. Most of our nonworking friends aren't there either, but nobody looks at it that way. The fact that they're on the tennis court or downtown shopping doesn't count. Anyway, if those missing twelve-and-one-half hours weekly nag at your conscience, then we suggest you make the most of the weekends.

Saturdays are a great time to take the kids shopping. If they are young, weekends can be spent going special places—the zoo, a museum, the library, visiting friends. The week's errands can be done on Saturday, with the little ones in tow. Pre-teens love to go to "their" places—the record store, the poster shack, the "with it" shops, the health-food store. Try exploring with your children. Stop in at an interesting shop or art gallery. Walk down a strange street in a different neighborhood. Go to a movie or out to lunch together. If you are athletically inclined, learn a sport such as tennis or golf together.

Weekends are a great time for a little togetherness with Daddy, too. Boys especially need the masculine example only your husband can supply. Suggest various building projects around the house. Most working couples we know tend to spend a good deal of time *en famille* on weekends. Many of our friends have boats or weekend cabins at the lake, and the whole family takes off for the weekend Friday afternoon. Camping is a fine family activity, if you like that sort of thing. We don't, but many of our acquaintances do.

You will find that your children really appreciate your company on the weekends, and we have found that they eagerly look forward to it. Because you're not just "there," all the time during the week, the events you do plan together become very important to all of you and the children seem to sense that you really enjoy being with them. We also look forward to it and we often plan during the week for the following weekend.

As the children grow up they will want to be with their friends more and with you less. That's one of life's inevitables and there is no sense fighting it, but we feel you should still be available on weekends to drive them to the bowling alley, tennis court, friends' houses, football field, and such places. In other words, if they know they can count on you some of the time, they are perfectly willing to accept your absence the rest of the time. If talked to honestly and sincerely, children are usually understanding and accepting—much more than often given credit for.

It's also a good idea to show your kids around your office. The weekend might be a perfect time. Let them see where you work. Show them what you do. Let them sit at your desk and try out all the equipment. They will probably be very impressed and will look at their mother in a new light. They will realize that you have another life away from them and the house, and although they might be awed it will be tinged with respect. We usually take our older children with us to the studio on holidays (Christmas and Thanksgiving are regular working days in broadcasting, although we do our show with just a skeleton staff.) They feel very important and they also get to see their mother at work. Many men take their children along if they have to run into the office for an hour or so on weekends. Why don't you do the same thing? The more familiar the kids are with what you do, the more they will accept and understand it as a perfectly natural part of you.

Our particular business offers some advantages to the children. We get press tickets to plays, movie premiers and amusements. We take our children to appropriate ones, and as they get older, they will accompany us more often. One of us was recently invited, along with husband and children, to one of President Nixon's Sunday Prayer Breakfasts at the White House. The whole family flew to Washington, spent the night and flew back Sunday night. The boys will have unforgettable memories of meeting the President and First Lady, along with cabinet members, congressmen and other dignitaries. That's one family weekend that will be hard to top!

A little common sense and planning will more than make up for your lack of togetherness during the week. In fact, we predict you will find your times together more relaxed, your enjoyment of your children heightened, and everyone's disposition pleasanter than when you were a full-time housewife.

Twenty Answers To Subdue the Opposition

Recently, we have been speaking before various women's groups on the subject covered in this book. Most of these women are full-time housewives and we purposely try to shake them up a little with our more "militant" ideas (which are really quite mild compared to those of many radical feminists).

The question and answer period afterward always brings forth some pointedly hostile questions and statements from women who find it difficult to face the truth about their lives. These women are middle-class wives like ourselves and it disturbs them to hear us, a reflection of them, admit that financial security and a comfortable life are not sufficient in themselves.

When you make the break and venture into the outside world, you will find most likely that you, too, face this sort of ambivalent attitude on the part of many women. A few years ago, the working wife who admitted she was working for pleasure and not out of dire financial need was an oddity and was constantly put on the defensive. Things have changed so radically that very often now it's the stay-at-home who feels she must defend *her* way of life.

These women always hit you where you're most vulnerable—your children and your marriage. You should be prepared for their negative questions and be ready with some snappy answers, because if they can pin you to the wall on one point, they will then feel very smug and righteous. Cocktail and dinner parties seem to spawn this kind of conversation, so to make your life easier, we have compiled a list of the twenty most asked questions and appropriate answers. Memorize them, if you can because, believe us, sooner or later you'll need them!

Q. What does your husband think of your working?
A. Would you ask me what I think of his working?

Q. How do you manage a job and homemaking?
A. I fake it.

Q. Doesn't working and rushing home to cook, mother, etc. exhaust you?
A. I thrive on it. It keeps me young.

Q. What about the children?
A. What *about* them?

Q. Aren't you missing your children's best years of growing up?
A. No. I enjoy less of them a lot more, and they feel the same.

Q. But, don't the children feel neglected?
A. They've never told me, if they do. In fact, they seem remarkably well adjusted.

Q. Doesn't your family mind your working?
A. I've never asked them.

Q. Don't you ever feel guilty?
A. Quite often, but I've learned to ignore it.

Q. What about carpooling after school?
A. I think carpooling is a Communist plot foisted off on the American housewife.

Q. But how do the children get to their activities?
A. They walk, run, or ride the bus. In an absolute emergency, I drive them, if possible.

Q. Do you like your children?
A. I adore them. But they are children and I am an

adult and our interests aren't always similar. Why inflict us on each other constantly?

Q. Does your husband ever feel neglected?
A. Probably, but he's kind enough not to tell me.

Q. Do you earn enough at your job to make it worthwhile?
A. If I *lost* money, it would be worthwhile.

Q. What if something happened to one of the kids and you weren't there?
A. I could get home from my office just about as fast as you could rush home from the tennis court.

Q. Isn't your child disappointed when he comes home from school and you're not there?
A. No, he's used to it, and he usually goes right out to play anyway.

Q. But what if he's bubbling over with something important to tell you?
A. Waiting until I get home teaches him self-control and if it's really that exciting, he can call me up at the office and I'll enthuse over the phone.

Q. I'd love to work, but I have no training or talent.
A. You have more than you think. Any woman who can run a home, juggle the bank balance, pay bills, keep household records, schedule a thousand varied appointments, keep up an active social life and personally supervise a host of household emergencies, can easily run a business or hold down a job in almost any field she chooses.

Q. I'm dying to go back to work, but what if my husband won't let me?

A. How can one grown adult stop another grown adult from living? You will have to decide whether subjecting your whole being to one man's ego is worth it. Are you going to live your life, or his?

Q. I tried going back to school/work once, but I just couldn't take it.

A. That's a cop-out. What you mean is, you weren't really committed to it.

Q. Oh, but your job is unique. I couldn't handle it.

A. How do you know? Have you tried?

PART IV

Keeping Your Perspective

The Twenty-Year Marriage Split-up

There has been a growing phenomenon the past few years that psychiatrists and family counselors call "The twenty-year marriage divorce syndrome." An increasing percentage of seemingly sound marriages are breaking up after twenty or more years of togetherness. These are not marriages that have been in obvious trouble for many years, or marriages that were in name only, held together for the sake of the children. Nor did the male partner feel the need to bolster a sagging libido by running off with a cute young thing twenty years his junior. These are the kinds of marital failings that happen to two seemingly nice, stable people — the kind of breakup always talked about with wonderment among their friends: "We can't imagine what got into Grace and Harry, they seemed such an ideal couple." "Harry's never looked at another woman — it can't be *that!*" "They seemed to have so much to look forward to with both the children gone now," and on ad infinitum.

What went wrong? Almost invariably, these couples found that the children and the demands of the home were the only glue holding the marriage together all these years. Take those away and all the supports come tumbling down. Most of these unions involved women who made their children their whole life. Many of the women never grew, never related to the larger world outside their homes and therefore had very little to offer the marriage when the children were gone. The husband had devoted most of his time to his profession and the social and economic demands of the family

130

structure. When the two were finally left alone together they found they were strangers. The husband grew increasingly restless and the wife became increasingly insecure. Both felt that things were falling apart and both felt powerless to stop it. Although counseling sometimes helps, one or the other of the partners finally gives up and another long-term marriage is severed. The woman is usually lonely and embittered. No longer young, she is thrown out into a world she never really knew and is frightened of coping with. Often, she has never worked prior to or during her marriage. She knows no life outside the security of the marital tandem and even though she might be financially secure, she feels abandoned and useless. These are the women from whom one often hears the refrain, "I gave him the best years of my life and this is the thanks I get."

One particularly sad case which comes to mind is a friend of ours who was constantly striving to make her kids the most popular on the block. She religiously attended every Little League game. She was the Girl Scout leader and the P.T.A. President. Her home was always open and nothing was too good for her children. She also prodded and pushed them beyond their limits because she wanted "her" children to excel. Her husband, a pleasant, but mild-mannered man, always sort of melted unobtrusively into the background. No one could have been more surprised than her close friends to find this shining example of suburban motherliness divorced after twenty-five years of marriage. Her friends were also astonished to learn that one child had disappeared into a commune in Colorado and another was last heard from in Canada where he had fled to escape the draft. This poor woman's world has come crashing down around her and she will never understand why.

Sometimes it's the wife who cuts the ties. Another woman we know asked her husband for a divorce after twenty-three years of wedded blahs, because of sheer boredom. She confessed to us she had been tied down all these years by the rigid role society had put her in and she had resented it more with each passing year. Her husband was a demanding man who expected unquestioning servitude and obedience from his wife. In return for abundant material goods, fine clothes and an elegant home, she was expected to fetch and carry, drop her interests if they conflicted with his, cater to his moods (with no regard to hers), and see to his general welfare. All of which she did with grace and charm while the children were young. A talented pianist before marriage, this woman broached the idea of taking her master's degree in music and then teaching part-time. Her husband said, "No," but this time, since the children were gone, our friend said, "The time has come," whereupon she divorced her husband and proceeded on what she calls, her "second life." Fortunately, her children were 100 per cent behind her, but she regrets those wasted years.

One psychologist puts it this way: "Women must be made to realize that there is no substitute for one's self. During the first twenty or so years of marriage, most women are too busy living their children's and husband's lives to think about the empty years ahead, but by the time they realize that life has passed them by, it's too late. The children leave and live their own lives, often with little thanks. The husband is increasingly immersed in his profession or business and has even less time for her. And what's ahead for the still young woman in her late forties? Twenty more years of playing bridge at the club? Twenty more years of meeting the "girls" for lunch? Twenty more years of emptiness and nonproductiveness? Twenty more years of living through her grandchildren?"

Don't let this happen to you. Don't become one of those faceless women who spend the best years of their lives in self-sacrifice and martyrdom to their families, who later look back and ask, "Where have the years gone? What have I done with them?" The time to start planning for your own future is now.

Where Do You Go From Here?

It must be pretty obvious by this point in the book that we feel the advantages of having a career outweigh the problems. We have also stressed the point that a large majority of women find that a career not only enriches their mind and soul, but also their marriage. This is usually the case, but don't overlook the possibility that you might outgrow your husband. You have probably heard the phrase, "he's outgrown his wife" applied to successful businessmen whose wives have become so entangled with the web of domesticity or so mentally lazy due to years of card games and shopping that they suddenly have nothing to say to each other. Well, the other side of the coin is the woman who suddenly finds life opening its doors to her, who finds herself accomplishing things she never dreamed she was capable of and, furthermore, realizes that she has the drive and ambition to push her way to even greater heights. All of a sudden her quiet, kind and steady husband seems dull, plodding and lacking ambition.

Often this new image of her mate is not merely a figment of her imagination. When a woman begins to develop into a fully functioning, productive human being her perspective changes and the man who was perfectly suited for her while she was in the role of full-time homemaker may no longer be on her wave length, nor she on his. There are also men who, for one reason or another, simply cannot adjust to a wife who is doing her own thing. They are conditioned to a traditional stay-at-home wife and come hell, high water or divorce, that's what they're going to get—whether or not it be you. When these problems arise you will have to make a decision and that's when the going gets rough.

There is also the possibility that you will find that in order to advance in your career you will have to move to another city where the opportunities are greater. This is a difficult crossroad to arrive at, especially if you're happily married. A woman we know faced this choice when she was offered the opportunity to audition for the Metropolitan Opera. After a lot of soul-searching she took the opportunity, leaving her family for a year, at which time they joined her in New York. We have been offered jobs in other cities paying far more than we now earn, but our decision has been in favor of our families. Another situation when the feathers hit the fan is when your husband gets transferred with a big promotion and you are faced with the decision of finding a new job or a new husband—neither of which is a picnic.

The chances of your being faced with these problems depend a lot on how ambitious and competitive you really are and how much responsibility you want to assume in your field. We have found that the higher up the ladder you go and the more important your position becomes the less responsibility you have time for at home—and something's gotta give. What gives is up to you. It may be that you stop climbing when you reach the vice-president level instead of pushing on toward the president's chair; or it may mean that you write a twice-a-week column in your local paper rather than reach for a daily syndicated column. It may mean you settle for a little less than you would like. We realize that the majority of women accept the premise that life is a series of compromises and that most career wives are aware of the fact that the demands of the chairman of the board and the lady of the house are very rarely compatible. Compromising your career may stick in your craw at times, but for the sake of marital harmony, to most women it's worth it. Please take heed, however, at this point—make darn sure it's worth it. We don't mean merely reaching the pinnacle of success in your field, as rewarding as that may be. What we do mean is reaching the pinnacle of yourself—being able to know you are a person in your own right, not because you are someone's wife or someone's mother. If when you look in the mirror, you're not quite sure of who you see, that's when the soul searching begins. We wouldn't attempt to advise you what direction to take if it comes down to this type of decision. You are completely on your own. Robert Townsend, author of *Up The Organization* said that men are a dime a dozen but a good job is hard to find. We don't necessarily go along with that. A good man is just as hard to find as a good job, and a lot more fun to cuddle up to. However, sitting at the head of that conference table does have its moments. If you're really lucky, you'll get both.

You Will Never Be the Same

Although much of this book has been written in a light-hearted vein, forgive us for turning serious in this, our final chapter. The freeing of woman's spirit and soul is a serious subject and cannot be treated lightly, even by those of us who look at life with a wry eye.

Throughout the book we've mentioned the Women's Liberation movement, sometimes critically, sometimes admiringly. Like all serious movements, it has its excesses and its comic aspects. It is, however, a very healthy move in the right direction for the woman of today—the woman you are or hope to become. We'd like to share with you our thoughts on what a woman's liberation really is and what we think it means to masses of women all over this country.

Forget the man haters, and the frumpy, no make-up "love us as we are, not as we're made-up to look like" set. Forget some of the angry rhetoric you've read and heard about male castration, sexual politics, Freudian fallacies, and revolution. That's the battle cry of a very few extremists whose rage at an insensitive society has caused them to overreact. We sympathize with their frustrations because those same feelings affect all of us. But for every one of them, there are thousands of women, like ourselves, doing quiet battle every day in the front lines of the business world. We, too, feel thwarted at times; we, too, chafe at the unfairness of a society that expects women to live solely through the accomplishments of other human beings—their husbands and children. We, too, feel like screaming at the pressures piled upon us, of coping not only with demanding careers, but with all the responsibility of running a home and tending to our family's many needs. Yet, although we are familiar with the problems, we think the answer lies not with slogans or even with sympathetic legislation—although the latter will help— but within yourself.

Every woman has the potential to become a fully functioning human being in our society. Every woman has the right, indeed the duty to think of herself, her future, and her role in life. If this role encompasses much more than her husband, her children and the four walls of her house, then she is obliged to follow her own particular path to wherever it takes her. She might stumble along the way, she may run into detours, but as long as she keeps travelling, she is being true to herself. This is what true woman's liberation is. A woman who does not need to rely on another human being for her existence, or her spiritual, economic or intellectual well-being, is truly free.

We can't begin to tell you the feeling of exuberance, almost of power, a woman who has attained this freedom experiences. Her life is then made up of choice, not chance. When a woman is freed from the shackles of dependency, her marriage is either going to crumble or grow much stronger. So many marriages are held together by fear, inertia, or economic dependency. Or they become battlegrounds where either the husband or wife is jockeying for power. We can't count the times women have called us on the air and said, "My husband won't let me," or "My husband would kill me if he knew what I did," or "I don't want to displease my husband by working because he would make my life miserable," or "I'm so unhappy, but my husband won't listen to anything I say." How can these be called adult relationships? They're more like father-daughter, or master-slave. We can assure you, that once you find your niche in the outside world and realize that you can be successful, respected and remunerated for your talents by strangers, your whole attitude about yourself, your life and your marriage will change.

If your marriage is sound, it will grow infinitely better. You and your husband will be able to treat each other as equals. Because you are no longer dependent on him for your every need he will be able to relax, too. Men feel guilty, too, you know. They realize that their wives depend on them for their very existence, and sometimes they resent the pressures. A hard-working man won't have to worry about coming home after an exhausting day and feeling that he is obligated to entertain his bored wife, if she's been out working, too. If he's tired and doesn't want to talk, chances are she'll be grateful, because she's tired, too. In any event, she'll certainly be more understanding of his moods. And we can guarantee you, a happily working wife will rarely be restless and will never need to force her husband to entertain her.

We hope this book has given you the courage and the knowledge to reevaluate your life and redirect it into more meaningful channels. It won't be easy, but you'll never regret it, and once set on your course you will find there's no turning back. Years later, when you look back on your former life as only a housewife-mother you'll wonder how you could have existed in such narrow confines. And you'll breathe a sigh of gratitude that you escaped in time.

All we have meant to say in this book is summed up in these ancient words from the Talmud:

> If I am not for myself, who will be for me?
> If I am for myself alone, what am I?
> If not now, when?

GOOD LUCK!

PART V

The Questionnaire

The Questionnaire

When we began writing this book, we felt it would be interesting to see if other working wives encountered the same problems and came up with solutions similar to ours or whether our situation was unique. We made up a questionnaire and sent it out to a cross-section of 100 acquaintances in various parts of the country. These women vary in age, interests, education, ethnic background and fields of endeavor. The only thing they have in common is that they have interesting careers and care for a husband and children in their spare time.

The youngest woman polled is twenty-five years old and the oldest is fifty. Their occupations include lawyer, doctor, assistant judge, teacher, French literature professor, journalist, economics consultant, art appraiser, editor for major publisher, industrial designer, lab technician, decorator, real-estate saleswoman, community service worker, plus several who have their own businesses.

Sixty percent said their present job related to their past education, training or work. Seventy-five percent worked prior to marriage, and about half of the women

142

either never stopped working or resumed almost immediately after marriage; the other half waited at least
ten years, and one respondent waited seventeen years
before starting her first year of college.

The percentage was 50–50 between full-time and
part-time work (although we must mention here that
these are not part-time jobs, but are careers handled on
a part-time basis by choice, which could at any time be
expanded into full-time careers). Every woman questioned said her career was permanent and she planned
to continue working indefinitely. They also were unanimous in answering YES! to the question, "Are you
happy working?" The unanimity hit a fever pitch in
reference to the question, "Would you prefer full-time
homemaking?"—eliciting such replies as, "You gotta be
kidding!!!!!," large "NO!," "Are you kidding?," and
"Over my dead body."

Sixty percent of the women said they had no trouble
combining homemaking and a career. The other 40 per
cent responded with such comments as, "If I could
only find reliable help," "I can't seem to get organized," and "I never have any time to myself." All but
two of the women polled say their husbands encourage
them in their careers or at least accept them gracefully. Several said their husbands pushed them into
developing their potential.

Most of the women have had to make changes in
their home life, such as employing more household
help and cutting back on entertaining. Most rely on at
least part-time help but would prefer full-time, and all
admit to relaxing their standards of housekeeping. As
for assistance from the male of the house, 85 per cent
said that their husbands helped in some areas, usually
carpooling, babysitting and occasional marketing. Only
one woman has managed to employ the new ethic,

saying, "I earn half the living—he halves the home-work with me."

Not one woman felt her marriage suffered due to her career. In fact, many emphasized that their marriage had improved, with such comments as "My husband thinks I am prettier, smarter and younger than ever!," "Days are not long enough to discuss our interests," "Working has made me more aware of my husband's family responsibilities, and more sensitive to his needs." Many of the respondents feel that their career has made them a better mate and a more interesting person.

The child-care arrangements varied, but most pre-ferred a combination of household help and nursery school facilities for preschoolers.

Every woman polled agreed that her main problem was time—time to relax, time for the kids, time for herself, time for her friends, time for her husband, time to just "be." "I feel the press of trying to catch up with unfinished business that chronically hangs over me." The short-cuts employed boil down to one word—"simplicity." Simple meals, simple entertaining, a lick and a polish for the house, and getting others to help out as much as possible.

All but two women say that her husband's career is the dominant one, but some couldn't resist adding "but I have always considered mine *equally* important," or "My husband's is first, but mine's a close second."

Every woman polled insists that her children are more self-reliant and happier than those of stay-at-home mothers.

Most of the women find that their friends accept their career as part of their personality and those who don't cease to be their friends. However, those who started working late in marriage find their friends ei-

ther surprised at their ability and awestruck or cool
and envious. One mother of six said her friends and
neighbors were shocked until they realized her
children were not left to roam around the streets unat-
tended.

Seventy-five per cent of the women admitted to feeling guilty about working at times—mostly in the area of
time spent with children.

The survey showed that 10 to 50 per cent of the
woman's income was absorbed directly by career requirements, the largest share going for child care. All
but two women feel that tax laws are unfair to working
women, mainly because of lack of child-care deduc-
tions in all but the lowest brackets.

All the respondents said that their children had
specific areas of responsibility—even the tiny ones. As
one mother said, "As soon as they can walk, they can
dress themselves and hang up their clothes."

Another unanimous loud and clear "YES" answered
the question, "Do you feel more fulfilled combining a
career with marriage?—eliciting such comments as:
"Definitely. I am a person. . . . I have interests other
than children, recipes (I hate to cook, anyway) and
wallpaper. I meet new, interesting people every day—
the dumdums, too, but that's what makes it so
fulfilling." "I could not survive without either. Having
only a marriage would starve my intellect, having only
a career would starve my emotions." "I've always been
an achiever. I'd go nuts if I had to sit home with my
mouth shut. . . . I have to feel a bit important." "I
would not have survived as only a housekeeper."

As for what advice the respondents would give other
women seeking a career, they all agreed on one—get
the right husband. Others encouraged "full steam
ahead, enjoy it," "You must want the thrills, chills, anx-

ieties and pleasures, or don't try it," "Try it. For some it's manna from heaven, for others unmitigated hell."

Not one woman questioned said she would change her life except in very minor areas. A few of those who hadn't struck out on their own before marriage wished they had, but basically all were content with their lot.

Although we in no way claim this to be a scientific study, this random sampling, along with the hundreds of other women we personally talked to, bear out our convictions that the problems, frustrations, joys and fulfillments of the truly committed working wife and mother are pretty much the same. They sometimes feel guilty, but not enough to quit. They have problems with time and organization, but they've learned to cope. Their husbands and children accept them for better or for worse. They love their life and are basically happy and fulfilled human beings.

Here is the questionnaire. It will give you an insight into the lifestyle of the woman you want to be.

Questionnaire From Mickie and Teddi
(*These answers will remain strictly confidential.*)

Please explain each answer where applicable. If you
need more space for your answers, just attach a plain
sheet and number the answer to corresponding question, or use other side of these pages.

NAME: ....

ADDRESS: ....

AGE: .... HOW LONG MARRIED: ....

COLLEGE ATTENDED: ....

DEGREE: .... OTHER: ....

PHONE: .... HUSBAND'S OCCUPATION: ....

AGES AND SEX OF CHILDREN: ....

1. Does your present job relate to your past work,
education or training?

2. Describe your present occupation:

3. Did you work prior to marriage? At what?

4. How soon after marriage did you resume work or
training toward present career?

5. Do you work full time? If not, what is your schedule?

6. How did you get your job?

7. Is it a permanent career?

8. Do you plan to continue working indefinitely?

9. Did you need extra training to continue career?
How long?

10. Are you happy working?   If not, why not?

11. Would you prefer full-time homemaking?

12. Do you find it difficult combining homemaking and a career?

13. What does your family think? Does your husband encourage or object?

14. What changes have you had to make in homelife because of career demands? Does husband help (cooking, shopping, children, etc.) ?

15. What are your household help arrangements?

16. What special arrangements have you had to make for older children because of job (carpools, lessons, activities, etc.) ?

17. If children are under school age, what day-care arrangements have you made? Are they satisfactory?

18. What are the major problems you face in trying to combine career and homemaking? Explain in detail.

19. What shortcuts have you personally employed to make life easier for you and your family (shopping, cooking, entertaining, etc.) ?

20. Has there ever been any conflict with your husband over whose career is dominant?

21. Since you began work are your children happier? Less happy? No different? Are they more or less self-reliant than children of nonworking mothers?

22. How do your friends react to your career?

23. Do you ever feel guilty because you don't spend more time at home?

24. What is approximate salary range for husband? $5 to $10 thousand_____$10 to $25 thousand_____ $25 to $40 thousand____ Over $40 thousand____.

25. What is approximate salary range for yourself: under $5 thousand ____$5 to $10 thousand ____$10 to $25 thousand ____ Over $25 thousand____.

26. What is the money you earn used for?

27. What percentage of your income is absorbed directly by career requirements (clothes, hair, extra help, child-care, travel, etc.) ?

28. Do you feel the tax laws are unfair to working wives?

29. Do your children have specific areas of responsibility to help you cope?

30. Do you feel more fulfilled combining a career with marriage? Explain.

31. Has your marriage suffered in any way due to your career? Or improved? Explain.

32. What advice would you give other women who are contemplating combining a serious career with motherhood and marriage?

33. If you had it all to do over would you conduct your life the same way, or would you do it differently? Explain.